GENERAL ROBERT E. LEE

*From a photograph taken just a few days
before the Battle of Chancellorsville*

The
Confederate Reader

How the South Saw
the War

Edited by

Richard B. Harwell

Dover Publications, Inc.
New York

Published in Canada by General Publishing Company, Ltd.,
30 Lesmill Road, Don Mills, Toronto, Ontario.

Published in the United Kingdom by Constable and Company, Ltd.

This Dover edition, first published in 1989, is an unabridged,
slightly corrected republication of *The Confederate Reader*,
originally published in 1957 by Longmans, Green and Co., Inc.,
New York. For this edition, several typographical errors have
been corrected, and three photographs have been moved from
their original pages to others.

Manufactured in the United States of America
Dover Publications, Inc., 31 East 2nd Street, Mineola, N.Y.
11501

Library of Congress Cataloging-in-Publication Data

The Confederate reader: how the south saw the war / edited by
Richard B. Harwell.
      p.   cm.
Previously published: New York : Longmans, Green, 1957.
Includes index.
ISBN 0-486-25980-3
    1. Confederate States of America—History—Sources.
2. United States—History—Civil War, 1861–1865—Sources.
I. Harwell, Richard B. (Richard Barksdale)
E488.C66 1989
973.7—dc19
                                        88-34891
                                        CIP

For
THOMAS H. ENGLISH
and
ROSS H. McLEAN
gentlemen scholars

Acknowledgment

Years of investigation into the printed records of the Confederacy have multiplied the thanks due to helpful scholars, librarians, and collectors in the compilation of *The Confederate Reader*. Several thousand Confederate publications have been closely examined and many, many of them read in their entirety. As some of these publications are rare (located perhaps in a single known copy), many libraries have been used to build the book. Chief among them are the Emory University Library, the Henry E. Huntington Library, the Boston Athenaeum, the Confederate Museum, and the Alderman Library of the University of Virginia.

The first tangible work on *The Confederate Reader* was made possible by a grant from the Huntington Library to work in its fine collection of Confederate material and by a corollary leave of absence from Emory University. My gratitude to both of these institutions is deep and sincere.

Individuals as well as institutions demonstrate the cooperative spirit of the scholarly world. My particular thanks are due Miss Margaret Jemison of Talladega, Alabama; Mr. Harold Mason of New Rochelle, New York; Miss Eleanor Brockenbrough, Miss India Thomas, Mr. McDonald Wellford, Mr. Louis Rubin, and Mr. Clifford Dowdey of Richmond; Miss Mary Isabel Fry, Miss Gertrude Ruhnka, and

Mr. Carey S. Bliss of San Marino, California; Mr. John Cook Wyllie of Charlottesville, Virginia; Mr. John L. B. Williams and Mr. Earl S. Miers of New York; Mr. Floyd M. Cammack and Mr. Ralph G. Newman of Chicago; Mr. Robert H. Woody of Durham, North Carolina; and Miss Marjorie Lyle Crandall and Mr. Walter Muir Whitehill of Boston: all these and many more.

RICHARD BARKSDALE HARWELL

September 2, 1957

Contents

1862

1863

The New Richmond Theatre   155

Mosby Makes a Night Raid   166

A Journey across Texas   177

The South Mourns Jackson   188

Defeat at Vicksburg   195

Mule Meat at the Hotel de Vicksburg   209

Gettysburg   213

1864

Illustrations

Introduction

THIS is *The Confederate Reader.* This is the story of
the Confederacy as the Confederates themselves
(and a few foreign sympathizers with the Confederates)
wrote it for one another. It is a roughly chronological
selection from the writings of the times, the writings that
were, theoretically at least, available to the Confederate
reading public. It does not exhaust the aspects of Confederate life, but it touches on most of them. It does not
attempt to give an over-all military history of the war,
but there is a generous sampling of battle reports and
general orders. Rather, it fills in the picture of Confederate life from a variety of sources (sources which were
nearly always heavily influenced by the military, though
not directly military)—from sermons, songs, humorous
sketches, novels, prison narratives, travel observations.
These are the living artifacts of the life of a Southerner
of the sixties, as important to the historian as the treas-
ured guns of Confederates and Federals are important to
the student of ordnance. Ink and paper survive with a
peculiar freshness, and the words of the Confederates
re-create their own era with an immediacy and truth that

bring new understanding of the period to the reader of nearly a century later.

The South is a state of mind. And the state of mind that was the South of the Confederacy is interwoven into the heritage and traditions of the modern South. Much of the continuing mental pattern of the South was established by the generation that preceded the Civil War. Its social pattern was solidified by the generation that followed the war. Its geographic pattern was established by the war itself. The war is the center of reference in the South's past. The thinking of the South, as opposed to that of the North, was set in the days of Calhoun. The modern social behavior of the South found its form when the Bourbons of the Reconstruction era succeeded in continuing, within a growing democracy, many of the features of the older plantation way of life. And the temporary geographic solidarity that united the South into the Confederate States of America is preserved in politics and in memory, so that Virginia's Northern Neck and the Texan Border have a common heritage which marks their citizens, in their own minds at least, as compatriots.

The heritage of a special past, or of a past that the romanticist likes to regard as special, needs understanding. The South is justly proud—and sometimes unjustly prideful—of its past. It loves to tell its history. Perhaps the best understanding of the present comes through understanding its relation to the past. The South's past can best be understood as the South explained its present of that day to itself.

The South is self-conscious. Now and historically, it is

self-conscious. The Nullification controversy between the
forces of Jacksonism and Calhounism imposed upon the
South a compulsion to explain itself. This compulsion has
never been thrown off and has, at times, been almost a
sectional monomania. It found its first region-wide expression in the slavery controversy. As tons of Northern
paper were filled with abolitionist sentiments, equal
amounts of Southern paper attempted to demonstrate
ethnographic, economic, and religious advantages of the
"peculiar institution." Concurrent with the expressions
on slavery was a growing propaganda for Southern nationalism that culminated in South Carolina's Ordinance
of Secession. After the war, the earlier memoirs of the
participants in the Confederacy are a treasury of Southern self-examination, but the generation of historians that
followed left, through their apologies for the South, a
stigma which has only recently been eliminated from
Southern writing. The Southerner is still self-conscious,
but the introspective examination of the region by Wilbur
J. Cash, Will Percy, and Ben Robertson; the perceptive
reporting of Jonathan Daniels, Ralph McGill, and Hod-
ding Carter; the distinguished historiography of Douglas
Southall Freeman, Charles S. Sydnor, Clement Eaton,
E. Merton Coulter, T. Harry Williams, and C. Vann
Woodward attest that the South can look fairly and
squarely at itself.

The history of the Civil War is the common heritage of
all Americans. No period in our history has been more
written about. The bibliography of those four years is
enough to fill volumes, the books themselves enough to

fill whole libraries. And here, more than about any other period, the South has felt it necessary to explain itself. Hardly was the ink dry on General Lee's farewell at Appomattox before the South began its attempts to vindicate in print its course during the war.

The flow of Confederate history has never ceased. First it was motivated by desire for vindication. Soon nearly every Confederate general was easily convinced that it would be a dereliction of his duty should he deny the public his memoirs. Unpretending reminiscences of private soldiers gradually filled in another side of the story. Regimental histories were published to gratify the pride of special units. Books about the war found a ready and continuing market. Women deprived of wealth and station by defeat could write and still preserve their social dignity. Personal diaries were given to the public. Material "written solely for the eyes of the author" found its way into print when tempted by the lure of financial gain. Publication of the official records of both armies by the United States government gave impetus to more and more serious histories. Over a generation had elapsed since the end of the war, but the game was not over when the course had been once run. A re-evaluation was due. Continued interest in the war has justified continued examination of it. Continued examination has turned up more and more of the facts of history, has presented more and more pictures of what the life of the South in the Confederacy was like, and has made the American Civil War the best documented of all wars.

It is a convenient war. It has a beginning and an end.

Its causes stretch back to the beginnings of our national life and its influences are still with us, but 1861–1865 is a tangible period. It was a war in which the same language was spoken on both sides and which, therefore, can be studied by one not trained in languages. It was a war in which the participants understood the ideology of one another (perhaps better than it has been understood since). By contrast to America's twentieth-century conflicts, it was a small war. It was a modern war in that in its theaters were developed many of the tactics which have since become standard military practice, in that it used modern weapons, and in that its armies were recruited and organized along lines similar to those of later American wars. Beyond all this, it was a romantic, sentimental, exciting war. Little wonder that the veterans of the Grand Army of the Republic loved to tell of the War of the Rebellion or that unreconstructed Confederates should recount again and again the glories of Southern Independence in the War for Separation.

The materials of the history of the Civil War have been worked over and over again—with one signal exception, the publications of the Confederates themselves. The Confederates were as self-conscious as any Southerners before or since. They were constrained to explain, not only to themselves but also to any other readers they could reach, the reasons for secession, their ambitions as an independent nation, and the glories of their heroic armies. The South was fighting for full independence—social, economic, and literary as well as political.

"Paper," wrote one Southerner in prefacing his narrative as a prisoner of the Yankees, "among other things, is scarce in the South, and paper may be turned into excellent account in the composition of cartridges, while metal that might be moulded into bullets is run into type. Yet newspapers and books are printed, and most of them eagerly read, especially any that have the most remote bearing upon the present contest." The Confederates realized the value of propaganda. It was important that paper be put to account to give a semblance of normalcy to existence in a nation fighting for its life, to bolster the morale of the people of the Confederacy, and to record for posterity a living record of the South's brief experiment in independence. The record left by these printed evidences of Confederate life is the truest record of the war. Prejudiced and incomplete as it is, it is nevertheless an accurate picture of the Confederacy.

Here, in their own words, written for their own people, is the story of the war as the Confederates knew, not remembered, it. Here is *The Confederate Reader*.

1860

To Dissolve the Union

THE FOCUS of growing tension throughout 1860 was Charleston. The question of secession had been close to the surface of political thinking in the Palmetto State since the Nullification controversy of President Andrew Jackson's administration. It had reached the boiling point in 1852, only to subside after the passage of an ordinance affirming the state's right to secede. Now it was ready to boil over. Continued affronts to the advocates of state rights had caused South Carolina in 1859 to forewarn Washington of secessive intentions by an invitation to her sister slaveholding states to consider measures for concerted action.

Positive action was deferred pending the results of the political canvass of 1860. The election of Abraham Lincoln was the signal for secession—and separation—and war to come.

The South Carolina Convention, originally convened in Columbia, adjourned to Charleston to escape a threatened epidemic of smallpox and proceeded to bring upon the state and upon the South the greater scourge of war. The proud little city, arrogantly conscious that she was

3

for the moment the center of national attention, awaited the passage of the Ordinance of Secession. After sober deliberation, feeling the responsibility of setting an example of dignity and reason, the delegates to the convention approved the ordinance early in the afternoon of December 20. Beneath the banner "The South Alone Should Govern the South" that stretched across Broad Street from the propaganda headquarters of the 1860 Association, crowds of citizens and militiamen streamed to the office of the *Mercury*, the fire-eating newspaper of secessionist Robert Barnwell Rhett, to confirm the news. And in scarcely fifteen minutes after its passage at St. Andrew's Hall copies of the Ordinance were rolling from the presses as a *Mercury* extra.

AN ORDINANCE

TO DISSOLVE THE UNION BETWEEN THE STATE OF SOUTH CAROLINA AND OTHER STATES UNITED WITH HER UNDER THE COMPACT ENTITLED "THE CONSTITUTION OF THE UNITED STATES OF AMERICA."

We, the People of the State of South Carolina, in Convention assembled, do declare and ordain, and it is hereby declared and ordained,

That the Ordinance adopted by us in Convention, on the twenty-third day of May, in the year of our Lord one thousand seven hundred and eighty-eight, whereby the Constitution of the United States of America was ratified, and also, all Acts and parts of Acts of the General Assembly of this State, ratifying amendments of the said Constitution, are hereby repealed; and that the union now subsisting between South Carolina and other States, under the name of "The United States of America," is hereby dissolved.

D. F. JAMISON, *Del. from Barnwell, and Pres't Convention.*

1861

Fort Sumter

S ENTIMENT in the lower South was overwhelmingly in favor of secession and separation. From the beginning the extremists in South Carolina counted on the early accession of Georgia, Florida, Alabama, Louisiana, Mississippi, and Texas to their ranks. In each of these states cool heads warned against the consequences of secession, but enthusiasm and emotion overrode wise admonition. The wisdom and love for the old Union of such as Alexander H. Stephens in Georgia, Benjamin F. Perry in South Carolina, and old Sam Houston in Texas could not prevail against the ambition-fired confidence and irresponsible claims of the fire-eaters. It mattered little that the South was not materially prepared for war. It was far too well prepared psychologically. What matter if there were not enough arms for a long war? What matter if there was no Southern navy? The war would be over in three months. Any Southerner could whip a dozen Yankees. Secession fever swept from Charleston to Montgomery, Jackson, Milledgeville, and Tallahassee. By February Louisiana had cast its lot with the secessionists, and the decision of Texas was a foregone conclusion.

"Hurrah, hurrah! for Southern Rights Hurrah," soon sang comedian Harry Macarthy as he plugged his own song "The Bonnie Blue Flag":

> First, gallant South Carolina nobly made the stand;
> Then came Alabama, who took her by the hand;
> Next, quickly Mississippi, Georgia and Florida,
> All raised on high the Bonnie Blue Flag that bears
>   a Single Star.

The secession of Texas was brought about after a bitter Unionist stand by her old patriot and governor, Sam Houston. But Houston could not hold back the hard-riding enthusiasm of the Texans for secession. The decision of the mammoth state, which remembered its own independence of less than a generation before, brought all the states of the great cotton belt into the new Confederacy and extended its territory from the Atlantic to ill-defined lines in the Western Territories.

The South moved in orderly and parliamentary fashion toward the formation of a new government. The *Star of the West* was fired on as she attempted to bring supplies to Major Robert Anderson's garrison at Fort Sumter in January, but the threat of immediate war subsided. Delegates were elected to a convention to be assembled in Montgomery. The Southern senators and representatives withdrew from the United States Congress. Secessionists in the army and navy resigned to place their services with their native states.

On February 4 the Montgomery convention began its sessions, and four days later a provisional government

had been established. The convention at first looked to
Georgia for the president of the new nation. But Bob
Toombs, on hearing that some of the delegations had decided to vote for Jefferson Davis of Mississippi, asked
that his name not be presented. The vote for Davis was
unanimous. The ex-senator received the news with apparent surprise. His ambition lay in military, not administra-
tive, duties. His first fame had come from his career in
the war with Mexico, and he had served a distinguished
term as President Franklin Pierce's Secretary of War.
But Davis resigned the appointment the new Republic of
Mississippi had given him as major general of its army
and left his plantation "Brierfield" for Montgomery.

William Lowndes Yancey, eloquent champion of secession in Alabama, introduced Davis to an assembled crowd
on the evening of February 17: "The man and the hour
have met." The next day, before an audience thoroughly
conscious of the historic importance, if not of the historic
implications, of the occasion they witnessed, Jefferson
Davis become the President of the Provisional Government of the Confederate States of America in a simple
and impressive ceremony. He delivered a short, dignified,
and well-reasoned statement of his position as head of a
new government. "We have changed the constituent
parts, but not the system of our government," he declared. "Sustained by the consciousness that the transition
from the former Union to the present Confederacy has
not proceeded from a disregard on our part of just obligations, or any failure to perform any constitutional duty—
moved by no interest or passion to invade the rights of

others—anxious to cultivate peace and commerce with all nations, if we may not hope to avoid war, we may at least expect that posterity will acquit us of having needlessly engaged in it. Doubly justified by the absence of wrong on our part, and by wanton aggression on the part of others, there can be no doubt that the courage and patriotism of the people of the Confederate States will be found equal to any measures of defence which honor and security may require."

Herman Arnold led his Montgomery Theatre band through the catchy strains of "Dixie," and the government of the Confederate States set about the task of establishing a new nation in fact as well as in name.

While the government in Montgomery burgeoned with red tape, appointments and bureaus, the military situation in Charleston Harbor was one of growing tension. Major Anderson had moved his garrison from Fort Moultrie to the unfinished, but more easily defended, harbor stronghold of Fort Sumter the day after Christmas. His position was an anomalous one, as both North and South were aware of the advantage to be gained by not striking the first blow.

The continued occupation by the Federals of a fort in sight of the birthplace of secession was particularly galling to Southern pride and patriotism, so it was here, on April 12, 1861, that war really began. It began in the fashion of a much-heralded theatrical event. All the niceties were complied with. Until the last, Major Anderson continued to exchange friendly notes with his acquaintances in Charleston. (The belief still existed that the problems of the day could be solved without violent interference with the personal lives of the participants.) The venerable Edmund Ruffin and the vigorous Roger Pryor came down from Virginia to share the honors of commencing hostilities. The people of Charleston lined the famous Battery to witness the spectacle of war. And, despite heavy artillery bombardment, not a single human life was lost during the battle for the fort. The only casualty occurred during Anderson's salute to the old flag at his surrender.

Friday, April 12, 1861.
The bombardment of Fort Sumter, so long and anxiously expected, has at last become a fact accomplished.

At about two o'clock, on the afternoon of Thursday, General Beauregard, through his Aides, Col. James Chesnut, Jr., Col. Chisolm and Capt. Lee, made a demand on Major Anderson for the immediate surrender of Fort Sumter. Major Anderson replied that such a course would be inconsistent with the duty he was required by his Government to perform. The answer was communicated by the General-in-Chief to President Davis.

This visit, and the refusal of the commandant of Fort Sumter to accede to the demand made by General Beauregard, passed from tongue to tongue, and soon the whole city was in possession of the startling intelligence. Rumor, as she is wont to do, shaped the facts to suit her purposes, enlarged their dimensions, and gave them a complexion which they had not worn when fresh from the pure and artless hands of truth.

A half an hour after the return of the orderlies it was confidently believed that the batteries would open fire at eight o'clock, and in expectation of seeing the beginning of the conflict, hundreds congregated upon the Battery and the wharves, looking out on the bay. There they stood, straining their eyes over the dark expanse of water, waiting to see the flash and hear the boom of the first gun. The clock told the hour of eleven, and still they gazed and listened, but the eyelids grew weary, and at the noon of the night the larger portion of the disappointed spectators were plodding their way homeward. At about nine o'clock, General Beauregard received a reply from President Davis, to the telegram in relation to the surrender of Sumter, by which he was instructed to inform Major Anderson that if he would evacuate the fort he held when his present supply of provisions was exhausted, there would be no appeal to arms. This proposition was borne to Major Anderson by the Aids who had delivered the first message, and he refused to accept the condition. The General-in-Chief forthwith gave the order that the batteries be opened at half-past four o'clock on Friday morning. Major Anderson's reply was decisive of the momentous question, and General Beauregard determined to apply the last argument. The stout soldier had resolved to make a desperate defence, and the bloody trial of strength must be essayed. The sword must cut asunder the last tie that bound us to a people, whom, in spite of wrongs and injustice wantonly inflicted through a long series of years, we had not yet utterly hated and despised. The last expiring spark of affection must be quenched in blood. Some of the most splendid pages in our glorious history must be blurred. A blow must be struck that would make the ears of every Republican fanatic tingle, and whose dreadful effects will be felt by generations yet to come. We must transmit a heritage of rankling and undying hate to our children.

The restless activity of Thursday night was gradually worn down; the citizens who had thronged the battery through the night, anxious and weary, had sought their homes, the Mounted Guard which had kept watch and ward over the city, with the first grey streak of morning were preparing to retire, when two guns in quick succession from Fort Johnson announced the opening of the drama. Upon that signal, at twenty-five minutes past four o'clock, A.M., the circle of batteries with which the grim fortress of Fort Sumter is beleaguered opened fire. The outline of this great volcanic crater was illuminated with a line of twinkling lights; the clustering shells illuminated the sky above it; the balls clattered thick as hail upon its sides; our citizens, aroused to a forgetfulness of their fatigue through many weary hours, rushed again to the points of observation; and so, at the break of day, amidst the bursting of bombs, and the roaring of ordnance, and before thousands of spectators, whose homes, and liberties, and lives were at stake, was enacted this first great scene in the opening drama of this most momentous military history. . . .

Steadily alternating, our batteries spit forth their wrath at the grim fortress rising so defiantly out of the sea. Major Anderson received the shot and shell in silence. And some excited lookers on, ignorant of the character of the foe, were fluent with conjectures and predictions, that revived the hope fast dying out of their hopeful and tender hearts. But the short-lived hope was utterly extinguished when the deepening twilight revealed the Stars and Stripes floating defiantly in the breeze. The batteries continued at regular intervals to belch iron vengeance, and still no answer was returned by the foe. About an hour after the booming began, two balls rushed hissing through the air, and glanced harmless from the stuccoed bricks of Fort Moultrie. The embrasures of the hostile fortress gave forth no sound again till between six and seven o'clock, when, as if wrathful from enforced delay, from casemate and parapet the United States officer poured a storm of iron hail upon Fort Moultrie, Stevens' Iron Battery and the Floating Battery. The broadside was returned with spirit by the gallant gunners at these important posts. The firing now began in good earnest. The curling white smoke hung above the angry pieces of friend and foe, and the jarring boom rolled at regular intervals on the anxious ear. The atmosphere was charged with the smell of villainous saltpetre, and as if in sympathy with the melancholy scene, the sky was covered with heavy clouds, and everything wore a sombre aspect.

About half past nine o'clock, Capt. R. S. Parker reported from Sullivan's Island to Mount Pleasant that everything was in fine condition at Fort Moultrie, and that the soldiers had escaped unhurt. The same dispatch stated that the embrasures of the Floating Battery were undamaged by the shock of the shot, and though the formidable structure had been struck eleven times, the balls had not started a single bolt. Anderson, after finding his fire against the Iron Battery ineffectual, had concentrated his fire upon the Floating Battery, and the Dahlgren Battery, both under command of Capt. Hamilton. A number of shells had dropped into Fort Sumter, and one gun *en barbette* had been dismounted. . . .

The venerable Edmund Ruffin, who, so soon as it was known a battle was inevitable, hastened over to Morris' Island and was elected a member of the Palmetto Guard, fired the first gun from Stevens' Iron Battery. Another son of the Old Dominion was appointed on General Beauregard's Staff on Thursday, bore dispatches to the General in com-

mand, from Brigadier-General James Simons, in command
of Morris' Island, during the thickest of the fight, and in the
face of a murderous fire from Fort Sumter. Col. Roger A.
Pryor, in the execution of that dangerous commission, passed
within speaking distance of the hostile fortress.

Fort Moultrie has fully sustained the prestige of its glorious name. Here, Col. Ripley, who was commandant of all the
artillery of Sullivan's Island and Mount Pleasant, made his
headquarters. The battery bearing on Sumter consisted of
nine guns, in command of Lieut. Alfred Rhett, with a detachment of seventy men, Company B. It fired very nearly gun
for gun with Fort Sumter. We counted the guns from eleven
to twelve o'clock, and found them to be forty-two to forty-six,
while the advantage was unquestionably upon the side of
Fort Moultrie. In that fort not a gun was dismounted, not a
wound received, not the slightest permanent injury sustained
by any of its defences, while every ball from Fort Moultrie
left its mark upon Fort Sumter. Those aimed at the barbette
guns swept with a deadly fire the parapet of the battery bearing on Cummings' Point, and also that against Sullivan's
Island, clearing the ramparts of men, striking the guns, or
falling with terrible effect upon the walls and roofing of the
quarters on the opposite side of the fortress. Many of its
shells were dropped into that fort, and Lieut. John Mitchell,
the worthy son of that patriot sire, who has so nobly vindi-
cated the cause of the South, has the honor of dismounting
two of its parapet guns by a single shot from one of the
Columbiads, which at the time he had the office of directing.
During the morning, Major Anderson had paid his respects
to all, and had tested the Floating Battery and the Iron Battery, and made nothing for the trouble. The last two or three
hours before dark, he devoted himself exclusively to Fort
Moultrie, and the two fortresses had a grand duello. Game to

the last, though much more exposed, Fort Moultrie held her own, and, it is believed, a little more than her own. Towards night, several rounds of red-hot shot were thrown into the barracks of the enemy. This battery has received universal applause and admiration.

A brisk fire was kept up by all the batteries until about seven o'clock in the evening, after which hour the guns boomed, throughout the night of Friday, at regular intervals of twenty minutes. The schooner Petrel, J. L. Jones, commanding, while lying off the mouth of Hog Island Channel, was fired into from Fort Sumter, about half-past eight o'clock. One shot took effect in the bow of the schooner, and several passed over her.

It were vain to attempt an exhibition of the enthusiasm and fearless intrepidity of our citizens in every department of this eventful day. Boats passed from post to post without the slightest hesitation, under the guns of Fort Sumter, and, with high and low, old and young, rich and poor, in uniform or without, the common wish and constant effort was to reach the posts of action; and amid a bombardment resisted with the most consummate skill and perseverance, and with the most efficient appliances of military art and science, it is a most remarkable circumstance, and one which exhibits the infinite goodness of an overruling Providence, that, so far as we have been able to learn from the most careful inquiry, not the slightest injury has been sustained by the defenders of their country.

It may be added, as an incident that contributed no little interest to the action of the day, that from early in the forenoon three vessels of war, two of them supposed to be the Harriet Lane and Pawnee, lay just beyond the bar, inactive spectators of the contest.

CLOSE OF THE BOMBARDMENT.

Second Day, Saturday, April 13, 1861.

We closed the account of the grand military diorama in progress on our Bay amidst the clouds and gloom and threatening perils of Friday night. The firing, abated in the early evening, as though for the concentration of its special energies, commenced again at ten o'clock, and amid gusts of rain, and clouds that swept the heavens, the red-hot shot and lighted shells, again streamed from the girt of batteries around, and concentrated in fearful import over Fort Sumter. Of the effects little was visible, of course, and anxious citizens, who from battery, spire and housetop, had bided the peltings of the storm, mute spectators of the splendid scene, could only wait the opening of the coming day for confirmation of the hopes and fears with which the changes in the scene successively inspired them. As dawn approached, the firing again abated, and when the rising sun threw its flood of light over the sparkling waters from a cloudless sky, it was but by random shots from outlying batteries, with scarce an answer from Fort Sumter, that spectators were assured the contest still continued, and that human feeling was not in harmony with the grace and glory of the scene. It was but a little while, however, before the energy of action was restored, and as the work of destruction still went on, it was feared that still another day of expectation and uncertainty was before us. A light issue of thin smoke was early seen at Sumter. At seven o'clock, a vigorous and steady fire was opened from Fort Moultrie, and a heavy cannonade ensued. But at eight o'clock the cry arose from the wharves, and rolled in one continuous wave over the city, "FORT SUMTER IS ON FIRE!" The watchers of the night before, who had retired for a few moments, were aroused, occupations were instantly suspended, and old and young, either mounted to their points of observation, or rolled in crowds upon the Battery, to look upon the last and most imposing act in this great drama. The barracks to the south had been three times set on fire during the bombardment of the day before, but each time the flames were immediately extinguished. Subsequently, however, a red-hot shot from Fort Moultrie, or a shell from elsewhere, found a lodgment, when the fact was not apparent, and the fire, smouldering for a time, at length broke forth, and flames and smoke rose in volumes from the crater of Fort Sumter. The wind was blowing from the west, driving the smoke across the fort and into the embrasures, where the gunners were at work, and pouring its volumes through the port-holes; the firing of Fort Sumter appeared to be renewed with vigor. The fire of the Fort, long fierce and rapid, however, was gradually abated, and although at distant intervals a gun was fired, the necessity of preserving their magazines and of avoiding the flames, left the tenants little leisure for resistance. But the firing from without was continued with redoubled vigor. Every battery poured in its ceaseless round of shot and shell. The enthusiasm of success inspired their courage and gave precision to their action; and thus, as in the opening, so in the closing scene, under the beaming sunlight, in view of thousands crowded upon the wharves and house-tops, and amid the booming of ordnance, and in view of the five immense ships sent by the enemy with reinforcements, lying idly just out of gun shot on the Bar, this first fortress of despotic power fell prostrate to the cause of Southern Independence.

About eight o'clock, Fort Moultrie had commenced to pour in hot shot, to prevent the extinguishment of the spreading flames, and to kindle new fires in all the quarters. The fight between the two forts was terrific. At this time, Sumter fired fifty-four shots at Moultrie in one hour, tearing the barracks to pieces. But the work was vain. Moultrie was too much for Sumter. In five minutes, she returned eleven shots. At about nine o'clock the flames appeared to be abating, and it was apprehended that no irreparable injury had been sustained; but near ten o'clock, a column of white smoke rose high above the battlements, followed by an explosion which was felt upon the wharves, and gave the assurance that if the magazines were not exploded, at least their temporary ammunition were exposed to the element still raging. Soon after the barracks to the east and west were in flames, the smoke rose in redoubled volume from the whole circle of the fort, and rolling from the embrasures, it seemed scarcely possible that life could be sustained. Soon after another column of smoke arose as fearful as the first. The guns had been completely silenced, and the only option left to the tenants of the fortress seemed to be whether they would perish or surrender. At a quarter to one o'clock, the staff, from which the flag still waved, was shot away, and it was long in doubt whether, if there were the purpose, there was the ability to re-erect it. But at the expiration of about twenty minutes, it again appeared upon the eastern rampart, and announced that resistance was not ended. In the meantime, however, a small boat started from the city wharf, bearing Colonels Lee, Pryor and Miles, Aides to Gen. Beauregard, with offers of assistance, if, perchance, the garrison should be unable to escape the flames. As they approached the fort, the United States' flag re-appeared; and shortly afterwards a shout from the whole circle of spectators on the islands and the main, announced that the white flag of truce was waving from the ramparts. A small boat had already been seen to shoot out from Cummings' Point, in the direction of the fort, in which stood an officer with a white flag upon the point of his sword.

This officer proved to be Col. Wigfall, Aid to the Commanding General, who, entering through a port-hole, demanded the surrender. Major Anderson replied, that "they were still firing on him." "Then take your flag down," said Col. Wigfall: "they will continue to fire upon you so long as that is up."

After some further explanations in the course of which it appeared, that Major Anderson's men were fast suffocating in the casemates, the brave commander of Sumter agreed that he would, unconditionally, surrender—subject to the terms of Gen. Beauregard, who, as was said by Col. Wigfall, "is a soldier and a gentleman, and knows how to treat a brave enemy." When this parley had been terminated, another boat from the city containing Major Jones, Cols. Chesnut and Manning, with other officers and the Chief of the Fire Department and the Palmetto Fire Company came up to the Fort. All firing had meantime ceased. The agreement to unconditional surrender was reiterated in the presence of new arrivals, and Messrs. Chesnut and Manning immediately came back to the city to bring the news, when it was also positively stated afterwards, that no one was killed on either side. It may seem strange, but it is nevertheless true. The only way to account for the fact is in the excellent protection offered by the unparalleled good works behind which the engagement was fought. The long range of shooting must also be taken into account. In addition to this, on each side, the men, seeing a discharge in their direction, learned to dodge the balls and to throw themselves under cover. A horse on Sullivan's Island was the only living creature deprived of life during the bombardment.

General Beauregard decided upon the following terms of Anderson's capitulation:

That is—First affording all proper facilities for removing

him and his command, together with company arms and property and all private property.

Secondly—That the Federal flag he had so long and so bravely defended should be saluted by the vanquished on taking it down.

Thirdly—That Anderson should be allowed to fix the time of surrender; to take place, however, some time during the ensuing day (Sunday).

These terms were the same as those offered before the contest. In pursuance of this programme, Major Anderson indicated Sunday morning as the time for his formal surrender.

The Tune of Dixie

THE AFFAIR at Sumter set off a chain of events that was to lead, irresistibly, to Appomattox. The first reaction was Lincoln's call for volunteers. This was immediately followed by the accession of Virginia to the Southern Confederacy and only a little later by the addition of Arkansas, Tennessee, and North Carolina to the group of seceding states.

It was apparent that Virginia would be the first great battlefield, and young Southerners nurtured in the righteousness of state rights and the belief in their military superiority to the Yankee foe were quick to volunteer—to join the army in time to participate in the glorious three months of warfare that would turn back the Northern invader. In the years immediately preceding the war volunteer companies had been formed in most of the Southern cities. As often as not essentially social organizations, these companies were little prepared for the kind of war that lay ahead. But the future of bloody battles and years of hardship did not worry them so long as the dangers were unforeseen, and the best of young Southern manhood marched defiantly, almost gaily, to Virginia.

One such company was the Mobile Cadets. They left Alabama in April, 1861, and proceeded to Virginia to be stationed in the vicinity of Norfolk for more than a year. In the summer of 1861 they felt keenly that they had not participated in the great battle of Manassas, but, before the war was over, they had taken part in nearly every other major engagement in Virginia and had amassed one of the bloodiest of regimental records.

Here, in a lighthearted excerpt from the contemporary account of one of its members, is a description of part of the journey of the Mobile Cadets to their post in Virginia and an account of the amazing rapidity with which "Dixie" was becoming the tuneful symbol of Southern nationalism. Its author, Henry Hotze, was a member of the Mobile Cadets at this time but was later detached and sent to London as commercial agent of the Confederacy. There he established and edited the remarkable propaganda organ of the Confederacy, *The Index*. It was in the columns of this paper that the following account appeared in the spring of 1862.

THE TUNE OF DIXIE

Norfolk, May 5, 1861.

We arrived here at daylight this morning in two special trains, after nearly twenty hours' continued but slow travelling. Our conveyances were again, as for the greater part of our many days' journey, cattle-cars, or box-cars, as they are termed; but these had been well aired and cleaned, a sort of rough benches fitted into them, and the sliding side-doors kept open, so that our situation, if not comfortable, was at least endurable. One passenger car was attached to each train for the officers and sick, of which latter we have already a goodly number, owing to the sudden change of climate, and of water and food, though no serious cases. The officers, for the most part, remained in the box-cars among the men, sharing their discomforts, and assisting in turning them into subjects of merriment.

The scenes on the way were a repetition of those we had witnessed in Georgia and Tennessee. Bevies of girls to greet us wherever the train stopped for wood and water, and gifts of flowers, cakes, and early fruit by the enthusiastic fair. Our "boys" have composed a set of doggerel rhymes to the tune of "Dixie," commemorative of the recent accession of Virginia and Tennessee to the Confederacy, and especially complimentary to the former. This they sing on every appropriate occasion, with marked effect upon the hearts of the Virginian beauties. Such was the popularity of the song at Norfolk, where it originated, that some considerate persons bethought themselves of having it printed on little slips of paper, as "The Song of Dixie, sung by the 3rd Regiment of Alabama Volunteers, on their passage through Virginia." These slips have been plentifully distributed on the road, and, I doubt not, will be preserved as historical relics, when the pretty girls who welcomed us shall have become grandmothers, and relate to the wondering little ones about the times when the first troops of Confederate volunteers came from the far South to fight the Yankees on Virginian soil.

> Oh, have you heard the joyful news?
> Virginia does old Abe refuse,
> 　　　Hurrah! hurrah! hurrah!

And Tennessee and brave Kentuck
Will show the North their Southern pluck,
Hurrah! hurrah!

and so on, through a dozen stanzas, each of which ends with
the patriotic refrain—

"We'ill die for old Virginia."

It is marvellous with what wild-fire rapidity this tune of
"Dixie" has spread over the whole South. Considered as an
intolerable nuisance when first the streets re-echoed it from
the repertoire of wandering minstrels, it now bids fair to become the musical symbol of a new nationality, and we shall
be fortunate if it does not impose its very name on our country. Whether by a coincidence simply accidental, or from
some of those mysterious causes which escape our limited
intelligence, its appearance in its present form was the knell
of the American Republic, and as such it seems to have been
instantaneously received by the masses in the South everywhere. What magic potency is there in those rude, incoherent
words, which lend themselves to so many parodies, of which
the poorest is an improvement on the original? What spell is
there in the wild strain that it should be made to betoken the
stern determination of a nation resolved to achieve its independence? I cannot tell.

Most persons believe it to be of recent origin, first introduced during the last Presidential contest by an "Ethiopian
minstrels'" troop performing in New Orleans. This is only
partially true; its real origin is of much older date. Those who
have travelled much on Western rivers must often have heard
it, in various forms, among the firemen and deck-hands of
the river steamers. For years the free negroes of the North,

especially those employed on board the steamers on the
Western rivers making periodical voyages South, have
cheered their labours with this favorite song:—

"I WISH I WAS IN DIXIE!"

PLAINTIVE AIR—Sung nightly in Washington by that Celebrated Delineator, ABRAHAM LINCOLN.

I wish I was in Dixie;
    In Dixie's land
    I'll take my stand,
And live and die in Dixie.
    Away, away,
Away down South in Dixie—

expressed the negro's preference for his more genial and sunny native clime, the land which is the negro's true home, and the only land where he is happy and contented, despite the morbid imaginings of ill-informed or misguided philanthropists.

The word "Dixie" is an abbreviation of "Mason and Dixon's line," as the line separating Maryland and Pennsylvania is called, and which both geographically and rhetorically, has expressed the Northern frontier of the South ever since the line was drawn by the surveyors whose names it immortalizes. Years before I heard the tune I have heard negroes in the North use the word "Dixie" in that sense, as familiarly as we do the more lengthy phrase from which it is derived.

A Visit to the Capitol at Montgomery

WILLIAM HOWARD RUSSELL, correspondent of the London *Times*, came to America in 1861 with an unsurpassed journalistic reputation gained as a reporter of the Crimean War. He was welcomed in both North and South and shown courtesies which allowed him to give a relatively full picture of the American scene. But generally scornful of American institutions, be they Northern or Southern, he soon managed to arouse the enmity of Confederate and Yankee partisans alike and was denied permission to accompany McClellan's army in its march on Richmond in 1862. He shortly returned to London and published his remarkably illuminating account of the first year of the war.

Although his letters were written as dispatches to the London *Times*, they were widely reprinted in both the United States and the Confederacy. His letter from Montgomery, for example, appeared in the Mobile *Advertiser & Register* for June 23, 1861.

Monday, May 6.—To-day I visited the capitol, where the Provisional Congress is sitting. On leaving the hotel, which is like a small Willard's, so far as the crowd in the hall is concerned, my attention was attracted to a group of people to whom a man was holding forth in energetic sentences. The day was hot, but I pushed near to the spot, for I like to hear a stump-speech, or to pick up a stray morsel of divinity in the *via sacra* of strange cities, and it appeared as though the speaker was delivering an oration or a sermon. The crowd was small. Three or four idle men in rough, homespun, make-shift uniforms, leaned against the iron rails enclosing a small pond of foul, green-looking water, surrounded by brick-work, which decorates the space in front of the Exchange hotel. The speaker stood on an empty deal packing case. A man in a cart was listening with a lacklustre eye to the address. Some three or four others, in a sort of vehicle which might either be a hearse or a piano van, had also drawn up for the benefit of the address. Five or six other men, in long black coats and high hats, some whittling sticks, and chewing tobacco, and discharging streams of discolored saliva, completed the group. "N-i-n-e h'hun'nerd and fifty dollars offered for him!" exclaimed the man, in the tone of injured dignity, remonstrance and surprise, which can be insinuated by all true auctioneers into the dryest numerical statements. "Will *no one* make any advance on nine hundred and fifty dollars?" A man near me opened his mouth, spat, and said, "twenty-five." "Only nine hundred and seventy-five dollars offered for him. Why, at's radaklous—only nine hundred and seventy-five dollars! Will no one," &c. Beside the orator auctioneer stood a stout young man of five-and-twenty years of age, with a bundle in his hand. He was a muscular fellow, broad-shouldered, narrow flanked, but rather small in stature; he had on a broad greasy, old wide-awake, a blue jacket, a coarse

cotton shirt, loose and rather ragged trowsers, and broken
shoes. The expression of his face was heavy and sad, but it
was by no means disagreeable, in spite of his thick lips, broad
nostrils, and high cheek-bones. On his head was wool instead
of hair. I am neither sentimentalist nor black republican, nor
negro-worshipper, but I confess the sight caused a strange
thrill through my heart. I tried in vain to make myself familiar with the fact that I could, for the sum of $975, become as
absolutely the owner of that mass of blood, bones, sinew,
flesh, and brains, as of the horse which stood by my side.
There was no sophistry which could persuade me the man
was not a man—he was, indeed, by no means my brother, but
assuredly he was a fellow-creature. I have seen slave markets
in the East, but somehow or other the Orientalism of the
scene cast a coloring over the nature of the sales there which
deprived them of the disagreeable harshness and matter-of-
fact character of the transaction before me. For Turk, or
Smyrniote, or Egyptian to buy and sell slaves seemed rather
suited to the eternal fitness of things than otherwise. The
turbaned, shawled, loose-trowsered, pipe-smoking merchants
speaking an unknown tongue looked as if they were engaged
in a legitimate business. One knew that their slaves would not
be condemned to any very hard labor, and that they would
be in some sort the inmates of the family, and members of
it. Here it grated on my ear to listen to the familiar tones of
the English tongue as the medium by which the transfer was
effected, and it was painful to see decent-looking men in
European garb engaged in the work before me. Perchance
these impressions may wear off, for I meet many English
people who are the most strenuous advocates of the slave
system, although it is true that their perceptions may be
quickened to recognize its beauties by their participation in
the profits. The negro was sold to one of the bystanders, and

walked off with his bundle, God knows where. "Niggers is cheap," was the only remark of the bystanders. I continued my walk up a long, wide, straight street, or more properly, an unpaved sandy road, lined with wooden houses on each side, and with trees by the side of the footpath. The lower of the two stories is generally used as a shop, mostly of the miscellaneous store kind, in which all sorts of articles are to be had if there is any money to pay for them; and, in the present case, if any faith is to be attached to the conspicuous notices in the windows, credit is of no credit, and the only thing that can be accepted in exchange for the goods is "cash." At the end of this long street, on a moderate eminence, stands a whitewashed or painted edifice, with a gaunt lean portico, supported on lofty lanky pillars, and surmounted by a subdued and dejected-looking little cupola. Passing an unkempt lawn, through a very shabby little gateway in a brick frame, and we ascend a flight of steps into a hall, from which a double starcase conducts us to the vestibule of the chamber. Any thing much more offensive to the eye cannot well be imagined than the floor and stairs. They are stained deeply by tobacco juice, which has left its marks on the white stone steps and on the base of the pillars outside. In the hall which we have entered there are two tables, covered with hams, oranges, bread and fruits, for the refreshment of members and visitors, over which two sable goddesses, in portentous crinoline, preside. The door of the chamber is open and we are introduced into a lofty, well-lighted and commodious apartment, in which the Congress of the Confederate States holds its deliberations. A gallery runs half round the room, and is half filled with visitors—country cousins, and farmers of cotton and maize, and, haply, seekers of places great or small. A light and low semicircular screen separates the body of the house, where the members sit, from the space under the gallery, which is appropriated to ladies and visitors. The clerk sits at a desk above this table, and on a platform behind him are the desk and chair of the presiding officer or Speaker of the Congress. Over his head hangs the unfailing portrait of Washington, and a small engraving, in a black frame, of a gentleman unknown to me. Seated in the midst of them, at a senator's desk, I was permitted to "assist," in the French sense, at the deliberations of the Congress. Mr. Howell Cobb took the chair, and a white-headed clergyman was called upon to say prayers, which he did, upstanding, with outstretched hands and closed eyes, by the side of the speaker. The prayer was long and sulphureous. One more pregnant with gunpowder I never heard, nor could aught like it have been heard since.

> "Pulpit, drum ecclesiastic,
> Was beat with fist instead of stick."

The reverend gentleman prayed that the Almighty might be pleased to inflict on the arms of the United States such a defeat that it might be the example of signal punishment forever—that this president might be blessed, and the other president might be the other thing—that the gallant, devoted young soldiers who were fighting for their country might not suffer from exposure to the weather or from the bullets of their enemies; and that the base mercenaries who were fighting on the other side might come to sure and swift destruction, and so on.

Are right and wrong mere geographical expressions? The prayer was over at last, and the house proceeded to business. Although each state has several delegates in Congress, it is only entitled to one vote on a strict division. In this way some curious decisions may be arrived at, as the smallest state is equal to the largest, and a majority of the Florida representatives may neutralize a vote of all the Georgia representatives. For example, Georgia has ten delegates; Florida has only three. The vote of Florida, however, is determined by the action of any two of its three representatives, and these two may, on a division, throw the one state vote into the scale against that of Georgia, for which ten members are agreed. The Congress transacts all its business in secret session, and finds it a very agreeable and commendable way of doing it. Thus, to-day, for example, after the presentation of a few unimportant motions and papers, the speaker rapped his desk, and announced that the house would go into secret session, and that all who were not members should leave.

As I was returning to the hotel there was another small crowd at the fountain. Another auctioneer, a fat, flabby, perspiring, puffy man, was trying to sell a negro girl, who stood on the deal box beside him. She was dressed pretty much like a London servant-girl of the lower order out of place, except that her shoes were mere shreds of leather patches, and her bonnet would have scarce passed muster in the New Cut. She, too, had a little bundle in her hand, and looked out at the buyers from a pair of large sad eyes. "Niggers were cheap;" still here was this young woman going for an upset price of $610, but no one would bid, and the auctioneer, after vain attempts to raise the price and excite competition, said, "Not sold to-day, Sally; you may get down."

Tuesday, May 7.—The newspapers contain the text of the declaration of a state of war on the part of President Davis, and of the issue of letters of marque and reprisal, &c. But it may be asked, who will take these letters of marque? Where is the government of Montgomery to find ships? The answer is to be found in the fact that already numerous applications have been received from the shipowners of New England, from the whalers of New Bedford, and from others in the Northern States, for these very letters of marque, accompanied by the highest securities and guaranties! This statement I make on the very highest authority. I leave it to you to deal with the facts.

To-day I proceeded to the Montgomery Downing street and Whitehall, to present myself to the members of the cabinet, and to be introduced to the President of the Confederate States of America. There is no sentry at the doors, and access is free to all, but there are notices on the doors warning visitors that they can only be received during certain hours. The President was engaged with some gentlemen when I was presented to him, but he received me with much kindliness of manner, and, when they had left, entered into conversation with me for some time on general matters. Mr. Davis is a man of slight, sinewy figure, rather over the middle height, and of erect, soldierlike bearing. He is about fifty-five years of age; his features are regular and well-defined, but the face is thin and marked on cheek and brow with many wrinkles, and is rather careworn and haggard. One eye is apparently blind, the other is dark, piercing, and intelligent. He was dressed very plainly, in a light-gray summer suit. In the course of conversation, he gave an order for the Secretary of War to furnish me with a letter as a kind of passport, in case of my falling in with the soldiers of any military posts who might be indisposed to let me pass freely, merely observing that I had been enough within the lines of camps to know what was my duty on such occasions. I subsequently was presented to Mr. Walker, the Secretary of War, who promised to furnish me with the needful documents before I left Montgomery. In his room were General Beauregard and several officers, engaged over plans and maps, apparently in a little council of war, which was, perhaps, not without reference to the intelligence that the United States troops were marching on Norfolk Navy-Yard, and had actually occupied Alexandria. On leaving the Secretary, I proceeded to the room of the Attorney-General, Mr. Benjamin, a very intelligent and able man, whom I found busied in preparations connected with the issue of letters of marque. Everything in the offices looked like earnest work and business.

On my way back from the State Department, I saw a very fine company of infantry and three field-pieces, with about one hundred and twenty artillerymen, on their march to the railway station for Virginia. The men were all well equipped, but there were no ammunition wagons for the guns, and the transport consisted solely of a few country carts, drawn by poor horses, out of condition. There is no lack of muscle and will among the men. The troops which I see here are quite fit to march and fight as far as their personnel is concerned, and there is no people in the world so crazy with military madness. The very children in the streets ape the air of soldiers, carry little flags, and wear cockades as they strut in the highways, and mothers and fathers feed the fever by dressing them up as Zouaves or Chasseurs.

Mrs. Davis had a small levee to-day in right of her position as wife of the President. Several ladies there probably looked forward to the time when their states might secede from the new Confederation, and afford them the pleasure of holding a reception. Why not Presidents of the State of Georgia, or Alabama? Why not King of South Carolina, or Emperor of Florida? Soldiers of fortune, make your game! Gentlemen politicians, the ball is rolling. There is, to be sure, a storm gathering at the North, but it cannot hurt you, and already there are condottieri from all parts of the world flocking to your aid, who will eat your Southern beeves the last of all.

One word more as to a fleet. The English owners of several large steamers are already in correspondence with the government here for the purchase of their vessels. The intelligence which had reached the government that their commissioners have gone on to Paris is regarded as unfavorable to their claims, and as a proof that as yet England is not disposed to recognize them. It is amusing to hear the tone used on both sides toward Great Britain. Both are most anxious for her countenance and support, although the North blusters rather more about its independence than the South, which professes a warm regard for the mother country. "But," say the North, "if Great Britain recognizes the South, we shall certainly look on it as a declaration of war." "And," say the South, "if Great Britain does not recognize our privateers' flag, we shall regard it as proof of hostility and of alliance with the enemy." The government at Washington seeks to obtain promises from Lord Lyons that our government will not recognize the Southern Confederacy, but at the same time refuses any guaranties in reference to the rights of neutrals. The blockade of the Southern ports would not occasion us any great inconvenience at present, because the cotton-loading season is over; but if it be enforced in October, there is a prospect of very serious and embarrassing questions arising in reference to the rights of neutrals, treaty obligations with the United States government, the trade and commerce of England, and the law of blockade in reference to the distinctions to be drawn between measures of war and means of annoyance.

As I write, the guns in front of the State Department are firing a salute, and each report marks a state of the Confederacy. They are now ten, as Arkansas and Tennessee are now out of the Union.

"Glorious, Triumphant and Complete Victory"

THE SPRING of 1861 was a readying time. The new government at Montgomery worked vigorously to put itself on a working basis, and finally removed to Richmond. Efforts were made to procure arms from Northern and foreign sources. In the South itself new manufactories were established to provide goods for home consumption and to create a military potential. The South was determined to assert industrial and commercial as well as political and military independence.

The first big military test did not occur until late July, when the Confederates met the Federal forces in the great amphitheater ringed by the hills near Manassas Junction, Virginia. Neither army was properly seasoned for a full-scale battle, and the fight at Bull Run had comic-opera as well as tragic aspects. What at first looked like a Northern victory was turned into a heavy defeat as reinforcements under Joseph E. Johnston joined the troops of Gustave Toutant Beauregard and routed the Yankees under McDowell.

Manassas was a memorable victory. Perhaps it created an overconfidence that eventually hurt the Confederacy. But it gave the South a hero in Thomas Jonathan Jackson. ("There stands Jackson like a stone wall," cried General Bee, and the name was evermore "Stonewall" Jackson.) It gave the South a martyr. ("They have killed me, but never give up the field" were the dying words of Francis Bartow.) And it gave the South a minor spoil, for if "Dixie" had not become Southern property by that time, the defeat of McDowell's troops, who had marched from Washington singing it as they crossed Long Bridge, made it Confederate and Southern forever.

Here is President Davis' telegram to General Samuel Cooper, Richmond's first word of the victory at Manassas. Following it is the address published by Generals Johnston and Beauregard to thank the soldiers for a "glorious, triumphant and complete victory." Though signed by both generals, the neo-Napoleonic rhetoric stamps it as actually written by the glamorous Creole. Frank Potts, a Virginia infantryman, recorded in his diary after the address was read to the troops: "It shows that our Beauregard not only wields the sword of Washington but the pen of Hamilton."

President Davis' telegram from the field of battle at Manasses[!], dated "July 21, at night," will become an important historical document. It is guarded in its statement, and thus falls far short of the facts as they afterward came out:

To General S. Cooper:

Night has closed on a hard-fought field. Our forces have won a glorious victory. The enemy was routed and fled precipitately, abandoning a very large amount of arms, munitions, knapsacks and baggage. The ground was strewn with their killed for miles and the farm houses and grounds around were filled with their wounded. The pursuit was continued along several routes toward Leesburg and Centreville until darkness covered the fugitives. We have captured several field batteries and regimental standards, and one United States flag. Many prisoners have been taken. Too high praise cannot be bestowed, whether for the skill of the principal officers, or for the gallantry of all the troops. The battle was mainly fought on our left several miles from our field works— our force engaged there not exceeding fifteen thousand; that of the enemy estimated at thirty-five thousand.

(Signed) Jeff. Davis.

Soldiers of the Confederate States:

One week ago, a countless host of men, organized into an army, with all the appointments which modern art and practiced skill could devise, invaded the soil of Virginia. Their people sounded their approach with triumphant displays of anticipated victory. Their Generals came in almost royal state; their great Ministers, Senators and women came to witness the immolation of our army and subjugation of our people, and to celebrate the result with wild revelry.

It is with the profoundest emotions of gratitude to an overruling God, whose hand is manifest in protecting our homes and liberties, that we, your Generals commanding, are enabled, in the name of our whole country, to thank you for that patriotic courage, that heroic gallantry, that devoted daring, exhibited by you in the actions of the 18th and 21st, by which the hosts of the enemy were scattered, and a signal and glorious victory obtained.

The two affairs of the 18th and 21st were but the sustained and continued effort of your patriotism against the constantly recurring columns of an enemy, fully treble your numbers; and these efforts were crowned, on the evening of the 21st, with a victory so complete, that the invaders are driven disgracefully from the field, and made to fly in disorderly rout back to their entrenchments—a distance of over thirty miles.

They left upon the field nearly every piece of their artillery, a large portion of their arms, equipments, baggage, stores, etc., etc., and amost every one of their wounded and dead, amounting, together with the prisoners, to many thousands. And thus the Northern hosts were driven from Virginia.

Soldiers! we congratulate you on an event which ensures the liberty of our country. We congratulate every man of you, whose glorious privilege it was to participate in this triumph of courage and of truth—to fight in the battle of Manassas. You have created an epoch in the history of liberty and unborn nations will rise up and call you "blessed."

Continue this noble devotion, looking always to the protection of a just God, and before time grows much older, we will be hailed as the deliverers of a nation of ten millions of people.

Comrades! our brothers who have fallen have earned undying renown upon earth, and their blood shed in our holy cause is a precious and acceptable sacrifice to the Father of Truth and Right.

Their graves are beside the tomb of Washington; their spirits have joined with his in eternal communion.

We will hold fast to the soil in which the dust of Washington is thus mingled with the dust of our brothers. We will transmit this land free to our children, or we will fall into the fresh graves of our brothers in arms. We drop one tear on their laurels and move forward to avenge them.

Soldiers! we congratulate you on a glorious, triumphant and complete victory, and we thank you for doing your *whole duty* in the service of your country.

(Signed) J. E. JOHNSTON,
General C. S. A.

(Signed) G. T. BEAUREGARD,
General C. S. A.

The Texans Leave for War

WHEN HE VISITED Texas in 1863, Englishman Sir Arthur James Lyon Fremantle commented: "At the outbreak of the war it was found very difficult to raise infantry in Texas, as no Texan walks a yard if he can help it. Many mounted regiments were therefore organized, and afterwards dismounted." The Texans were probably wise in their prejudice against infantry service; perhaps they knew the hardships that would await them on a long march to Virginia. But they were no less patriotic, no less eager to join the Southern armies, than troops in other states.

Out of Texas came the famous Hood's Texas Brigade. Chaplain of Hood's Texans was Nicholas A. Davis, a devout Presbyterian and a determined advocate of the glory of his soldier charges. In 1863 he had printed in Richmond a small volume that was one of the first of Confederate regimental histories. In this little book he recounts the difficulties which beset the Texans on their march to the Virginian theater of war, experiences in strong contrast to the journey of Henry Hotze's Cadets from Mobile to Norfolk.

Hundreds of Texans flocked to the Camps of Instruction set up by the state government in April, 1861, but only four companies could be formed when the Confederate government announced that it would accept their enlistments only as Confederate, not Texas state, troops. After weeks spent in the miasmic camps of a Texas summer the troops were finally dispatched toward Richmond by General Earl Van Dorn. Here is Chaplain Davis' story of the start of that long journey.

The hour of departure was hailed with rejoicing by the men, and all countenances were beaming with animation; all hearts were high with hope and confidence, and every bosom seemed warmed by enthusiasm;—the last greetings among friends were interchanged, the last good-byes were said, and away we sped over the flowery prairies, with colors fluttering in the breeze, each hoarse whistle of the locomotive placing distance between us and our loves at home . . .

The men of whom we are now writing had come together from the hills and valleys of Texas, at the first sound of the tocsin of war. The first harsh blast of the bugle found them at their home, in the quiet employment of the arts and avocations of peace. It is a singular fact, but no less singular than true, that those men who, at home, were distinguished among their fellows as peculiarly endowed to adorn and enrich society by their lives and conversation, who were first in the paths of social communion, whose places when they left were unfilled, and until they return again must be deserted shrines, should be the first to leap from their sequestered seats, the first to flash the rusty steel from its scabbard, and to flash it in the first shock of battle. But so it is, and we venture to assert, that of all those whom this war has drawn to the field, and torn away from the domestic fireside, there will be none so much missed at home as those who left with the first troops for Virginia. They were representative men from all portions of the State—young, impetuous and fresh, full of energy, enterprise, and fire—men of action—men who, when they first heard the shrill shriek of battle, as it came from the far-off coast of South Carolina, at once ceased to argue with themselves, or with their neighbors, as to the why-fores or the where-fores—it was enough to know that the struggle had commenced, and that they were Southrons.

Where companies had not been formed in their own counties, they hastened to adjoining counties, and there joined in with strangers. Some came in from the far-off frontier. Some came down from the hills of the North, and some came up from the savannahs of the South—all imbued with one self-same purpose, to fight for "Dixie."

Among them could be found men of all trades and professions—attorneys, doctors, merchants, farmers, mechanics, editors, scholastics, &c., &c.—all animated and actuated by the self-same spirit of patriotism, and all for the time being willing to lay aside their plans of personal ambition, and to place themselves on the altar of their country, and to put themselves under the leveling discipline of the army.

On the evening of the 17th, we were embarked at Beaumont on the steamer Florilda, a large and comfortable steamer, upon which we glided off from the landing, and set sail for the Bluff, the terminus of navigation, and from whence our journey had to be made by land. The trip was unattended by any feature of particular interest, and all arrived at Nibletts Bluff, on the morning of the 18th, at an early hour, and after debarking and getting all the baggage ashore, the men went into camp in the edge of the town.

Here we had the first realization of the fact, that we were *actual soldiers*, and had the first lesson illustrated to us, that a soldier must be patient under wrong, and that he is remediless under injustice—that he, although the self constituted and acknowledged champion of liberty, has, nevertheless, for the time being, parted with that boon, and, that he is but the victim of all official miscreants who choose to subject him to imposition.

The poor soldier receives many such lessons, and his fortitude and patriotism is often taxed to bear them without open rebellion, but as this was the first instance in which we had an opportunity of seeing and feeling such lessons experimentally, we here chronicle the circumstances for the benefit of all concerned. Gen. Van Dorn had entered into a contract with one J. T. Ward to transport these troops from Texas across to Louisiana, and Ward had undertaken as per agreement to furnish transportation in wagons across the country. He had been going back and forth for weeks, looking at the different roads, preparing the means of transportation; had delayed us getting off from Texas until all his vast arrangements were systematized, and until all his immense resources could be deployed into proper order, and concentrated at Niblett's Bluff for this grand exodus of two thousand soldiers, who were but awaiting his movements to begin their own pilgrimage to the great Mecca of their hopes, the "Old Dominion." To hear this man, Ward, spout and splutter among the streets of Houston about his teams and his teamsters, his wagons and his mules, one would have thought that the weight of the whole Quartermaster's Department of the Confederate Army rested upon his shoulders, and that his overburdened head was taxed with the superintendence of trains from California to the Potomac. Be this as it may, on arriving at the Bluff, whatever may have been the resources of our quartermaster, Ward, on this special occasion he fell short of an approximation of our necessities. We had started on the trip with clothing, camp-equipage, medical stores, and commissary supplies, all complete. The citizens of Texas had left nothing undone on their part to send their sons into the field well supplied with everything essential for their comfort, and, in addition, many things that had just been drawn from the agent of the Government, at Houston, which it was important should be carried with us. The troops were new to service, and unaccustomed to marching. It could not be expected that they could make the tedious trip through the swamps of Louisiana, unaided by liberal transportation. Van Dorn had unwisely and unjustly kept them in the sickly miasma of Buffalo Bayou until disease had already fallen in the veins of many, and all of them were suffering more or less from the enervating effects of that confinement. Such was the condition of the men now thrown into a thin and sparsely settled region of Louisiana, dependent alone upon others for every necessity to their new condition.

Under this state of affairs we found *seven wagons*, with indifferent teams, which Ward had procured for the purpose of transporting five hundred men, with the equipments and outfit mentioned. Ward had come to the Bluff with us on the steamer, but had gone immediately back, after leaving assurances that his preparations for our conveyance were ample. It is said that the wagons that he did furnish, were gathered up in that immediate vicinity, and that he engaged some of them even at so late an hour as our arrival at the Bluff.

The consequences were, that the officers in command had to rely upon themselves for the means of prosecuting the march. Tents, cooking utensils, clothing, medical stores, &c.,

to a large amount, were stowed away with whosoever would promise to take care of them for us until they could be sent on. Our sick men were left behind, and our journey commenced with what few things could be carried in these wagons.

Such an inauspicious introduction to the service, was far from being encouraging to the patriotic ardor, and many vented their curses against Ward, Van Dorn, and all concerned; but so earnest were the men in their devotion to the cause in which they had engaged, and so deep the confidence that all things would work right when we once got fairly along under the protecting aegis of our new Government; that soon all mutinous mutterings or complainings were suppressed, and the men set about relieving themselves of their difficulties as soon as possible.

A Skirmish of the Horse Artillery

THE TEXANS did not reach Virginia in time for the battle at Manassas, but their force was to be felt many times later in the war.

As the summer of 1861 wore into fall there were no more decisive battles. The Federals withdrew toward Washington to reorganize the "On to Richmond" march. General Beauregard went into camp at Centreville, where he undertook to train further his relatively raw Confederate soldiers. It was here that he received a visit from the famous Baltimore belles Hetty and Jennie Cary and their magnetic cousin Constance, the future wife of Jefferson Davis' private aide, Burton Harrison. The Misses Cary inspected the recent battlefield at Manassas and enlivened camp life generally. But they will be remembered for their introduction to the Confederate troops gathered at Centreville of "My Maryland," the stirring song written by James Ryder Randall and set to the tune of "Lauriger Horatius" by Jennie Cary. In a mock ceremony at Beauregard's headquarters Constance, Hetty, and Jennie were made, respectively, "captain-general," "lieutenant-colonel," and "first lieutenant" of the "Cary Invincibles." The South was still enjoying its war.

A few weeks later the three girls were called upon by a committee of the Confederate Congress to execute the design for the new battle flag. (The "Stars and Bars" had been difficult to distinguish from the "Stars and Stripes" in battle.) The young ladies soon dispatched their flags of the new design—"The Southern Cross," as this battle flag came to be known—to their heroes along the battle front in Northern Virginia, Generals Beauregard, Johnston, and Van Dorn.

But all was not socializing and playing at war. There were constant skirmishes as Yank met Rebel. Out of the skirmishes and small battles was emerging a new Southern hero, the dashing J. E. B. Stuart. In a family of torn loyalties, Jeb Stuart had no doubt on which side his duty lay. A trained soldier, and a good one, he entered the Confederate Army determined to inflict disaster on the enemy.

Here is his report of a small but typical engagement in the fall of 1861—the skirmish at Lewinsville, Virginia, September 11.

REPORT OF THE ENGAGEMENT AT LEWINSVILLE, VIRGINIA, J. E. B. STUART, COL. COMMANDING.

Headquarters Munson's Hill,
September 11th, 1861.

General:

I started about 12 o'clock, with the 13th Virginia Volunteers, commanded by Maj. Terrill, 305 men, one section of

Rosser's Battery, Washington Artillery, and a detachment of First Cavalry, under Captain Patrick, for Lewinsville, where I learned from my cavalry pickets, the enemy were posted with some force. My intention was to surprise them, and I succeeded entirely. Approaching Lewinsville by the enemy's left and rear, taking care to keep my small force an entire secret from their observation, I, at the same time, *carefully provided* against the disaster to myself which I was striving to inflict upon the enemy, and felt sure, that if necessary, I could fall back successfully before any force the enemy might have, for the country was favorable to retreat and ambuscade. At a point, nicely screened by the woods from Lewinsville, and a few hundred yards from the place, I sent forward, under Maj. Terrill, a portion of his command, stealthily to reach the woods at a turn of the road and reconnoitre beyond; this was admirably done, and the Major soon reported to me that the enemy had a piece of artillery in position, in the road just at Lewinsville, commanding our road. I directed him immediately to post his riflemen so as to render it impossible for the cannoniers to serve the piece, and if possible, capture it. During subsequent operations, the cannoniers tried ineffectually to serve the piece, and finally, after one was shot through the head, the piece was taken off. While this was going on, a few shots from Rosser's section, at a cluster of the enemy, a quarter of a mile off, put the entire force of the enemy in full retreat, exposing their entire column to flank fire from our pieces. Some wagons and a large body of cavalry first passed in hasty flight, the rifle piece and howitzer firing as they passed; then came flying a battery, eight pieces of artillery, (Griffin's,) which soon took position about six hundred yards to our front and right, and rained shot and shell upon us during the entire engagement, but with harmless effect, although striking very near. Then passed three regiments of infantry, at double quick, receiving in succession as they passed, Rosser's unerring salutation—his shells bursting directly over their heads and creating the greatest havoc and confusion in their ranks. The last infantry regiment was followed by a column of cavalry, which at one time, rode over the rear of the infantry in great confusion. The Field, General and Staff-Officers were seen exerting every effort to restore order in their broken ranks, and my cavalry videttes, observing their flight, reported that they finally rallied a mile and-a-half below, and took position there, firing round after round of artillery from that position up the road, where they supposed our columns would be pursuing them. Capt. Rosser having no enemy left to contend with, at his own request, was permitted to view the ground of the enemy's flight, and found the road plowed up by his solid shot, and strewn with fragments of shells—two men left dead in the road, one mortally wounded, and one not hurt, taken prisoner. The prisoners said the havoc in their ranks was fearful, justifying what I saw myself of the confusion.

Major Terrill's sharp-shooters were by no means idle, firing wherever a straggling Yankee showed his head, and capturing a Lieutenant, (captured by Maj. T., himself,) one Sergeant and one private, all belonging to the Nineteenth Indiana, (Col. Merideth's).

The prisoners reported to me that General McClellan himself was present, and the enemy gave it out publicly that the occupancy of Lewinsville was to be permanent. Alas for human expectations!

The officers and men behaved in a manner worthy of the General's highest commendations, and the firing done by the section, under direction of Capt. Rosser and Lieut. Slocumb, all the time under fire from the enemy's battery, certainly, for accuracy and effect, challenges comparison with any ever made.

Valuable assistance was rendered me by Chaplain Ball, as usual, and Messrs. Hairston and Burke, citizens attached to my staff, were conspicuous in daring. Corp'l Hagan, and Bugler Freed, are entitled to special mention for good conduct and valuable service.

Our loss was not a scratch to man or horse. We have no means of knowing the enemy's, except it must have been heavy from the effects of the shots. We found in all four dead and mortally wounded, and captured four. Of course they carried off all they could. . . .

Please forward this report to General Johnston, Gen. J. Longstreet.

Most respectfully,
Your obed't serv't.
(Signed.)   J. E. B. Stuart.
Colonel Commanding.
(Official.)   R. H. Chilton, A. A. General.

A Prayer for Our Armies

THE PRAYERS of the people, as well as their material support, were with the armies of the Confederacy. Here is "A Prayer for Our Armies" written for the use of the Confederate soldiers in 1861 by Bishop William Green of Mississippi.

Almighty God, whose Providence watcheth over all things, and in whose hands is the disposal of all events, we look up to Thee for Thy protection and blessing amidst the apparent and great dangers with which we are encompassed. Thou hast, in Thy wisdom, permitted the many evils of an unnatural and destructive war to come upon us. Save us, we beseech Thee, from the hands of our enemies. Watch over our fathers, and brothers, and sons, who, trusting in Thy defence and in the righteousness of our cause, have gone forth to the service of their country. May their lives be precious in Thy sight. Preserve them from all the dangers to which they may be exposed. Enable them successfully to perform their duty to Thee and to their country, and do Thou, in Thine infinite wisdom and power, so overrule events, and so dispose the hearts of all engaged in this painful struggle, that it may soon end in peace and brotherly love, and lead not only to the safety, honor and welfare of our *Confederate States,* but to the good of Thy people, and the glory of Thy great name, through Jesus Christ our Lord. Amen.

Winter in Virginia

A S SOLDIERS OF FORTUNE, unofficial observers, or reporters a number of foreigners fought with the Confederate Army. Their accounts of the war are sometimes
particularly illuminating as they wrote from a vantage
point conditioned by neither Yankee nor Confederate
prejudices and preconceptions. Though most of their accounts were printed only in England or on the Continent,
copies of them (particularly of the English books) found
their way back to the Confederacy, for the Southerners
were intensely interested in what impression they made
on such outsiders.

A brief glimpse of winter in a Confederate Army camp
in northern Virginia and a short description of the bustle
that had descended on Richmond as the capital of the
Confederacy are contained in the following account ex-
cerpted from the anonymous *Battle-fields of the South.*

For the next two weeks scarcely any sound was heard but
that of axe-men engaged in felling trees; and within a very

short time we were all well housed in log-huts, covered with layers of straw and mud. The fire-places being large, admitted 'sticks' of wood four feet long; and sometimes ten logs of this length constituted a fire. Some bought stoves to cook on, and built additional dwellings for their servants; but within the fortnight all were comfortably provided for. Our commanders occupied some princely residences owned by Union men in Maryland, who had been large lottery dealers, and possessed of immense wealth. The various regiments were placed on the east side of the forts, ready to occupy them within five minutes' notice.

Amusements of all kinds were soon introduced, but chiefly cock-fighting, as in summer. Men were sent out in all directions to buy up game fowl; and shortly there rose up a young generation of "trainers," versed in every point of the game, and of undisputed authority in the settlement of a quarrel. These, for the most part, were gentlemen from the Emerald Isle, not a few of whom were in every regiment in the service. In the matches, regiment fought against regiment, and company against company, for stakes varying from 5 dols. to 2,000 dols. a side; and such was the mania for "roosters" that the camps sounded like a poultry show, or a mammoth farmyard. "Snow-balling" was also a favourite pastime with the Southerners, and, together with skating and sledging, much delighted them; the majority had never seen snow or ice, except when the latter was used with "sherry-cobblers," "whisky-skins," "cocktails," &c.

I was loth to leave the brigade; but service called me to Richmond. So, having partaken of all the enjoyments of "singing clubs," "negro minstrels," "debating clubs," and the like, I departed for Manassas by a quartermaster's waggon, and soon arrived at Centreville. The outposts and guards at the latter place were extremely vigilant—annoyingly so, I thought

—and for the slightest irregularity in our 'passes' and papers would have sent us back to Leesburg. Fortifications of immense strength and extent arose on every hand, and were all well mounted. Though I could not comprehend the half of what fell under my notice, I felt strongly impressed that no army in the world could capture the place by an assault in front or flank. For miles these earthworks could be seen stretching through the country; and I counted not less than five hundred heavy pieces, without numbering them all.

The troops were comfortably quartered in well-built framehouses, placed in lines of streets, with parade grounds in front; sinks, gutters, and other sanitary arrangements seemed complete. The care and forethought displayed by our generals for the comfort, health, and convenience of the men surprised and delighted me: large bakeries, wash-houses, infirmaries, blacksmiths' shops, numerous sutlers' establishments (where no liquors were sold), chapels, parade and drill grounds, head-quarters, chiefs of departments, immense stables, warehouses and State depots—even a railroad connecting the place with Centreville to facilitate communication and send supplies.

The only drawback here—and this was sufficient to mar the whole—was the incredible quantity and tenacity of the mud. Locomotion in rainy or damp weather baffles all description; and to say that I have seen whole waggon trains fast in the road, with mud up to the axles, would afford but a faint idea of the reality. If timber had been plentiful, the roads might have been "corduroyed," according to the Yankee plan, viz., of piling logs across the road, filling the interstices with small limbs, and covering with mud; but timber was not to be procured for such a purpose; what little there might be was economically served out for fuel.

On arriving at Richmond a wonderful contrast to the well-disciplined order of Manassas presented itself. The Government offices were quiet and business-like, but no other part of the capital was so. The hotels were crowded to excess, as they always are; and great numbers of officers in expensive uniforms strutted about on "sick leave," many of whom had never been in the army at all, and after running up bills with all classes of tradesmen would suddenly depart for parts unknown. The marvel was, that people could be so deceived, for it is no exaggeration to say that every third man was dignified with shoulder-straps, and collectively they far out-numbered all the officers at Manassas! In theatres, bar-rooms, and shops, on horseback or on foot, all wore the insignia of office. Not one was to be found of less rank than captain, and as for colonels—their name was legion! I was measured by a youth for a pair of boots, and bought some dry-goods of another, one morning: in the evening I saw both of them playing at billiards at the "Spottswood," dressed out in bran-new uniforms, with insignia belonging to the rank of major! This was sufficient explanation; and it did not at all surprise me afterwards to hear that nearly all the thousand and one gambling hells were kept by captains, majors, and colonels. General Winder, the provost-marshal, subsequently made it a punishable offence for any to assume uniforms except soldiers. The change was sudden and ludicrous in effect.

The floating population of Richmond was made up of the strangest elements. Some came to see friends, others with wonderful inventions or suggestions for Government. Not a few were impressed with an idea that the Cabinet needed their advice and counsel; but the majority of these strangers came with the modest determination to offer their services at large salaries, pretending that if they were not accepted for this or that office, some State or other would feel humbled, perhaps secede from the Confederacy, and I know not what. It was laughable indeed to hear the self-sacrificing Solons holding forth in bar-rooms or in private. Their ideas of all things military were decidedly rich, and would have astonished poor Johnston or Beauregard, who were put down as mere schoolboys beside them. General Washington Dobbs, who had been engaged all his life in the leather business somewhere in Georgia, had come up to proffer his valuable services as brigadier; but being unsuccessful, his patriotism and indignation electrified the whole private family where he boarded. Colonel Madison Warren, some poor relation of the English blacking-maker, had lived in some out-of-the-way swamp in the Carolinas; he came to Richmond to have a private talk with the President, to let him know what *he* thought about General M'Clellan and old Scott. Not getting an audience, he offered himself for the vacancy of quartermaster-general, and not being accepted was sure that Jefferson Davis was a despot, and that the Southern Confederacy was fast going to the devil.

Smith had a self-loading, self-priming field-piece, that would fire a hundred times a minute, and never miss. Each gun would only weigh twenty tons, and cost 10,000 dols. He had asked a commission to make a thousand of them only, was willing to give Government the patent right gratis; and they would not listen to him! How *could* the South succeed when neglecting such men as Smith? Jones was another type of a numerous class of patriots. Tracts were necessary food for the soldiers. He (Jones) "only" wanted the Government to start a large Bible and Tract house, give him the control of it, and he would guarantee to print as many as were needed, and sell them as cheaply as anybody else, considering the high price of everything. Jones, like a thousand others, did not succeed with any of the departments, and after being

jammed and pushed about in the various lobbies and stair-
cases for a whole month, arrived at the conclusion that the
Confederate Government was not "sound" on the Bible
question, and, therefore, ought not to be trusted in this
enlightened and Gospel-preaching age!

When the high price of every necessary is considered, it
appears strange that the city should be so crowded. Boarding
averaged from 2 dols. to 5 dols. per day at the hotels, and
not less than 10 dols. per week in any family. Boots were 35
dols. per pair; a suit of clothes (civil), 175 dols.; military,
200 dols., or more; whisky (very inferior), 5 dols. per quart;
other liquors and wines in proportion; smoking tobacco, 1.50
dols. per pound; socks, 1 dol. per pair; shoes, 18 dols. to 25
dols.; haircutting and shaving, 1 dol.; bath, 50c.; cigars
(inferior) four for 1 dol., &c. The city, however, knew no
interruption to the stream of its floating population, and
balls, parties, and theatres, made a merry world of it; and
Frenchmen say, it was Paris in miniature. Four in the afternoon was grand promenade hour; and, in fine weather, the
small park and principal streets were crowded. Military and
naval officers would sun themselves on balconies, or stretch
their limbs elegantly at hotel doors.

1862

Naval Victory in Hampton Roads

THE CONFEDERACY had virtually no navy when the war began in 1861. President Davis wasted no time in issuing letters of marque to ships which would request them, but more effective methods were needed to build an adequate navy. Congress authorized the building of ships abroad, and enterprising men undertook the construction and outfitting of vessels at Selma, Alabama; Columbus, Georgia; and New Orleans. The capture of the Yankee warships in the Gosport Navy Yard at Norfolk eased the situation, but the Confederacy was never able to keep pace with the Union in adding ships to its fleet. Though the blockade was, indeed, often hardly more than a paper blockade, the Confederate Navy was just as often hardly more than a paper navy.

One of the Confederate prizes at Gosport was the USS *Merrimac*, a relatively new cruiser. She was repaired and re-outfitted for the Confederates as the CSS *Virginia*. Her duel with the USS *Monitor* was one of the turning points of naval history. Their battle spelled the end of wooden navies. Before she met her doom against the revolutionary *Monitor*, the *Virginia* threw terror into the hearts of the Federal Navy by her audacious and victorious foray against the frigates *Cumberland* and *Congress*.

Here is Flag Officer Franklin Buchanan's official account of the Battle of Hampton Roads, March 8 and 9, 1862. It is worthy of note that the Lieutenant Parker mentioned was William Harwar Parker who had previously made a long Pacific voyage as an officer of the U.S. Navy aboard the *Merrimac*. Although he comes off none too well in Buchanan's report, he subsequently had a distinguished career in the Confederate Navy and served as commandant of the Confederate States School-Ship *Patrick Henry*, the Confederate naval academy which conducted its courses on board ship in the James River.

Naval Hospital ⎱
Norfolk, March 27th, 1862 ⎰

Sir: Having been confined to my bed in this building since the 9th inst., in consequence of a wound received in the action of the previous day, I have not had it in my power at an earlier date to prepare the official report, which I now have the honor to submit, of the proceedings on the 8th and 9th insts., of the James River Squadron under my command, composed of the following named vessels: Steamer Virginia, Flag Ship, ten guns; steamer Patrick Henry, twelve guns, Commander John R. Tucker; steamer Jamestown, Lieut. Commanding J. N. Barney, two guns; and gunboats Teazer, Lieut. Commanding W. A. Webb; Beaufort, Lieut. Commanding W. H. Parker, and Raleigh, Lieut. Commanding J. W. Alexander, each one gun. Total 27 guns.

On the 8th inst., at 11, A. M., the Virginia left the Navy-Yard, Norfolk, accompanied by the Raleigh and Beaufort, and proceeded to Newport News to engage the enemy's frigates Cumberland and Congress, gunboats and shore batteries. When within less than a mile of the Cumberland, the Virginia commenced the engagement with that ship with her bow gun, and the action soon became general, the Cumberland, Congress, gunboats and shore batteries concentrating upon us their heavy fire, which was returned with great spirit and determination. The Virginia stood rapidly on towards the Cumberland, which ship I had determined to sink with our prow, if possible. In about fifteen minutes after the action commenced we ran into her on her starboard bow; the crash below the water was distinctly heard, and she commenced sinking, gallantly fighting her guns as long as they were above water. She went down with her colors flying. During this time the shore batteries, Congress, and gunboats kept up their heavy concentrated fire upon us, doing us some injury. Our guns, however, were not idle; their fire was very destructive to the shore batteries and vessels, and we were gallantly sustained by the rest of the squadron.

Just after the Cumberland sunk, that gallant officer, Commander John R. Tucker, was seen standing down the James River under full steam, accompanied by the Jamestown and Teazer. They all came nobly into action and were soon exposed to the heavy fire of shore batteries. Their escape was miraculous, as they were under a galling fire of solid shot, shell, grape and canister, a number of which passed through the vessels without doing any serious injury, except to the Patrick Henry, through whose boiler a shot passed, scalding to death four persons, and wounding others. Lieut. Commanding Barney promptly obeyed a signal to tow her out of the action. As soon as damages were repaired, the Patrick

Henry returned to her station and continued to perform good service during the remainder of that day and the following.

Having sunk the Cumberland, I turned our attention to the Congress. We were some time in getting our proper position, in consequence of the shoalness of the water, and the great difficulty of managing the ship when in or near the mud. To succeed in my object, I was obliged to run the ship a short distance above the batteries on James River, in order to wind her. During all the time her keel was in the mud; of course she moved but slowly. Thus we were subjected twice to the heavy guns of all the batteries in passing up and down the river, but it could not be avoided. We silenced several of the batteries, and did much injury on shore. A large transport steamer alongside the wharf was blown up, one schooner sunk, and another captured and sent to Norfolk. The loss of life on shore we have no means of ascertaining.

While the Virginia was thus engaged in getting her position for attacking the Congress, the prisoners state it was believed on board that ship that we had hauled off; the men left their guns and gave three cheers. They were soon sadly undeceived, for a few minutes after we opened upon her again, she having run on shore in shoal water. The carnage, havoc and dismay caused by our fire compelled them to haul down their colors, and to hoist a white flag at their gaff, and half mast another at the main. The crew instantly took to their boats and landed. Our fire immediately ceased, and a signal was made for the Beaufort to come within hail. I then ordered Lieut. Commanding Parker to take possession of the Congress, secure the officers as prisoners, allow the crew to land, and burn the ship. He ran alongside, received her flag and surrender from Commander Wm. Smith and Lieut.

Pendergrast, with the side-arms of those officers. They delivered themselves as prisoners of war on board the Beaufort, and afterwards were permitted, at their own request, to return to the Congress, to assist in removing the wounded to the Beaufort. They never returned, and I submit to the decision of the Department whether they are not our prisoners. While the Beaufort and Raleigh were alongside the Congress, and the surrender of that vessel had been received from the commander, she having two white flags flying, hoisted by her own people, a heavy fire was opened upon them from the shore and from the Congress, killing some valuable officers and men. Under this fire the steamers left the Congress; but as I was not informed that any injury had been sustained by those vessels at that time, Lieut. Commanding Parker having failed to report to me, I took for granted that my order to him to burn her had been executed, and waited some minutes to see the smoke ascending from her hatches. During this delay we were still subjected to the heavy fire from the batteries, which was always promptly returned.

The steam frigates Minnesota and Roanoke, and the sailing frigate St. Lawrence, had previously been reported as coming from Old Point, but as I was determined that the Congress should not again fall into the hands of the enemy, I remarked to that gallant young officer, Flag Lieut. Minor, "that ship must be burned." He promptly volunteered to take a boat and burn her, and the Teazer, Lieut. Commanding Webb, was ordered to cover the boat. Lieut. Minor had scarcely reached within fifty yards of the Congress, when a deadly fire was opened upon him, wounding him severely and several of his men. On witnessing this vile treachery, I instantly recalled the boat and ordered the Congress destroyed by hot shot and incendiary shell. About this period

I was disabled and transferred the command of the ship to that gallant, intelligent officer, Lieut. Catesby Jones, with orders to fight her as long as the men could stand to their guns.

The ships from Old Point opened their fire upon us. The Minnesota grounded in the north channel, where unfortunately the shoalness of the channel prevented our near approach. We continued, however, to fire upon her until the pilots declared that it was no longer safe to remain in that position, and we accordingly returned by the south channel, (the middle ground being necessarily between the Virginia and Minnesota, and St. Lawrence and the Roanoke having retreated under the guns of Old Point,) and again had an opportunity of opening upon the Minnesota, receiving her heavy fire in return; and shortly afterwards upon the St. Lawrence, from which vessel we also received several broadsides. It had by this time become dark and we soon after anchored off Sewell's Point. The rest of the squadron followed our movements, with the exception of the Beaufort, Lieut. Commanding Parker, who proceeded to Norfolk with the wounded and prisoners, as soon as he had left the Congress, without reporting to me. The Congress having been set on fire by our hot shot and incendiary shell, continued to burn, her loaded guns being successively discharged as the flames reached them, until a few minutes past midnight when her magazine exploded with a tremendous report. . . .

While in the act of closing this report, I received the communication of the Department, dated 22d inst., relieving me temporarily of the command of the squadron for the naval defences of James River. I feel honored in being relieved by the gallant Flag Officer, Tattnall.

I much regret that I am not now in a condition to resume

my command, but trust that I shall soon be restored to health, when I shall be ready for any duty that may be assigned to me.

Very respectfully,
FRANKLIN BUCHANAN,

Flag Officer.

Hon. S. R. Mallory,
    Secretary of the Navy.

The Texans Invade New Mexico

THE BATTLE OF GLORIETTA, or Pigeon's Ranch, was a small but important battle in the course of the war in the West. Texan troops under Brigadier General H. H. Sibley moved into New Mexico Territory during January and February, 1862, with signal success. The Federals retired from the principal settlements at Albuquerque and Sante Fe, and the Confederates were victorious in a series of minor engagements. The Battle of Glorietta was fought the last of March in a canyon twenty-three miles east of Santa Fe. Both Confederates and Federals reported it as a victory. Actually the Confederates won the field, but the loss of their supply train (which occurred as a corollary of the battle) was fatal to their New Mexican campaign.

The two Confederate reports here printed are typical of the hyperbole of which the Confederates were often guilty in their official claims. In his informal report to the President, Tom Ochiltree, aide to General Sibley, called accurately the losses on his own side but exaggerated by many score the Yankee losses. His "met, attacked, whipped and routed" is Texan for "*Veni, vidi, vici.*" In his address to his soldiers Colonel Scurry is dramatic enough, yet he surpassed himself in his official report of the battle in which he declares: "The intrepid Ragnet, and the cool, calm, courageous Pyron, had pushed forward among the rocks, until the muzzle[s] of the opposing forces guns passed each other."

San Antonio, Texas, April 27th, 1862

His Excellency President Davis:

I have the honor to inform your Excellency of another glorious victory achieved by the Confederate army of New Mexico.

On the 27th March, Lt. Col. Scurry, with 1,000 men from 2nd, 4th, 5th and 7th Texas volunteers, met, attacked, whipped and routed 2,000 Federals, 23 miles east of Santa Fe.

Our loss was 33 killed and 35 wounded—among the killed was Major Ragnet, and Capt. Buckholtz, of the 4th, and Major Shropshire of the 5th Texas mounted volunteers, Lt. Col. Scurry, commanding was twice slightly wounded, and Major Pyron, commanding battalion T. M. R., had his horse blown from under him by a shell.

The enemy's loss was over seven hundred killed and wounded—five hundred being left on the field. Their rout was complete, and they were scattered from the battle field to Fort Union.

The Confederate flag flies over Santa Fe and Albuquerque. At the latter place, the flag was made of a captured United States flag, raised upon a United States flag-staff—the salute fired by a captured United States battery, and Dixie played by a captured United States band.

The Federal force defeated at Glorietta, consisted of 1,600 Pike's Peak volunteers and 600 regulars, under command of Col. Slough. I have the honor to inform your excellency, that I will wait upon you with important despatches in a few days.

Very respectfully,
Tom P. Ochiltree.
Assistant Adjutant General,
Army of New Mexico

HEAD-QUARTERS ADVANCE DIVISION ARMY OF
NEW MEXICO
Canon Glorietta, March 29, 1862.

GENERAL ORDER
No. 4.

Soldiers— You have added another victory to the long list of triumphs won by the Confederate *armies.* By your conduct you have given another evidence of the daring courage and heroic endurance which actuate you in this great struggle for the independence of your country. You have proven your right to stand by the side of those who fought and conquered on the red field of San Jacinto. The battle of Glorietta—where for six long hours you steadily drove before you a foe of twice your numbers—over a field chosen by themselves, and deemed impregnable, will take its place upon the rolls of your country's triumphs, and serve to excite your children to imitate the brave deeds of their fathers, in every hour of that country's peril.

Soldiers— I am proud of you. Go on as you have commenced, and it will not be long until not a single soldier of the United States will be left upon the soil of New Mexico. The Territory, relieved of the burden imposed on it by its late oppressors, will once more, throughout its beautiful valleys, "blossom as the rose," beneath the plastic hand of peaceful industry.

By order of

    Lieut. Col. WM. R. SCURRY, Commanding.

ELLSBERRY R. LANE, Adjutant.

The Drummer Boy of Shiloh

D URING EARLY 1862 the Federal forces moved steadily
into Tennessee. Confederate fortunes reached their
lowest ebb since the war began. The key point of the
campaign was the Battle of Shiloh, one of the bloodiest
fights of all time. The Confederates won an initial victory
but failed to follow it up, and the net result to the South
was a crushing defeat and the loss of one of their ablest
general officers, Albert Sidney Johnston.

Out of the Battle of Shiloh came a folk hero for all
America. The drummer boy of Shiloh was a Yankee
drummer who is supposed to have met his death in the
battle. His story was put in rhyme and set to music by
Will Shakespeare Hays, who wrote music for a publishing
firm in Louisville. The sentimentality of the piece brought
it immediate popularity in a period of the war when the
folks at home wanted just such outlets for their emotions.
As the words of the song avoided identifying its hero as
either Yankee or Confederate, it was easy for it to cross
the battle lines, and it enjoyed wide popularity in the
South as well as in the North.

76

THE DRUMMER BOY OF SHILOH

On Shiloh's dark and bloody ground, the dead and wounded
lay.
Amongst them was a drummer boy, that beat the drum that
day.
A wounded soldier raised him up, His drum was by his side.
He clasped his hands and raised his eyes and prayed before
he died:
Look down upon the battle field, Oh Thou, our Heav'nly
friend,
Have mercy on our sinful souls. The soldiers cried, "Amen."
For gather'd round a little group, Each brave man knelt and
cried.
They listen'd to the drummer boy who prayed before he
died.

"Oh, Mother!" said the dying boy, "Look down from Heav'n
on me,
Receive me to thy fond embrace, Oh take me home to thee.
I've loved my country as my God, To serve them both I've
tried."
He smiled, shook hands. Death seized the boy who prayed
before he died.

Each soldier wept then like a child, Stout hearts were they
and brave.
The flag his winding sheet, God's book the key unto his
grave.
They wrote upon a simple board these words "This is a guide
To those who mourn the drummer boy who prayed before
he died."

Stealing the Telegraph

DURING THE SUMMER of 1862 Confederates read with glee of the daring raids of John Hunt Morgan and his men into Kentucky. On Morgan's staff was an efficient and resourceful young telegrapher called George Ellsworth. His report of how he tapped the Union telegraph lines to send spurious messages and generally confound the Federal forces chasing Morgan was widely printed in the newspapers of the South and stands as one of the most amusing spots in the often laborious official records of the war.

Morgan's dashing raids and his much-publicized romance with a "secesh lady" of Kentucky captured the imagination of the South. Mrs. Sally Rochester Ford wove the story of Morgan and his men (as far as it had gone) into a novel published by Sigmund H. Goetzel in Mobile in the spring of 1863. Here is her adaptation of Ellsworth's account of his manipulations of the Union telegraph as told in her chapter "Paris, Richmond, Crab Orchard, Somerset."

The alarm and uncertainty which pervaded the Federal forces in Central Kentucky at the brilliant exploits of Colonel Morgan, and the rapidity of his movements, can scarcely be conceived. Lexington and Paris both threatened, Cynthiana taken, no one could decide which would be the next point of attack. Lexington called upon Paris for reinforcements—Paris in reply demanded succor of Lexington. But the condition of the latter city became so hazardous, menaced as it was from the direction of Georgetown and Richmond, that it was finally decided to concentrate the troops within its limits for its defence. Accordingly, the forces were ordered from Paris to Lexington, leaving the former town wholly at the mercy of the advancing foe.

On the 19th of July, the day following the capture of Cynthiana, Colonel Morgan moved upon Paris, now entirely undefended. When within a few miles of the city, he met a flag of truce, tendering him the peaceful and quiet possession of the place, and when he entered the streets, cheers and welcomes rang out on the air. Remaining here through the night, Colonel Morgan understood through his scouts that very nearly the entire force from Lexington was being moved upon Paris, for the purpose of attacking him. Not desiring an engagement, when it could be avoided, Colonel Morgan determined to fall back upon Richmond, preparatory to leaving the State. Accordingly, orders were issued to the men to be ready to march early the following morning. Meanwhile, pickets kept watch, lest at any time they should be surprised.

As the Confederates were setting out the next day towards Richmond, they discovered the Federals moving towards the town from Lexington. Colonel Morgan called a halt, and by a little manœuvering so scared the Yankees, who supposed he intended to flank them, that they wheeled about and made a quick retreat. Thus relieved of their presence, Colonel Morgan was enabled to bring off all his guns and stores without molestation or detriment. The only loss sustained was that of one picket, who, it was supposed, was surprised and captured by the enemy in their advance.

From Paris the Confederate force moved to Richmond. Here the warmest enthusiasm greeted them on all sides. Their passage through the town to their encampment beyond was a grand ovation, each individual vieing with his neighbor in his endeavors to manifest his delight and approbation. Ladies showered bouquets and waved handkerchiefs —children waved handkerchiefs and smiled—men, old and young, smiled, and bowed, and hurraed. Ample provision was made for a luxurious repast for the whole command, who partook of the kindly cheer with right good zest, their appeties being well developed by their long and weary ride. Several recruits joined them here, who were furnished with arms and mounted.

It had been Colonel Morgan's intention to remain in Richmond several days, thereby giving an opportunity for the enrollment of many who were desirous to enlist under his standard, but being informed that a large cavalry force had been sent out by way of Danville to intercept and cut off his retreat, he determined to thwart their plans by pushing forward to Crab Orchard, which point he reached the 22d of July, at day-break.

There he found about one hundred and twenty wagons and one million dollars' worth of stores, all of which was given into the hands of his men to be destroyed, as it was impossible to remove anything over that rugged, broken country. The boys gave themselves to the work of burning and breaking with great zest, and soon the gigantic task was accomplished and the whole column again on the advance towards Somerset, which was reached at sun-down of the same day. This point was the depot of the Federal army at Cumberland Gap, and contained large stores. Colonel Morgan feeling entire safety, took possession of the telegraph office, and countermanded every order of Gen. Boyle with regard to the movement of the troops still in pursuit of him. There another million dollars' worth of Federal property was destroyed, and a thousand stand of arms recaptured that had been taken from Gen. Zollicoffer's forces at the memorable and disastrous engagement of Fishing Creek.

Having here rested his troops, Col. Morgan moved forward to Sparta, which point he reached July 24th, having been absent on his expedition just twenty days, during which time he "captured (and parolled) over twelve hundred prisoners, seven thousand stand of arms, one gun and destroyed, at lowest computation, seven and a half million dollars' worth of stores, arms and subsistence, besides hospital buildings, bridges and other property. Besides this, with the loss of only ninety men, he dispersed over seventeen hundred Home Guards, captured seventeen towns, in which he destroyed war material, and marched above one thousand miles, and recruited his force of eight hundred and seventy men, to twelve hundred."

After Col. Morgan's return from Kentucky into Tennessee, the latter part of July, he removed his headquarters to Hartsville, a small town on the north bank of the Cumberland, some twelve or fifteen miles from Gallatin, in a direct line, but much farther than this by the river.

There was a Federal force, mostly Kentuckians, in possession of Gallatin, commanded by Col. Boone. Col. Morgan determined to capture the town, Yankees and all, and to this end sent a force under Capt. Desha to execute his purpose. This was on the morning of the 12th of August. The detachment was accompanied by George A. Ellsworth, telegraph operator, who had, on so many occasions, rendered Col. Morgan valuable assistance while in Kentucky. The morning was beautifully bright; the sun had scarcely risen when the party found themselves within two miles of the town. Dashing forward so as to catch the Federal Colonel unawares, the Confederates were demanding the surrender of the place before the Yankees knew aught of their unwelcome presence in their vicinity. The movement was *comme il faut*. The Federals were completely surprised. No resistance whatever was offered, but surrender came as if it had been a premeditated thing. The men, with their Colonel was parolled by Captain Desha. When, however, the parolled Colonel and his men reached Louisville, a few days afterwards, they were arrested on a charge of cowardice, and sent forward to Camp Chase for imprisonment.

Col. Boone was severely reprimanded for yielding his command into the hands of the enemy without a struggle; but he argued that resistance under the circumstances, was wholly useless. They were surrounded by the Confederates without a moment's warning. His men were not under arms, there was no organization, nor could any be effected before the rebels were upon them.

While Captain Desha, assisted by Captain McCann of the Cheatham Rifles, was scaring the Yankee Kentuckians out of all sense of propriety by marching upon them *sans cérémonie*, and claiming them as prisoners, Mr. Ellsworth was playing his part of the game by annoying the enemy with despatches. Dashing into Gallatin, on his fine chestnut sorrel steed, booted and spurred like any other brave knight of the Southern cross, he rode quickly up to the principal hotel and inquired in quite a peremptory tone, for the telegraph office.

"At the depot, sir," replied the waiter of the public house looking at him in blank astonishment.

Ellsworth hesitated no longer. Spurring his horse he galloped off at full dash to the depot. Alighting, hurriedly, and throwing the rein over his horse's head, he burst open the door, and sprung up stairs to the bed-room of the sleeping operator, who, aroused by the dreadful noise, looked up from his bed to see—oh horror!—a "rebel" standing over him with a six-shooter presented to his head.

Pale with affright at this most fearful apparition, he sat stark upright in the bed. Could it be so? He rubbed his eyes and gazed wildly up. There it stood. Was it ghost or de'il, or what was tenfold worse than either—an avenging rebel? His hair stood on end. His eyes stared fearfully from their sockets; his lips were pale and motionless; he trembled from head to foot, like one suddenly seized with a strong ague.

"Why are you so scared, man?" said Ellsworth to him. "I do not want your life—behave yourself, and you have nothing to fear. Resist, and you are a dead man. Dress yourself and come with me; Colonel Morgan needs your services in the room below."

The poor affrighted operator, somewhat reassured, sprung from his bed at the word of command and hastily donned his apparel. As he gave the last of a few hurried strokes to his hair, Ellsworth, impatient of waiting, turned upon him and said:

"Now, follow me, sir, to the room below."

The man seized his hat and obeyed the command with alacrity.

"Now, show me all your signals. Mind, no cheat. I will not be imposed on," said Ellsworth, sternly, as the two reached the room and stood beside the desk.

Had the operator thought for a moment of deception, the

blood-thirsty look of the huge revolver which Ellsworth still held in his hand, would have dissipated any such intention.

"Now, let me test the line to Nashville and Louisville."

The Yankee, with a gracious smile, stepped aside.

"O. K.," said Ellsworth; "what is your earliest office hour?"

"Seven thirty minutes, sir," responded the operator, bowing obsequiously.

"And it is now just five," said Ellsworth, taking out his watch and looking at the time; "two hours and a half before I can begin my work."

Ellsworth ordered breakfast for himself and prisoner, and the two sat down side by side to the steaming coffee and smoking rolls as if they had always been the veriest cronies.

"Seven o'clock! we must to our work, sir!" and Ellsworth escorted his new-found friend from the breakfast table back to the office.

Placing Mr. Brooks outside the office under guard, Ellsworth entered and took possession, feeling that he sufficiently understood matters to communicate with any point.

The signal was given at seven and ten minutes. It was from the depot office in Nashville.

"Train left here for Louisville on time."

Another signal, and the operator at Franklin, Kentucky, informed Gallatin that the train had left *on time* for the South.

Ellsworth stepped to the door.

"Tell Captain McCann I wish to see him at this place immediately," he said to a Confederate soldier, who was standing near.

In a few minutes the Captain rushed into the room.

"Any trouble, Ellsworth?"

"The train from Franklin will be due, Captain, in a very

little while. Had you not as well prepare to take charge of her?"

"Certainly, certainly, Ellsworth. I will do so with pleasure"; and the Captain dashed out, called together his men and posted them in proper position for the proposed business.

Soon the train came steaming on, all unconscious of danger. She had scarcely reached the water tank, just outside the town, when the Confederates very politely made known their desire to take her in charge.

This was readily assented to by the engineer and conductor, who saw that resistance or escape was not for a moment to be thought of.

The train from Nashville was due, but there was no indication yet of her arrival.

Ellsworth seating himself, asked of the Nashville operator: "Train No. 6 not yet arrived. What can be the trouble with her?"

The reply soon came. "Guess Morgan's got her; she left on time with twenty-four cars, six loaded."

Bowling Green called Gallatin. "Where is the Nashville train? Heard anything from her?"

"Not yet arrived," responded Ellsworth.

Bowling Green then called Nashville. "Gallatin says No. 6 not yet arrived; have you heard from it?"

Nashville, in reply, said: "No; they left on time."

Bowling Green, quite perturbed and beginning to suspect foul play, called to Nashville: "Any rumors of the enemy between Nashville and Gallatin?"

"Nary rumor!" was the laconic answer.

Gallatin was then informed by Nashville that the passenger train had left on time, bound north.

Inquiry after inquiry was made of Gallatin with regard to

the two trains, both by Nashville and Bowling Green. The invariable response of Gallatin was, "Not yet arrived."

Eleven o'clock came. Nashville, as if aroused by some sudden fury, began to call on Gallatin with great earnestness.

Ellsworth suspected the cause. The cars, having obtained information of the occupancy of Gallatin by the Confederates, had suddenly put back to Nashville and given the alarm. Questions were asked which Ellsworth did not dare to answer, for fear of betrayal.

He stepped to the door and invited in the Federal operator, Mr. Brooks.

"Now, sir," said Ellsworth to him, "I want you to answer Nashville in the most satisfactory manner. I shall listen to your replies, and if there is anything wrong, it will have to be atoned for by a life during the war in a Dixie prison."

"All shall be right, sir," responded the accommodating operator, glad to be at his old work again.

Nashville, with suspicions highly aroused, called to Gallatin: "What was the name of that young lady you accompanied to Major Foster's?"

"Be careful," enjoined Ellsworth, leaning over the shoulder of the operator. "Give a correct reply!"

"I don't remember of going to Major Foster's with any young lady," was the response.

"What about that nitric acid I sent you the other day?" asked Nashville.

"You sent me no nitric acid."

"Is that correct?" and Ellsworth eyed the operator sternly.

"Correct, sir."

Nashville, yet suspicious: "Mr. Marshall, the Superintendent of Railroads, is not yet satisfied that you are not Morgan's operator, and wished you to tell him who you desired to take your place while you were gone on leave of absence, how long you wished to be gone, and where did you wish to go?"

Gallatin responded: "Tell Mr. Marshall that I wished Mr. Clayton to take my place, while I got a week's leave to go to Cincinnati."

Nashville was convinced, and soon there came over the wires the following order:

"*To Murphy, Conductor, Gallatin:*

"You will run to Edgefield Junction to meet and pass trains Nos. 4 and 6, and pass them both at that point. Answer how you understand.

B. MARSHALL."

The answer was promptly returned, that the instructions would be obeyed.

Nashville informed Ellsworth that "trains Nos. 4 and 6 had left again at eleven fifteen minutes."

About 4 o'clock in the afternoon, Nashville again called lustily on Gallatin: "Trains Nos. 4 and 6 are back again, the second time. We have positive information that the enemy is in possession of Gallatin. Where is Murphy?"

It was unnecessary to practice the deception farther. The cars would not come.

At five o'clock Ellsworth sent the following to George D. Prentice:

"GALLATIN, August 12, 1862.

"*George D. Prentice, Louisville, Ky.:*

"Your prediction, in yesterday's paper, regarding my whereabouts, is like most of the items from your pen. You had better go to Jeffersonville to sleep to-night.

"JOHN H. MORGAN,

"Commanding Brigade."

A lady, beautiful and sprightly, accompanied by Capt. McCann, and two other ladies, made her appearance in the office, and was introduced to Mr. Ellsworth.

"Will you, Mr. Ellsworth, send a message to Prentice for me?" she said, laughing.

"Assuredly I will, with pleasure."

She turned to the desk, and hurriedly write her dispatch:

"GALLATIN, August 12, 1862.

"*George D. Prentice, Louisville, Ky.:*

"Your friend, Colonel John H. Morgan, and his brave followers, are enjoying the hospitalities of this town, to-day.

"Wouldn't you like to be here? The Colonel has seen your $100,000 reward for his head, and offers $100,000 better for yours, at short range.

"Wash. Morgan, whom you published in your paper some time ago, when he was in Knoxville, accompanies his cousin John, with four hundred Indians. He seeks no scalp but yours.

"A SECESH LADY."

Mr. Brooks, who was now released from his military position, as prisoner, joined in the conversation of the merry party, with as much zest as any one. He seemed to enjoy highly the whole day's proceedings, and even jested over his morning's fright.

The party repaired to the house of the lady, where, with the assembled fair of the good town of Gallatin, the heroes of the day passed the evening with song and dance, and the graphic recital of thrilling adventure. Every manifestation of joy that the citizens of Gallatin could give at their release from Yankee thraldom, was displayed by all classes.

Captains Desha and McCann, and their men, were welcomed to the best cheer the town could offer— were feted and toasted—and smiled upon by bright eyes, until they were made to appreciate, in some degree, at least, the great favor they had bestowed on the grateful inhabitants.

A Scout for Stuart

A BOUT THIS TIME another new hero was becoming known to the Army of Northern Virginia. The fabulous character of William D. Farley became a living legend in the camps of Jeb Stuart. His activities were greatest in the campaigns of 1862, and he fell in the Battle of Fleetwood, June 9, 1863. But the impress of his bravery and ability had been felt by his companion-in-arms John Esten Cooke, and the Virginian novelist wrote an article about him for a later issue of *The Southern Illustrated News* that gave his memory of Farley to the whole South.

In the old "Army of the Potomac," and then in the "Army of Northern Virginia," there was a man so notable for daring, skill and efficiency as a partisan, that all who valued those great qualities honored him as their chiefest exemplar. He was known among the soldiers as "Farley, the Scout," but that term did not express him fully. He was not only a scout, but a partisan leader; an officer of excellent judgment and magnificent dash; a soldier born, who took to the work with all the skill and readiness of one who engages in that occupation for which, by Providence, he is especially designed.

He served from the beginning of the war to the hard battle of Fleetwood, in Culpeper, fought on the 9th of June, 1863. There he fell, his leg shattered by a fragment of shell, and the brave true soul went to rejoin its Maker.

One of the "chiefest spites of fate," says an elder poet, "is that oblivion which not seldom submerges the greatest names and events." The design of this brief paper is to put upon record some particulars of the career of one of these men— so that, in "the aftertime," which sums up the work and glory of the men of this epoch, his name shall not be lost to memory.

Captain William Downs Farley was born at Laurens village, South Carolina, on the 19th of December, 1835. He was descended, in a direct line, from the "Douglas" of Scotland, and his father, who was born on the Roanoke river, in Charlotte county, Virginia, was one of the handsomest and most accomplished gentlemen of his time. He emigrated to South Carolina at the age of twenty-one, married, and commenced there the practice of law. To the son, the issue of this marriage, he gave the name of William Downs Farley, after his father-in-law, Colonel William F. Downs, a distinguished lawyer, member of the Legislature, and an officer of the War of 1812. The father of this Colonel Downs was Major Jonathan Downs, a patriot of the times of '76; his mother, a daughter of Captain Louis Saxon, also distinguished in our first great struggle; thus our young partisan of 1863 had fighting blood in his veins, and, in plunging into the present contest, only followed the traditions of his race.

From earliest childhood he betrayed the instincts of the man of genius. Those who recollect him, then, declare that his nature seemed composed of two mingled elements—the one gentle and reflective, the other ardent and enthusiastic. Passionately fond of Shakespeare and the elder poets, he loved to wander away into the woods, and, stretched beneath some great oak, pass hour after hour in dreamy musing—but if, at such times, he heard the cry of the hounds and the shouts of his companions, his dreams were dissipated, and, throwing aside his volume, he would join in the chase with headlong ardor.

At the age of seventeen, he made, in company with a friend, the tour of the Northern States, and then was sent to the University of Virginia, where his education was completed. The summer vacation gave him an opportunity of making a pedestrian excursion through Virginia; and thus, having enlarged his mind by study and travel through the North and a portion of the South, he returned to South Carolina. Here he occupied himself in rendering assistance to his father, who had become an invalid, and, we believe, commenced the practice of the law. His love of roving, however, did not desert him, and his father's business required repeated journeys into the interior of the State. The scenery of the mountains proved a deep and lasting source of joy to him, and, standing on the summits of the great ranges, he has been seen to remain in such rapt contemplation of the landscape, that he could scarcely be aroused and brought back to the real world. These expeditions undoubtedly fostered in the youthful South Carolinian that ardent love of every thing connected with his native State, which, with his love of wild adventure, constituted the controlling elements of his being.

"He had now attained," a friend writes, "the pride and maturity of manhood. There were few handsomer or more prepossessing men. As a young man, after the battle of Culpeper, in speaking of the loss of Farley and Hampton, said, 'two of the handsomest men in our State have fallen.' His figure was of medium height, elegantly formed, graceful, well knit, and, from habitual exercise on the gymnasium, possessing a remarkable degree of strength and activity. His hair was dark brown, his eyebrows and lashes were so dark, and so shaded the dark grey eyes beneath, as to give them the appearance of blackness. His manner was, generally, quiet, polished and elegant; but let him be aroused by some topic which awoke his enthusiasm (Secession and the Yankees, for instance), and he suddenly stood transformed before you; and in the flashing eye and changing cheek you beheld the dashing 'Hero of the Potomac!' "

The same authority says:

"His moral character was pure and noble—'Sans peur et sans reproche.' It is a well-known fact among his friends and associates, that ardent spirits of any kind never passed his lips until the first battle of Manassas, being sick with measles, he fought until almost fainting, and accepted a draught from the canteen of a friend. This was the *first* and *last* drink he ever took.

"His father, whose last hours he watched with untiring care and attention, died just before the opening of the war. Captain Farley had, from an early age, taken great interest in the political affairs of the country; he was a warm advocate of State Rights, and now entered into the spirit of Secession with eagerness and enthusiasm. He was very instrumental in bringing about a unanimity of opinion on this subject in his own district.

"He made frequent visits to Charleston, with the hope of being in the scene of action should an attack be made on the city, and was greatly chagrined that the battle of Sumter was fought during a short absence, and he only reached the city on the day following. He was the first man in his district to fly to the defence of Virginia, whose sacred soil he loved with a devotion only inferior to that which he bore his own State. He joined Gregg's regiment, in which he served three months, and on the disbanding of which he became an independent fighter."

From this time commences that career of personal adventure and romantic exploits which made him so famous. Shouldering his rifle—now riding, then on foot—he proceeded to the far outposts nearest to the enemy, and was indefatigable in penetrating their lines, harassing detached parties, and gaining information for Generals Bonham and Beauregard. Falling back with the army from Fairfax, he fought—though so sick that he could scarcely stand—in the first battle of Manassas, and then pursuing the flying enemy, he entered permanently upon the life of the scout, speedily attracting to himself the unconcealed admiration of the whole army. To note the outlines even of his performances at this time, would require thrice the space we have at our disposal. He seemed omnipresent on every portion of our lines; and if any daring deed was undertaken—any expedition which was to puzzle, harass or surprise the enemy, Farley was sure to be there. With three men he took and held Upton's Hill, directly in face of the enemy; on numberless occasions he surprised and shot the enemy's pickets, and with three others, waylaid and attacked a column of several hundred cavalry led by Colonel (afterwards General) Bayard, whose horse he killed, slightly wounding the rider.—This audacious attack was made some ten or fifteen miles beyond our lines, and nothing but a passionate love of the most desperate adventure could have led to it. Farley ambushed the enemy, concealing his little band of three men in some pines; and although they might easily have remained *perdus* until the column passed, and so escaped, Farley determined to attack, and did attack—firing first upon Bayard, and nearly stampeding his whole regiment.

After a desperate encounter he and his little party were all captured or killed, and Farley was taken to the Old Capitol in Washington, where he remained some time in captivity. General Bayard mentioned this affair afterwards in an interview with General Stuart, and spoke in exalted terms of the courage which led Farley to undertake so desperate an adventure.

Released from prison, Farley hastened back to his old "stamping ground" around Centreville, reaching that place in the winter of 1861. He speedily received the most flattering proposals from some eminent officers who were going to the South-West, but chancing to meet General J. E. B. Stuart, that officer took violent possession of him, and thenceforth kept him near his person, as volunteer aid-de-camp. With this arrangement Farley soon became greatly pleased. He had already seen Gen. Stuart at work, and that love of adventure and contempt of danger—the coolness, self-possession and mastery of the situation, however perilous—which characterized both, proved a lasting bond of union between them.

Thenceforth, Farley was satisfied. His position was one which suited his peculiar views and habits admirably. Untrammeled by special duties—never tied down to the routine of command, or the commonplace round of camp duty—free as the wind to go or come whenever and wheresoever he pleased, all the instincts of his peculiar organization had "ample room and verge enough" for their development; and his splendid native traits had the fullest swing and opportunity of display. It was in vain that Gen. Stuart, estimating at their full value his capacities for command, repeatedly offered him position. He did not want any commission; he said his place suited him perfectly, and he believed he could do more service to the cause as scout and partisan, than as a regular line-officer. He had not entered the army, he has often declared to me, for place or position; promotion was not his object; to do as much injury as possible to the hated foe was his sole, controlling sentiment, and he was satisfied to be where he was.

His devotion to the cause was indeed profound and almost passionate. He never rested in his exertions, and seemed to feel as if the success of the struggle depended entirely on his own exertions. A friend once said to him: "If, as in ancient Roman days, an immense gulf should miraculously open, and an oracle should declare that the honor and peace of the country could only be maintained by one of her youths throwing himself into it, do you believe you could do it?" He looked seriously, and answered earnestly and with emphasis, "*I believe I could.*"

This devotion he proved by his tireless energy, his wonderful adventures, his contempt for danger, and the concentration of every faculty of his soul and being upon the pursuit of the enemy. He seemed to hunt Yankees as he had formerly done wild animals in the mountains of South Carolina, and more than once told me that he did not feel as if they were human beings; they were *wolves* that had come to attack our homes, and ought to be dealt with as such, hunted down and destroyed on all occasions. "My principle is," he said one day, "to kill a Yankee wherever I find him. If they don't like that, let them stay at home." He had probably killed a hundred with his own hand.

Thus permanently attached as volunteer aid to Gen. Stuart, Farley thereafter took part in all the movements of the cavalry. He was with them in that hot falling back from Centreville, in March, 1862; in the combats of the Peninsula, where, at Williamsburg, he led a regiment of infantry in the assault; in the battles of Cold Harbour and Malvern Hill, at the second Manassas, Sharpsburg, Fredericksburg, and the scores of minor engagements which marked almost every day upon the outposts. He missed the battle of Chancellorsville, greatly to his regret, having gone home, after an absence of two years, to witness the bombardment of Charleston, and see his family.

It was soon after his return in May, that the fatal moment came which deprived the service of this eminent partisan. At the desperately contested battle of Fleetwood, in Culpeper county, on the 9th of June, 1863, he was sent by Gen. Stuart to carry a message to Col. Butler, of the 2d South Carolina cavalry. He had just delivered his message, and was sitting upon his horse by the Colonel, when a shell, which also wounded Col. Butler, struck him upon the right knee and tore his leg in two at the joint. He fell from the saddle, and was borne to an ambulance, where surgical assistance was promptly rendered. His wound was, however, mortal, and all saw that he was dying.

At his own request the torn and bleeding member, with the cavalier's boot still on, was put in the ambulance, and he was borne from the field. His strength slowly declined, but his consciousness remained. Meeting one whom he knew, he called him by name, and murmured "I am almost gone." He lingered but a few hours, and at twilight of that day, the writer of these lines looked on him in his shroud; the pale, cold features calm and tranquil in their final sleep.

He was clad in his new uniform coat, and looked every inch the soldier, taking his last rest. He had delivered this coat to a lady of Culpeper, and said, "*If anything befalls me, wrap me in this and send me to my mother.*"

Such was the end of the famous partisan. His death has left a void which can scarcely be filled. I believe that this is the sentiment of thousands who never saw him, but who feel acutely the loss which we have experienced in his death. His extraordinary career had become fully known, and a writer some months before his death gave utterance to the sentiment of everyone when he wrote: "The story—the plain, unvarnished story of his career since the war began, is like a tale of old romance. Such abnegation of self! Office and money both spurned, because they seemed to stand in the way of his duty. What thrilling incidents! What strength and courage! and what wonderful escapes! No wonder, as he rides by, we so often hear it exclaimed, 'There goes the famous scout, Farley! The army has no braver man, no purer patriot!' "

We put on record here the following passage from the letter of a lady in Culpeper to his mother, giving, as it does, an outline of the man, and bearing testimony in its simple words, warm from a woman's heart, to the affection which was felt for him:

"My dear madam, I want you to know how we in Virginia admired, appreciated and loved your son. Had he been *her own*, Virginia could not have loved him more; certainly she could not *owe* him more—and so long and so bravely had he fought upon her soil. He was particularly well known in this unfortunate part of the State, which has been, sometimes for months, overrun by our foes. Many families will miss his coming, so daring was he, and so much depended on by General Stuart. He scouted a great deal alone in the enemy's lines, and was often the bearer of letters and messages from loved ones, long unheard from. Often, when we have been cut off from all communication from our own people, he has been the first to come as the enemy were leaving, often galloping up when they were scarcely out of sight—always inspiring us with fresh hope and courage, his cheerful presence itself seeming to us a prophecy of good.

"On Tuesday night, just one week before the battle in

which he fell, he came here, about one o'clock at night. We
were surprised and alarmed to see him, as a large party of
the enemy had passed our very doors only a few hours before.
When my aunt opened the door she found him sitting on the
steps, his head resting on his hands, as if tired and sleepy.
We asked him if he did not know the Yankees were near.
'O yes,' he replied; 'they have been chasing me, and compelled me to lengthen my ride considerably.' He came in,
but said, 'I cannot rest with you long, as I must be riding all
night.' We gave him some bread, honey and milk, which we
knew he loved (he said he had been fasting since morning.)
—'Ah,' said he, 'this is just what I want.' He buckled on his
pistols again before sitting down, and said laughingly to me,
'Lock the doors and listen well, for I'll never surrender.' We
stood in the porch when he left, and watched him walk off
briskly (he had come on foot, having left his horse in the
woods). We hated to see him go out in the dark and rainy
night time, but *he* went cheerfully, so willing was he to
encounter danger, to endure hardships, 'to spend and be
spent' in his country's service."

To "spend and be spent" in the great cause of the South,
was truly this brave spirit's chief delight. These are not idle
words, but the truth in relation to him. The writer of this
piece was long and intimately associated with him, and so far
from presenting an exaggerated picture of him, the incidents
and extracts above given do him only partial justice. I never
saw a braver man, nor one more modest. He had a peculiar
refinement of feeling and bearing which stamped him a
gentleman to the inmost fibre of his being. This delicacy of
temperament was most notable; and it would be difficult to
describe the remarkable union of the most daring courage
and the sweetest simplicity of demeanor in the young partisan. Greater simplicity and modesty was never seen in

human bearing—and so endearing were these traits of his character that children and ladies—those infallible critics—were uniformly charmed with him. One of the latter wrote:

"His death has been a great sorrow to us. He was with us frequently the week before the battle, and won our entire hearts by his many noble qualities, and his superiority to all around him. He talked much about his family; he loved them with entire devotion. He read to us some of your poems and repeated one of his own. I close my eyes and memory brings back to me the thrilling tones of that dear voice, which though heard no more on earth, has added to the melody of heaven."

His manner was the perfection of good breeding, and you saw that the famous partisan, whose exploits were the theme of every tongue, had not been raised, like others of his class, amid rude associates and scenes, but with gently nurtured women, and surrounded by the sweet amenities of home. His voice was a peculiar one—very low and distinct in its tones; and these subdued inflections often produced upon the listener the impression that it was a habit acquired in scouting, when to speak above a murmur is dangerous. The low, clear words were habitually accompanied by a bright smile, and the young man was a favorite with all—so cordial was his bearing, so unassuming his whole demeanor. His personal appearance has already been described, but it may interest some of his friends in the far South to know how he appeared when "at work." He dressed uniformly in a plain suit of gray, wearing a jacket, and over this a dark blue overcoat, with a belt, holding his pistol, tightly drawn around the waist. In his hat he wore the black cavalry feather, and his boots were of that handsome pattern which are worn by Federal officers, with patent leather tops and ornamental thread work. Boots, saddles, sabres, pistols—none of these things cost him or the Confederate States a single dollar. They were all captured—either from sutlers' wagons or the enemies he had slain with his own hand. I never knew him to purchase any portion of his own or his horse's equipment —saddle, bridle, halter, sabre, pistols, belt, carbine, spurs, were all captured from the enemy. His horses were in the same category, and he rarely kept the same riding horse long. They were with great regularity shot under him; and he mounted the first he found running riderless, or from which his pistol hurled one of the enemy.

I have spoken of his modest, almost shy demeanor. All this disappeared in action. His coolness remained unaffected, but he evidently felt himself in his proper element, and entitled to direct others. At such moments his suggestions were boldly made, and not seldom resulted in the rout of the enemy. The cavalry once in motion, the quiet, modest gentleman was metamorphosed into the fiery partisan. He would lead a charge with the reckless daring of Murat, and cheer on the men, with contagious ardor, amid the most furious storm of balls. The thought that there was danger at such moments evidently never crossed his mind. His disregard of personal exposure was supreme, and the idea that he was surrounded by peril never occurred to him. He has repeatedly told the present writer, with that simplicity and sincerity which produce conviction, that in action he was scarcely conscious of the balls and shells flying and bursting around him—that his interest in the general result was so strong as to cause him to lose sight of the danger from them. Those who knew him did not venture to doubt the assertion.

He delighted in the wild charge, the clash of meeting squadrons, and the roar of artillery. All these martial sights and sounds ministered to the passionate ardor of that temperament which made him most at home where balls were whistling and the air oppressive with the odor of battle. But, I think, he even preferred the life of the scout—the long and noiseless hunt for his foe—the exercise of those faculties by means of which an enemy is surprised and destroyed—the single combat with sabre and pistol, often far off in the silence of the woods, where a dead body half concealed amid the grass is all that remains to tell the tale of some desperate hand-to-hand encounter. The number of such contests through which Farley had passed would seem incredible to those who did not know him, and thus comprehend how the naked truth of his career beggared romance. He rarely spoke of these affairs, and never unless to certain persons and under peculiar circumstances. He had a great horror of appearing to boast of his own exploits, and so greatly feared securing the reputation of coloring his adventures that he would rarely speak of them. Fortunately for his memory, many persons witnessed his most desperate encounters, and still live to testify to the reckless daring of the young partisan. With these his eventful career will long remain the subject of fire-side tales; and in the coming days of peace, when years have silvered the hair of his contemporaries, old men will tell their grandchildren of his strange adventures and those noble traits which made his name so famous.

To the world at large, he will always thus appear—as the daring partisan and high-souled lover of his country—as one who risked his life in a hundred desperate encounters, and in all those bloody scenes never quailed or shrunk before a foe, however powerful or dangerous. But to those who lived with him—heard his low, friendly voice, and saw every day his bright, kindly smile—he appears in a different character. To such the loss we have sustained is deeper—it seems irreparable. It was the good fortune of the writer of these lines to thus see the brave young man—to be beside him in the field, and, at home, to share his confidence and friendship. Riding through the summer forests, or wandering on across the fields of broom-straw, near Fredericksburg, last autumn—better still, beside the good log fire of winter—we talked of a thousand things, and I saw what a wealth of kindness, chivalry and honor he possessed—how beautifully the "elements were mixed" in his character. Brave and true—simple and kind—he has passed away; and among those eminent natures which the writer has encountered in this struggle, few are remembered with such admiration and affection as this noble son of Carolina.

The best conclusion of this brief and inadequate sketch will be the mention of the brave partisan in General Stuart's report of the battle of Fleetwood. It is as follows:

"Captain W. D. Farley, of South Carolina, a volunteer aid on my staff, was mortally wounded by the same shell which wounded Colonel Butler, and displayed, even in death, the same loftiness of bearing and fortitude which has characterized him through life. He had served, without emolument, long, faithfully and always with distinction. No nobler champion has fallen. May his spirit abide with us."

What nobler epitaph!

Beauregard Answers Butler

UNION GENERAL BEN F. BUTLER had earned the unsavory nickname of "Bethel Failure" at the battle of Big Bethel, Virginia, in the spring of 1861. In success at New Orleans the next year he earned an even more unsavory reputation as a tyrannical ruler of conquered territory.

Butler's General Orders were anathema to the people of New Orleans, who felt that the bounds of civilized warfare had been passed in the stringency and vindictiveness of his regulations. Most reprehensible of a series of reprehensible edicts was his famous "Women of the Streets" order of May 15, which aroused public opinion of the whole world against him. In issuing such an order Butler served well the propaganda mills of the Confederacy.

Here is General Beauregard's answer to it.

YOUNG LADIES WANTED

IN THE

ENGINEER CORPS

→ • • ← →

A Few Places Yet Left!

→ • • ←

GREAT INDUCEMENTS!

Are offered YOUNG LADIES in the Engineers.

TRY IT!

→ • • ←

COME INTO THE ENGINEERS & BE HAPPY!

→ • • → ← — · · ·

NO HUMBUG!

The ENGINEER CORPS are stationed exclusively on the SEABOARD ! Young ladies fond of *Oysters! Crabs! Eels! Turtles! Catfish! or Clam Soup!* may enjoy this diet all the year round by securing a husband in the ENGINEERS!! LARGE FORTUNES considered *no objection* in the Engineer Corps! Consumptive and delicate YOUNG LADIES of large means, *try the Engineer Corps and the Sea Air!* YOUNG LADIES mourning the loss of wealthy and indulgent parents, and with no sympathising brothers and sisters, *seek consolation in the Engineer Corps.* A hearty welcome is offered; the pleasures of a home by the sounding sea are secured; sympathising hearts are found, and true happiness is warranted only in the ENGINEER CORPS! TRY IT! TRY IT!

APPLY EARLY. Offers received for a few days only.

☞ N B Grass and California Widows need not apply.

104

Head Quarters Western Department,
Corinth, Mississippi, May 19th, 1862.

GENERAL ORDERS,⎱
    No. 44.   ⎰

For the information of this army, the following General Orders No. 28, of the Federal Officer, Major General Butler, ("the Haynau of the North,") commanding at New Orleans, will be read on dress parade:

NOTICE.

HEADQUARTERS DEPARTMENT OF THE GULF,
NEW ORLEANS, May 15, 1862.

General Orders, No. 28.

As the officers and soldiers of the United States have been subject to repeated insults from the women (calling themselves ladies) of New Orleans, in return for the most scrupulous non-interference and courtesy on our part, it is ordered that hereafter when any female shall, by word, gesture or movement, insult or show contempt for any officer or soldier of the United States, she shall be regarded and held liable to be treated as a woman of the town plying her avocation.

By command of

MAJOR GENERAL BUTLER.

GEO. C. STRONG, A. A. G., Chief of Staff.

Men of the South! shall our mothers, our wives, our daughters and our sisters, be thus outraged by the ruffianly soldiers of the North, to whom is given the right to treat, at their pleasure, the ladies of the South as common harlots? Arouse friends, and drive back from our soil, those infamous invaders of our homes and disturbers of our family ties.

(Signed,)   G. T. BEAUREGARD,
                                  General Commanding.

Behind the Lines in Carolina

WILLIAM WYNDHAM MALET was an interested and interesting visitor to the South in the summer of 1862. He left his vicarage at Ardeley, Hertfordshire, England, to go to South Carolina and break to his sister the news of a death in their family. He spent the summer there at the plantations of patrician Plowden C. J. Weston and visited most of the rest of South Carolina as well as Richmond and the mountain country of western North Carolina. His comments on the South are colored with the impressions of an enjoyable visit, but he presents an interesting picture of life behind the lines in an area not yet too much disturbed by the progress of the war.

Perhaps the Southerners were on their best behavior for the Rev. Mr. Malet. Mary Boykin Chesnut in her charming *Diary from Dixie* commented that "everybody has his best foot foremost at McMahon's because the stray Englishman there is supposed to be writing a book." Mrs. McMahon's was the choicest boardinghouse of Columbia and it was there that Malet met Mrs. Chesnut, the poet Paul Hamilton Hayne, Governor Francis Pickens, and others of the most prominent citizens of South

Carolina. He had little reason to form any but a favorable opinion of what he saw.

In the first of the following passages the Englishman describes his arrival at Conwayboro and gives some details about plantation life. Here is a picture of slavery at its paternalistic best. His references to the making of saltpeter is reminiscent of the famous vulgar poem which was later circulated from Selma, Alabama, concerning the making of saltpeter for use in manufacturing gunpowder from the "chamber-lye" from Selma homes. Columbia is described in the next excerpt from Malet's *An Errand to the South in the Summer of 1862*. Here the reference to the bells is to the church bells which had been collected to melt into Confederate cannons. The idea was the subject of a Confederate poem and of an etching by Adalbert J. Volck, but the donation of the bells was more of a patriotic gesture than the fulfillment of a real military need.

On Friday the 13th of June I arrived at the place of refuge. Here was an English lady with her little maid, both from the peaceful vale of Taunton, "dwelling among her own people," the sable descendants of Canaan, as safely as if in their native land, protected by county police—yea, safer; for they slept with their doors and windows unbolted, and did not feel afraid.

The county is called Horry (after some colonial governor), in the north-east corner of the State of South Carolina, which is 500 by 450 miles. Conwayboro' is the county town, having the county courthouse and gaol, with its sheriff and mayor, &c.; the population about 350. There are two churches —one Presbyterian, one Methodist; the houses are never more than two stories high—most of them only one—all built of wood, with brick chimneys; raised on brick or wooden piers two feet or more high. Every negro hut is built in this way, keeping the floors very dry, and free from snakes, which rather abound at Conwayboro': from the earth under every house, saltpetre is obtainable. A contractor told me he found fifteen pounds under a negro's house built ten years; and a house of that size—say thirty feet square—would yield one pound and a-half per annum. About three inches of earth is scraped up, and water percolated in casks, evaporation developing the saltpetre: by this means, and by sulphur from the north-west part of South Carolina, and charcoal which the endless woods supply, the army is provided with abundance of gunpowder. The houses are far apart, placed in their own gardens—like the compounds of our Indian bungalows—with their negro huts nearly all surrounded by neat fences. Thus Conwayboro', though of small population, is of considerable extent, fields lying between some of the houses. The court-house and gaol are of brick, the former having the usual façade of Doric pillars. Evergreen oaks cast their welcome shade in all directions; fig-trees and vines cool the houses; peach orchards yield their delicious fruit. The treatment for these peach-trees is very simple; viz., baring the roots in winter, and just before spring covering them with a coat of ashes and then with earth: with this they beat any wall-fruit I ever saw in England. The gardens produce abundance of tomatos, okras, egg-plants, &c. Tomatos in soup and stewed are the standard dish; and they are also eaten as salads.

Every house was full; many refugees from the coast about

George-Town, fifty miles distant, having obtained lodgings. The house I came to is on a bluff, looking over a "branch" of the Wakamaw river: the negroes' huts formed quite a little hamlet of itself, the number of souls being forty; these buildings being ready, besides stabling, &c. for four horses, and about fifty acres of land, made it convenient for Mrs. W——'s purpose, whose plantation too was within a drive, about forty-two miles down the river, where 350 negroes used to be employed; but a fresh estate of 800 acres was just bought about 300 miles inland, to which 150 were removed by rail. Never did I see a happier set than these negroes. For six months had this lady been left with them alone. Her husband's regiment had been ordered to the Mississippi, about 1000 miles west. In this army the officers are all elected; the men of each company choose the lieutenants and captains, and the captains choose the field-officers from themselves, the colonel appointing his adjutant. This gentleman had procured Enfield rifles from England for 120 men of his regiment, the 10th South Carolina, before the Queen's proclamation came out, and cloth for their clothing, but he himself served for several months as a private: he has since refused promotion beyond captain. All his ambition is with his company, which is said to be a pattern of discipline and dash—indeed the whole regiment commanded by Lieutenant-Colonel Manigault is General Bragg's "pet regiment." The negro servants watched for tidings from their master by the tri-weekly mails as anxiously as their mistress. This gentleman, and some other masters, deemed it the best policy to be open with their negroes, and let them know the real cause of the war; and that probably the Abolitionists would try and induce them to desert. On the 30th December this Mr. W—— appointed a special prayer and fast-day at his plantation church, and after service addressed the negroes, previous to his leaving for the House of Representatives, of which he was a member (elected for George-Town). Not only women, but the men wept: they said they would never leave him—they loved their "massa and missis:" and not one of them has left. Lately two Southern gentlemen, on their way to George-Town, met one of them, and pretending to be Yankees, to try the man, asked him if he would go with them to the United States fleet, and be free. He asked, how he could leave his master and mistress?—"No! he would never do that!" Fifteen negroes were bringing up a "flat" (i.e., a river barge) load of rice to Conwayboro'; en route they heard of the approach of some Yankee gunboats, when they ran the flat up a creek till they were clear away, and then continued their course. They declared they would have swamped the flat and its cargo, if the Yankees had discovered it, and would themselves have taken to the swamps, where no white man could follow them: 300 barrels of rice were thus brought up and sold by Mrs. W——, at the Boro', for eleven and a-half dollars a barrel (the half-dollar going for commission) retail to the inhabitants; the usual price before the war being sixteen to eighteen dollars, and from four to six dollars a cwt.; for this boon the neighborhood was most grateful.

Now I hear the sounds peculiar to this region, the land of sand, of woods, of "branches," of creeks, and swamps:—the hollow bark of the crocodile; the bellowing of the bull-frog, all night long—the note of summer, just as the cuckoo's is in England; also, breaking the silence of the night, the mournful cry of the "whip-poor-will." I had feared, from this latitude being about that of Morocco, it would be too hot for singing-birds; but, on the contrary, the mocking-bird, plain to eye but charming to ear, sent forth its varied song by night and by day; the nightingale's notes at night, and the thrush and the blackbird's warble by day. Some told me they imitate caterwauling, but I was glad not to hear that phase of their song. It is a plain bird, having black, brown, and white feathers, about the size of our thrush; it is heard everywhere in North and South Carolina and Virginia, and all through the spring and summer. On the 19th June the thermometer at Conwayboro' was 80° at eleven A.M., and 76° at nine P.M.: during the day a heavy thunderstorm echoed through the forests; the wind here blowing over lofty pines, sounds like the wind at sea.

There are seven negro cottages around the bungalow. Mrs. W—— gives out supplies of food weekly, viz., corn flour, rice and bacon, and salt;—molasses, of which they are very fond, is now scarcely to be had; but they have a little, and plenty of honey and milk, and they are well clothed. In all the houses of negroes the boys and girls have separate bed-rooms. After dark the court-yard in front of the cottages is illuminated with pine-wood bonfires, which destroy the mosquitoes, and the children dance round the blaze; never a company of negroes, but some one plays a fiddle, and often tambourine or banjo to accompany. Here the coachman, "Prince," is a capital fiddler; his favourite tunes are "Dixie Land" and country dances. Just before bed-time more solemn sounds are heard: the negro is demonstrative in his religion, and loud and musical were heard every evening the hymns, many of them meeting in one of the houses. Remarkable for correctness are their songs, and both men and women's voices mingled in soft though far-sounding harmony. Some old church tunes I recognised. Sometimes they sent forth regular "fugues;" then, after a pause, would come the prayer, offered up by "Jemmy," or some "gifted" man. I could over-hear some of the words; e. g. "O Lord, in whose palm of his hand be the waters of the ocean—who can remove moun-

tains—who weighs the earth in a balance—who can still the
waves of the storm—who can break the pines of the forest
—who givest us a land of rivers of waters—O Jesus! who died
on the cross for us—O forgive us our sins; O help us in this
time of trial and need. Protect our massa far away; protect
our brothers 'Hector' and 'Caesar' with him; defend us now
we are away from home; defend our friends and relatives
at home, &c." All the 350 negroes (except old Pemba, about
70 years of age, who had been brought from Africa, when a
little girl) were born on the estate: like Abraham's servants,
"born in his own house." The smile and voice of the negroes
are most agreeable, and their manners very polite. The
names are curious: "Prince," the capital coachman, a regular
Jehu, not afraid of any horse, drove me out; his assistant-
groom is "Agrippa." Prince always has a book with him on
the box, which he reads directly he stops at a visit; his favourite book is "Pilgrim's Progress." Prince has a son, "Napoleon.". . .

On 3rd July I started for Columbia and Winsboro'. The
train from Wilmington arrived at Fairbluff at 12.30 night;
cars full of wounded men from Richmond, reached Kingsville, 100 miles, at 7. A.M. Near this place the Wateree River
and its tributaries and swamps are traversed by a viaduct
raised on timber tressel-work for five miles. Kingsville is the
junction of the branches to Augusta and Columbia; therefore many of the poor wounded soldiers got out. It was sad
to see them. The station hotel, by no means adequate to
the demand now put upon it by the war, did not meet their
wants; the hot fries and beefsteaks of the American breakfast
they could not taste. I asked "mine host" if there was nothing
else. "No—only pay 75 cents, and sit down." Several of them
said, "We only want a little milk and water and a biscuit,"—
which were not to be had; water was indeed scarce! They

covered the station, some on stretchers, some on crutches— no one to attend to them. It was twenty miles to Columbia, which we did in the luggage-car of a freight train. On 4th July I arrived at Columbia, capital of South Carolina, a very pretty city, called the "Garden City." Every street has an avenue of trees and one long street, a double one. I was provided with a letter to the Governor, Mr. Pickens, by the kindness of Mr. Mason; and I lost no time in making use of it. Found him at his office, and, luckily, the general of the district with him. I reported the state of things at Kingsville, and orders were issued then and there for an assistant surgeon to be stationed there, and a wayside hospital erected, with all the needments for the sick and wounded. I avoided the crowded hotels, and put up at Mrs. McMahon's boarding-house. These houses are to be found in every town, and very nice they are, having the table-d'hote system well carried out; the drawing-room, pianoforte, &c. Never was there a cleaner house than Mrs. McMahon's; and most agreeable society. She had Colonel Hayne, aide-de-camp to the general, a poet and a friend of poets; Mrs. Bartow, the widow of one of the brave men who fell at the battle of Bull Run, 1861; and Colonel Chesnut (one of the State Council), with his lady, and several others. Our good hostess gave us a great treat in real tea and coffee; but her supply was nearly out.

On the 5th of July, Governor Pickens took me a drive round and through the city. It stands high, looking down South on the Congeree River, which runs from west to east; the Congeree and Wateree meeting a few miles off make the Santee. The country is pretty, healthy, and undulating; they call it a "rolling" country. The soil is good; substratum rocky. The gardens and fields are very productive. The water is excellent.

The Governor was for three years United States Minister at St. Petersburg. He showed his determination to stand up for the state rights in the affair of Fort Sumter in April, 1861. Of course we talked about that. . . .

The hanging gardens and public park of Columbia, with fountains playing among beautiful shrubberies, slope down towards the rapid and winding Congeree. Every evening they were crowded with the promenaders and beautiful children, enjoying the cool vesper breeze. Many are the gardens here, but for elegance and beauty, and sweetness of flowers, I suppose Colonel Preston's is equal to any in the world. It is a land redolent with fruit and flowers, and milk and honey abound.

In the evening, at a veritable tea, I was introduced to Mrs. Pickens, one of the fairest of the fair daughters of Louisiana. Great was the luxury of high-flavoured tea from Russia, and coffee from Mocha, after weeks of burnt rye for coffee, and water bewitched with short supply of tea; and, while travelling, only sassafras, or holly tea at the best. In these warm latitudes the custom of paying visits in the evening is most agreeable, and this is the thing to do. Dinner is done from two to four; then I daresay many a siesta is taken, to string the bow for the soiree quivers of conversation. . . .

I was rejoiced to hear, that of the hundreds of bells which had been sent to the Columbian depot from churches and plantations, to be made into cannon, not one had been melted. "How so?" said I. The answer was, "We are foundering our own cannon from our own iron mines, and we have taken a great many from the enemy."

General Robert Edward Lee

THE CONFEDERACY produced two undying heroes. And the first of these was Robert E. Lee. Posterity has made of him truly a knight beyond compare. But Lee's fame is no myth. At the beginning of the war his services were as eagerly sought by the Union as by the Confederacy. How he followed his state into the war as his conception of his highest patriotic duty and led the Confederate armies to their greatest glories is an oft-told tale, but it resumes a new freshness in the words with which it was freshly told in Richmond in 1864 in a booklet called *The War and Its Heroes*.

The achievements of this distinguished officer form the most remarkable chapter, not only in the history of the present gigantic war, but, in some respects, in the entire annals of war. To detail them minutely would fill a volume even larger than this, and we, therefore, leave this agreeable task to the future historian. In the halcyon days, which we opine are not far distant, the student of history will delight to dwell upon them, even as we delight to find rescued from oblivion any little circumstance of early youth in which Napoleon or Washington was concerned.

Robert Edward Lee is a member of the old historical family of Westmoreland Lees. He is the youngest son, by a second marriage of General Henry Lee, better known to history by his *soubriquet* of "Light Horse Harry," the friend and confidant of Washington, and the author of one of the most pleasant histories ever written by a Virginian. He was born at Stratford, in Westmoreland county, in 1806 [*sic*], in the same house and in the same chamber in which Richard Henry Lee and Francis Lightfoot Lee, two signers of the Declaration of Independence, were born.

He entered West Point, as a cadet from his native State, in 1825. On the first day of his entrance he took the head of his class, and kept it until he graduated in 1829, having never been marked with a demerit, or been subjected to a reprimand, or received any other species of punishment whatever, during the whole time of his residence. Having graduated at the head of his class, he was, of course, selected for service in the corps of topographical engineers, which was always filled from the ranks of the highest graduates. He entered upon his new field of duty in July, 1829, with the brevet rank of second lieutenant. We hear no more of him until 1835, when he was appointed assistant astronomer for fixing the boundary line between Ohio and Michigan. He became first lieutenant in September, 1836, and captain in July, 1838. In 1845, he was chief engineer in the army of General Wool, in Mexico. In 1847, he was brevetted major, for "gallant and meritorious conduct" in the battle of Cerro Gordo, fought April 18th, 1847. He received a second brevet for "gallant and meritorious conduct" in the battles of Contreras and Cherubusco, and was now lieutenant-colonel by brevet. For gallant and meritorious conduct in the battle of Chapultepec, where he was wounded, on the 1st September, 1852, he was appointed superintendent of the Military Academy. How long he continued in that post we do not know; but we find him, in 1858, lieutenant-colonel of the famous regiment of cavalry of which Albert Sydney Johnston was colonel, and as such highly distinguishing himself in the desperate fight with the Indians on the prairies of Texas, which created so much excitement at the time. Nor do we know how he came to be at Washington at the time of John Brown's attempt at insurrection; but we *do* know that he was sent by President Buchanan, with a body of marines, to capture the outlaw, and that he did it.

Such is a brief outline of the services rendered to the old United States by Robert E. Lee during the long period of thirty years.

In the old army he was believed by all officers, almost without exception to be, by many degrees, the most accomplished soldier in the whole army. His superiority, indeed, was so incontestable, that it excited no jealousy whatever in any quarter. When his reputation had been somewhat impaired for the time, by his campaign in Western Virginia, a distinguished officer, now in the service of Virginia, but heretofore for many years an officer in the old army of the United States, observed that injustice was done to General Lee—that in the old army, each officer perfectly understood the calibre of every other—that Lee was, by the acknowledgment of all, the first man in the service—and that, if an opportunity were afforded him, he would prove what he was, in a way that would silence scepticism forever. The opinion entertained of him by General Scott is well known. "Lee," said that vain and self-sufficient old coxcomb, "is the greatest military genius in America, myself not excepted." He might very well say so, if it be true, as has often been said, that to the genius of Lee he owed the laurels he had reaped in Mexico. Whether this anecdote, however, be true or false, it is well known that he regretted the loss of Lee more than that of all the other officers, when Lee determined to stand by the land that gave him birth, and that he made the most strenuous efforts to retain him. He might as well have attempted to roll back the earth in its daily revolution upon its axis. General Lee is the most thorough of all Virginians. Virginian in sentiment and feeling, his father's son could scarcely avoid being; but he is more thoroughly Virginian than could be expected even from a person born and connected like himself. So intense is this feeling, that he has been heard to say, even since his wonderful successes have placed him at the very head of his age, that he had but one ambition, and that was to be Governor of Virginia. It was, therefore, as certain as any future event could be, that as soon as Virginia seceded, he would go along with her. She did secede in April, 1861, and a few days after, her Convention appointed him Commander-in-Chief of her forces. He arrived in Richmond about the 25th of April, having sent in his resignation of his commission in the old army some time before.

General Lee immediately entered upon the duties of his office. It may be presumed that they were of the most arduous character; but difficulties disappeared beneath his fingers, as though they had been dissolved by magic. He had an army to organize and drill, the materials of war to create almost out of nothing, the troops to arm, clothe and feed, after they had been collected, and all the duties of a minister of war to discharge, in addition to his more immediate duties of General-in-Chief. It is impossible, for the want of materials, to furnish an account of his administration between the time of entering upon his office and that of turning the army of Virginia over to the Confederacy. When the difficulties with which he was surrounded are taken into consideration, we feel convinced that his services will bear a comparison with those of Carnot, or any other war minister that ever existed. When President Davis made his appointments of generals, he was the third on the list; General Cooper being first and General Sydney Johnston second. The appointments were made with reference to the rank held by each officer in the old army.

After the defeat and death of General Garnett, General Lee was appointed by President Davis to take command of our forces in Western Virginia. In the early part of August he repaired to his command, carrying with him reinforcements enough to swell his force to 16,000 men. On the short campaign which ensued it is not our purpose to dwell. It is well known to have failed, whether through any fault of the General it is impossible, among conflicting statements, to decide. The hopes of the people were very high when he took command, and their confidence in his skill unbounded. When, therefore, the campaign resulted in a failure, there was no measure to the indignation of the country. President Davis, however, who is himself a military man, and had the whole facts in his possession, formed a very different opinion of the case from any that had been formed by those who knew nothing but what had been gathered from the newspapers. He acquitted General Lee thoroughly, and that acquittal must be considered decisive. It was not so considered at the time, however, by the people. General Lee's military reputation fell immeasurably, and from one of the most popular generals in the service he became decidedly unpopular. His case presents one of the strongest examples on record of the folly and injustice of judging any man by the standard of popular appreciation. Had he not had an opportunity afforded him of proving what he really was, he would have gone down to posterity as an inefficient officer, entirely unequal to the command of even a brigade.

Immediately on his return from this unsuccessful campaign, General Lee was appointed to command in the military district of which Charleston is the centre. His skill as an engineer had never been doubted, notwithstanding his ill success as Commander-in-Chief; and he was expected to put it in practice in fortifying the city and harbor of Charleston. He succeeded completely. Having accomplished this object, General Lee returned to Richmond. It was soon after this that our disasters in Kentucky and Tennessee began to occur. Their effect upon the country was depressing in the extreme. Congress, at that time in session, passed a joint resolution appointing General Lee Commander-in-Chief. Whether this act was vetoed by the President we do not know, but he seems of his own accord to have placed General Lee in a position almost equivalent; in one which gave him, in fact, the largest share in the control and direction of the war, It was probably owing to his advice that the policy of concentration was adopted as the only one that could enable our inferior forces to contend successfully with the huge levies of the Yankees.

We now come to the *real* commencement of General Lee's career, a career so brilliant as to establish his claim to be reckoned among the greatest captains that have risen in the world. The army of McClellan was around Richmond. It had been, at the commencement of the Peninsula campaign, 168,000 strong. It had suffered severely in battle, and more severely still from disease. Still it numbered, according to the best estimate we have been able to make, at least 130,000 men. General Johnston had gained a great victory at Seven Pines, but the country was deprived of his services at this critical juncture by the severe wound which he had received in that battle. President Davis believed that nobody could so well supply his place as General Lee, and he was accordingly ordered to take the command. He did so on the 1st of June. He saw, at a glance, that the seige of Richmond could not be raised without beating the enemy out of the formidable works in which they had entrenched themselves, and he immediately set about devising the means to accomplish it. How it was done we leave to the future historian to describe. It suffices our purpose to chronicle the result. In the course of one week, General Lee, by a series of combinations unsurpassed in the history of war, had succeeded in beating the enemy out of a succession of fortifications of the most formidable character, had driven him from around Richmond, to a place thirty miles below, and had relieved all fears for the safety of the capital. That he did not completely destroy the enemy was no fault of his.

General Lee is the most successful general of the age. His exploits are brilliant almost beyond example. When we say this of a man who commands an immense army, it is supererogatory to say anything of his talents. Nothing but genius of the highest order can conceive the combinations necessary to insure the uninterrupted success of so large a host, over an enemy greatly superior in force. In all departments of science his acquirements are great, and has besides an uncommon stock of general information. His judgment is as quick as his military glance, and it rarely deceives. Withal he is one of the most unpretending men in the world —a thorough gentleman in his manner—very affable to all who approach him—and extremely amiable in private life. He is about five feet ten inches high, was eminently handsome in his youth, is still one of the finest looking men in the army, rides like a knight of the old crusading days, is indefatigable in business, and bears fatigue like a man of iron.

Morgan in Kentucky

THE RAIDS of the romantic Morgan thrilled Southerners throughout the Confederacy. What matter the numerical superiority of the North, what matter the blockade, what matter the output of thousands of Yankee factories if a small body of partisans could outwit and outfight the enemy?

Here is Morgan's own proclamation to his men praising them for their actions in late August, 1862.

Proclamation.

Headquarters Morgan's Brigade,
Hartsville, Tenn., *August 22,* 1862.

Soldiers: Your gallant bearing during the last two days will not only be inscribed in the history of the country and the annals of this war, but is engraven deeply in my heart.

Your zeal and devotion on the 20th, at the attack of the trestle-work at Saundersville, and of the Springfield Junction Stockade—your heroism during the two hard fights of yesterday, have placed you high on the list of those patriots who are now in arms for our Southern rights.

All communication cut off betwixt Gallatin and Nashville —a body of 300 infantry totally cut up or taken prisoners— the liberation of those kind friends arrested by our revenge-ful foes—for no other reason than their compassionate care of our sick and wounded, would have been laurels sufficient for your brows. But, soldiers, the utter annihilation of Gen. Johnson's brigade—composed of twenty-four picked com-panies of regulars, and sent on purpose to take us, raises your reputations as soldiers, and strikes fear into the craven hearts of your enemies. General Johnson and his staff, with 200 men taken prisoners, sixty-four killed and 100 wounded, attests the resistance made, and bears testimony to your valor.

But our victories have not been achieved without loss. We have to mourn some brave and dear comrades. Their names will remain in our breasts, their fame outlives them. They died in defence of a good cause. They died like gallant soldiers—with their front to the foe.

Officers and men! Your conduct makes me proud to com-mand you! Fight always as you fought yesterday, and you are invincible.

John H. Morgan,
Colonel Commanding Cavalry

A Hit at Everybody

B UT NO ARMY has ever been all heroes and heroics. Like all other large bodies of men, the Confederate Army had its shirkers, its malcontents, its cowards, and its criminals. Officers, especially during the first years of the war when company grade officers were generally elected, were not always of the highest caliber. It speaks well, however, of the army as a whole that there was so little of misconduct that the Confederates could freely poke fun at it.

The following piece was intended for a soldier paper, *The Army Argus*, but reached first the editors of the Mobile *Register* and was published in that paper. It appears here as later reprinted, for a wider audience, in the columns of *The Southern Literary Messenger*.

The following document, intended for the "Army Argus," while that paper was published at Corinth, having lost its way, has fallen into our hands. If its generalities hit anybody in particular, it is their fault, and those who are not hurt by it, who, we are sure, must constitute the great majority in the different classes enumerated, cannot fail to be amused by it, and perhaps instructed as to the errors into which they may be in danger of falling unsuspiciously.

<*Mobile Register.*

MILITARY CATECHISM.

By Col. T. C. J****

Scene—School-room—Class in Military Affairs stand up.

Question. What is the first duty of a Brigadier General?

Answer. To swear by note.

Q.—What is the second duty?

A.—To drink every day a large quantity of bad whiskey.

Q.—What is the third duty?

A.—To be constantly astonished that these and other feats do not bring him a Major General's commission.

Q.—What is the first duty of a Colonel?

A.—To put three stars on his collar.

Q.—What is the second duty?

A.—To see that his regiment is never put to such useless work as drilling in the School of the Battalion.

Q.—What is the third duty?

A.—To imitate the Brigadier Generals in a small way, especially in the fine arts of swearing and drinking.

Q.—What is the first duty of a Captain?

A.—To forget all the promises he made to the boys when he was elected, and put on dignified airs in the presence of his old associates.

Q.—What is the second duty?

A.—To get a finer uniform than his Colonel.

Q.—What the third duty?

A.—To become the best poker-player in the army.

Q.—What is the first duty of an Adjutant General?

A.—To become so huffish that every one will dislike to do business with him.

Q.—What is the second duty?

A.—To fill his office with young squirts, as clerks and assistants, to look fiercely at visiters.

Q.—What is the third duty?

A.—To perpetually intrigue for a higher position in the line, provided it is not attended with personal danger.

Q.—What is the duty of a regular aid?

A.—To make himself important.

Q.—What is the second duty?

A.—To make himself very important.

Q.—What is the third duty?

A.—To look upon those gentlemen who, through patriotic motives, or admiration of his chief, volunteer to serve the country without compensation, in the capacity of an aid, as a sort of interloper that interferes with his importance.

Q.—What is the first duty of a Quartermaster?

A.—A great Captain has laid down the three great duties of this officer. He says the first duty is to make himself comfortable.

Q.—What does he say is the second duty?

A.—To make himself damned comfortable.

Q.—What does he lay down as his third duty?

A.—To make everybody else damned uncomfortable.

Q.—What is the first duty of a Commissary?

A.—To take all the delicacies provided in the army for his own use.

Q.—What is the second duty?

A.—To share sparingly said delicacies with his friends, and never let them go into such vulgar places as the mouths of sick soldiers.

Q.—What is the third duty?

A.—To be very particular to see that the requisitions for rations are in proper form—all the t's crossed and i's dotted —when presented by soldiers who are sick or who have had nothing to eat for three or four days.

Q.—What is the first duty of a Medical Director?

A.—To permit the sick and wounded to take care of themselves.

Q.—What is the second duty?

A.—To learn the sick and wounded to be of little trouble to the medical department, and to this end to constantly ship those mortally wounded, or *in extremis*, to distant points, without attendants, and without any thing to eat or drink.

Q.—What is the third duty?

A.—To employ a good part of his time in cursing the physician, in charge of those distant hospitals, for letting so many of the sick and wounded die.

Q.—What is the first duty of a surgeon?

A.—Under the names of drugs and medicines, to purchase a full supply of good liquors.

Q.—What is the second duty?

A.—To cause all private cellars to be searched, and all the good brandies found there to be confiscated, lest the owners should smuggle them to the soldiers, give them away and make the whole army drunk.

Q.—What is the third duty?

A.—To see that he and his assistants drink up all of said liquors.

Q.—What is the fourth duty?

A.—To wear the largest amount of gold lace, and be always absent from the post of danger and of duty.

Q.—What is the first duty of a Chaplain?

A.—Never to mention the subject of religion to the soldiers.

Q.—What is the second duty?

A.—To preach to the regiment only once a year, and not that unless specially requested by the Colonel.

Q.—What is the third duty?

A.—To grumble all the time about the smallness of his pay.

Q.—What is the first duty of pickets?

A.—To go to sleep on their posts.

Q.—What is the second duty?

A.—To wake up when the enemy's pickets invite them to come over and take a drink.

Q.—What is the third duty?

A.—To be "driven in" upon the explosion of the first shell.

Q.—What is the first duty of an army?

A.—To destroy as much private property as possible, particularly that belonging to its friends.

Q.—What is the second duty?

A.—To parole all prisoners taken from the enemy who are known to have burned houses, stolen negroes or murdered women.

Q.—What is the third duty?

A.—Always to act on the defensive and never to invade the enemy's territory however good may be the opportunity, although he may be ravaging yours all the time.

Q.—What is the first duty of the Government?

A.—To fill all its important posts with Yankees and foreigners.

Q.—What is the second duty?

A.—To deliver its chief cities without striking a blow.

Q.—What is the third duty?

A.—Never to learn from experience.

Q.—What is the first duty of the Southern people?

A.—To keep out of the army.

Q.—What is the second duty?

A.—To make all the money they can out of the Government and the soldiers, as wars come seldom.

Q.—What is the third duty?

A.—To surrender the entire trade in shoes and clothing—on which trade the army is dependent—to that patriotic class of men known as Jews, who are too conscientious to charge the government or the army a profit exceeding two thousand per cent.

Q.—What is the fourth duty?

A.—To let success cause a relaxation of their exertions, and see in every little reverse the ruin of our cause.

That will do—take your seats.

Richmond Views of the News

THE SOUTH was conscious that not only its political independence, but its independence in every type of endeavor, must be won to give the Confederacy a truly national existence. "The South must not only fight her own battles," admonished a Mobile music publisher on sheets of his music, "but sing her own songs & dance to music composed by her own children." She must make her own ordnance, build her own ships, and publish her own books and papers.

The Southern Illustrated News was established in Richmond in the late summer of 1862. Frankly patterned after *The Illustrated News* of London, this new weekly was designed to fill the void left by the inaccessibility of papers formerly received from the North and to provide reading matter more acceptable than the Yankee publications in both quality and point of view. Despite the lack of professional authors, trained engravers, and adequate supplies of paper, *The Southern Illustrated News* was a resounding success and was soon the leading weekly in the South. Here are four excerpts from the columns of its early issues: an editorial comment on the invasion of Maryland, an explanation of British failure to recognize the Confederacy, a report of President Lincoln's Emancipation Proclamation, and a sketch of Belle Boyd, the most famous of Confederate women spies.

THE INVASION OF MARYLAND

The movement which has placed our troops upon the soil of Maryland has electrified the country, already exulting in the glory achieved by the unrivalled couraged of our noble army and the high skill of its great commander. The loftiest hopes are entertained, and not a shadow of doubt seems to obtrude itself for a moment upon the enlivening prospect. Criticism, abashed by the brilliant successes that have cleared Virginia of the Yankees in a space of time so brief that we can hardly recognize its existence, is silent for the time, and no voice is heard but that of approbation. The public, indeed, has, all along, been ahead of the government in regard to this particular matter. It eagerly desired to march into Maryland immediately after the battle of Manassas in July of last year. Its wishes were not gratified then for reasons which, no doubt, appeared sufficient to the government, but it has never abandoned that favorite project, or ceased to hope that the day might come when it would be gratified. It has come at last, and the advance has been made under the most favorable circumstances that it is possible to imagine. The veteran forces of the enemy have been either destroyed or demoralized by the battles of July and August. To meet our troops in Maryland, they have little else than raw recruits, many of them averse to the service and all of them cowed and over-awed by the ill-success of the last three months and the high reputation of the enemy they are brought to oppose. Be the numbers of these recruits as large as they may, they will still be no match for our veterans. Indeed, the larger the force, the greater the confusion and the more certain and more fatal the defeat. But our Generals have it in their power, by breaking up the railways, to prevent a very great accumulation even of raw recruits.

It is evident that this movement has either taken the enemy entirely by surprise, or that if he anticipated it, he was utterly unable to prevent it. As late as the 6th of September, when our troops were already, if not in actual possession of Fredericktown, at least within a few miles of it, a Philadelphia paper assured its readers that all the passages of the Potomac were securely guarded, and that it would be impossible for the "Rebels" to cross that river. A day or two before, the Washington Star expressed the most scornful incredulity upon the same subject, declaring that it wished nothing better than for them to make the attempt. It hoped General McClellan would not interrupt them, but suffer them to pass over without molestation, that he might cut off their retreat and capture the whole of them. We were inclined, at first, to believe that this was mere empty braggadocio— mere whistling to keep up courage—but from the entire absence of all precautions to delay our passage, we are induced to think that it was spoken in earnest, and that it was not believed at Washington any more than at Philadelphia, that the attempt would be made. The inhabitants, thus far, have shown themselves highly favorable to our cause, which is, indeed, their own. It is reported—with what degree of truth we know not—that the county of Frederick has already furnished a brigade of infantry and 150 cavalry. As it has been generally believed that the Western portion of Maryland was that which was least disposed to join with the South, this fact, if it be a fact, is of the greatest significance. The Eastern counties and the city of Baltimore have long been known to be unanimous, or nearly so, in our favor, and the sign thus given in Frederick indicates a very feeble party in favor of the Yankee rule.

Mighty events—mightier than any that have yet occurred —are evidently on the wing. Before another issue of this paper, a great battle may have been fought, and the fate of Washington, possibly of the war, have been determined. We wait with anxiety, yet without the smallest fear, for the result. Our brave boys are not to be beaten by any force the Yankees can bring against them.

THE REASONS WHY WE HAVE NOT YET BEEN ACKNOWLEDGED BY GREAT BRITAIN

A great deal of indignation has been felt and expressed in certain quarters because we have not been acknowledged as an independent nation by Great Britain, and not a little astonishment. For indignation, we cannot but think there is great reason. The old Government of the United States, taking warning from the events of the Revolution, established a rule from which it never departed with respect to such matters. It was to acknowledge the Government *de facto* of every country with which it had political relations. This was a wise rule, instituted by the great Southern Presidents who ruled the destinies of the country for so many years, and made for it all of its history which is not absolutely contemptible. Of late years this has also been the policy of Great

Britain, borrowed, no doubt, from the practice of the United States, and founded on the plainest dictates of justice and common sense. Great Britain had suffered awfully from having pursued the opposite course, and she seemed to have taken warning from the past. She had entered into a war of five years' standing with France for acknowledging the independence of the thirteen colonies, and had come out of it with a beggared exchequer, a defeated army, and an empire sundered in twain. She had refused to acknowledge the independence of the French Republic, and the bloodiest and most dangerous war she had ever been engaged in to that time was the consequence. She refused to recognise the French Empire, and a war more bloody and dangerous still had been the consequence. The practice which she borrowed from the United States was a wise and a safe practice. It committed her to no discussion of the right of the government she recognised to rule the country which it professed to rule, and to no interference with the internal affairs of such country. It disclaimed, indeed, all pretension to knowledge upon that head. It merely addressed itself to the Government which it found in power, without asking any questions whatever. Thus, when Louis Philippe established the throne of July upon the ruins of the throne of the elder Bourbon dynasty, Great Britain at once recognised the new Government. When the Orleans dynasty was overthrown, she made haste to acknowledge the Republic. When Louis Napoleon established his Presidency, she did the same thing, as she did likewise when he made himself Emperor. She recognised all the Republics of South America, and the Empire of Iturbide in Mexico, though, to the best of our belief, Spain has never acknowledged their independence to this day. She recognised and assisted to set up Greece. She not only recognised Belgium, but contributed to get Prince Leopold made

King. But two years ago, when the King of Naples was driven from his throne, she immediately recognised his successor, Victor Emmanuel. The Confederate States are the only new power she has refused to recognise, and yet they have manifested a degree of strength greater than all those we have enumerated put together. We have, under these circumstances, we think, some right to be indignant. We have not the smallest right to be astonished.

Great Britain has been trying to bring about the very state of things now existing here ever since the United States became a recognised power of the earth. She never could find it in her heart to forgive the successful revolt of the colonies. During Mr. Madison's first term, disclosures were made by the celebrated John Henry, which, although attempts of the most strenuous kind were made to discredit the witness, proved, beyond a doubt, that a deeply laid plot had been concocted by the Government of Canada and certain traitors in New England to separate that part of the country from the Union and annex it to the British Empire. In the war which followed shortly after, the people and press of New England were almost unanimous in favor of Great Britain, and opposed to those whom they ought to have regarded as their countrymen. In latter days England has been jealous of the growing power of the United States to an inordinate degree. She has clearly foreseen that, if they continue united, they must become, before the close of this century, the first nation of the world, with an invincible army, a navy that must assume the empire of the seas, and a commerce that must swallow up all the commerce of the Old World. Thus, in addition to the old grudge, she has been stimulated by the fear of losing her position among the powers of the earth. Cost what it might, she has felt that for her the greatest of all objects has been to destroy the Union.

She has succeeded at last, and it is not wonderful that she should desire to see the war carried on as long as both parties may have the strength to maintain themselves. She feels that intervention would follow recognition, and this she is by no means disposed to undertake, because it might have the effect of shortening the war.

The war in question, besides removing a powerful rival from her path, is useful to her in another respect. If it should last long enough, it may be the means of getting her cotton from India into demand, and it may stimulate the production in Australia. When we consider that cotton constitutes the very basis upon which her enormous power is built, we shall see at once the importance of having it all under her own control. This she hopes to accomplish by destroying the culture in this country, which can only be done by destroying the labor which produces it. The abolition of slavery in her West Indian possessions was but the preliminary step to the abolition of slavery in this country. . . . She cares nothing for the slave in Brazil, where his condition is infinitely worse than it is here, or in Cuba, where it is worse even than it is in Brazil. All her sympathy is reserved for the slave in the Southern States of this Confederacy, who cultivates the products of which she wishes to preserve a monopoly.

In addition to these causes, it may be that the British Government feels itself in no condition to intervene, because of the present condition in Europe. Affairs are far from satisfactory in Italy, and any moment may witness the outbreak of a general war. As we have already observed, recognition might bring on intervention as a necessary consequence, and intervention would be sure to bring on war. This the British Government will avoid if it can. It already has a most exaggerated opinion of the strength of the Yankee Government, and is evidently very unwilling—we might almost say afraid—to come into collision with it. A late debate in Parliament plainly revealed an extraordinary degree of alarm on the subject of Canada. Entangled as it already is in a war which it supports with difficulty, the Ministry apparently think Yankeedom yet strong enough to tear that noble province from their grasp.

These, we think, are the reasons why Great Britain—meaning the British Government—is averse to recognise us. That the majority of the people sympathise with us, while they detest the Yankees, we do not doubt.

A NOTE ON THE EMANCIPATION PROCLAMATION

Lincoln seems to be in a state of desperation. He has issued a proclamation, declaring all negroes belonging to rebels free. As his armies have freed the negroes wherever they have been, this proclamation does not at all alter the character of the war. He has issued another, in which he proclaims martial law all over the United States. As he has no authority in the Southern States, of course it is altogether inoperative there. But it does operate in the Yankee States, and was no doubt designed for them. The Democratic party has of late begun to show itself very formidable in those States, and there was fair prospect of their beating the Abolitionists proper, at the next elections. This proclamation is intended to keep them quiet, or to dispose of them in the most summary manner, if they should succeed in their ticket. Opposition is not tolerated north of the Potomac, and any man who attempts it will be dealt with as a traitor. The government there is a military despotism, as absolute as that of Russia. The old Constitution of the United States has sunk into absolute contempt. Those who express a wish to see it respected, are forthwith clapped into jail on a charge of treason.

MISS BELLE BOYD

This young lady, who has, by her devotion to the Southern cause, called down upon her head the anathemas of the entire Yankee press, was in our city last week. Through the politeness of Mr. Cowel[l], the artist at Minnis's gallery, we are enabled, in this issue of our paper, to present her picture.

Miss Belle is the daughter of Benjamin B. Boyd of Martinsburg, at which place he was for a long time prominently engaged in the mercantile profession. He afterwards removed to Knoxville, Tennessee, where he lived about three years, but returned to Martinsburg about two years previous to the breaking out of the present war. Her mother was the daughter of Captain Glenn of Jefferson county. Miss Belle is the oldest child of her parents, and is about 23 years of age. An uncle of Miss Belle, James W. Glenn, of Jefferson county, commanded a company during the present war, known as the "Virginia Rangers," until recently, the captaincy of which he resigned on account of ill-health. James E. Stuart, a prominent politician of the Valley, and who was a member of the Virginia Convention of 1850, married a sister of Miss Belle's mother.

During her early years Miss Belle was distinguished for her sprightliness and the vivacity of her temper.

That our readers may have an opportunity of seeing what the Yankee correspondents say about this young lady, we extract the following article from the columns of the Philadelphia "Inquirer," which was written by the army correspondent of that sheet:

"These women are the most accomplished in Southern circles. They are introduced under assumed names to our officers, so as to avoid detection or recognition from those to whom their names are known, but their persons unknown. By such means they are enabled to frequently meet combinedly, but at separate times, the officers of every regiment in a whole column, and by simple compilation and comparison of notes, they achieve a full knowledge of the strength of our entire force. Has modern warfare a parallel to the use of such accomplishments for such a purpose? The chief of these spies is the celebrated Belle Boyd. Her acknowledged superiority for machination and intrigue has given her the leadership and control of the female spies in the valley of Virginia. She is a resident of Martinsburg, when at home, and has a pious, good old mother, who regrets as much as any one can the violent and eccentric course of her daughter since this rebellion has broken out. Belle has passed the freshness of youth. She is a sharp-featured, black-eyed woman of 25, or care and intrigue have given her that appearance. Last summer, whilst Patterson's army lay at Martinsburg, she wore a revolver in her belt, and was courted and flattered by every Lieutenant and Captain in the service who ever saw her. There was a kind of Di Vernon dash about her, a smart pertness, a quickness of retort, and utter abandonment of manner and bearing which were attractive from the very romantic unwontedness.

"The father of this resolute black-eyed vixen is a paymaster in the Southern army, and formerly held a place at Washington under our Government. She has undergone all that society, position and education can confer upon a mind suited to the days of Charles the Second, or Louis the Fourteenth— a mind such as Mazarin or Richelieu would have delighted to employ from its kindred affinities.

"Well, this woman I saw practicing her arts upon our young lieutenants and inexperienced captains, and in each case I uniformly felt it my duty to call them aside and warn them of whom she was. To one she had been introduced as Miss Anderson, to another as Miss Faulkner, and so to the end of the chapter. She is so well known now that she can only practice her blandishments upon new raw levies and their officers. But from them she obtains the number of their regiments and force. She has, however, a trained band of coadjutors, who report to her daily—girls aged from 16 upward—women who have the common sense not to make themselves as conspicuous as she, and who remain unknown, save to her, and are therefore effective. The reports that she is personally impure are as unjust as they are undeserved. She has a blind devotion to an idea, and passes far the boundary of her sex's modesty to promote its success.

"During the past campaign in the Valley this woman has been of immense service to the enemy. She will be now if she can."

The Battle of Fredericksburg

THE BATTLE OF FREDERICKSBURG on December 12, 1862, was one of the great victories of the Confederacy and one of the first great winter battles of the war. Here is the account of it which appeared in the weekly review of military events in *The Southern Illustrated News.*

⁂

We have had stirring times since our last issue—important movements, resulting in a great pitched battle and a glorious victory. — On Thursday, the 11th, the Yankees opened a tremendous fire of shot and shell upon the devoted town of Fredericksburg. No less than 173 pieces of the heaviest artillery were in action at once, from the hills of Stafford, which completely overlook and command the place. Under cover of this fire, the Yankees attempted to construct two pontoon bridges opposite the city, but were repeatedly driven off by our sharpshooters in the rifle pits along the shore and in the houses. About 4 o'clock, however, they succeeded in crossing. Instantly the event was announced by the telegraph to all

Yankeedom as a glorious victory, the New York Herald next morning proclaiming the movement to have been "decisive and victorious." At nearly the same moment, two bridges were thrown over below, and the Yankees crossed there also. Our men fell back, and the Yankees became certain of victory. The Baltimore American's correspondent said next morning, "A battle is predicted to day, but we think it doubtful whether the Rebels design to fight us in their present position." It is evident that they had not the remotest conception of what was in store for them. All day Friday, the enemy were engaged in passing over their troops. There was some skirmishing along the line, but nothing of serious moment occurred. On Saturday, at an early hour, Gen. Lee drew up his forces on the heights beyond Fredericksburg. Gen. Jackson, on the right, farthest down the river, and Gen. Longstreet on the left. The Confederate army then drawn up presented the appearance of a huge crescent, concave to the front. Its line was five miles long, and its artillery was posted in such a manner as to command all the approaches with a cross fire.

About 9 o'clock, under cover of a dense fog, a heavy body of the enemy advanced against the right of our line, where Gen. Jackson commanded. Gen. Stuart, who was stationed on the extreme right with two brigades of cavalry, immediately moved up two sections of his horse artillery and opened a heavy fire on his flank. The enemy, in advancing, was met by the division of Gen. A. P. Hill of Jackson's corps, and assailed with such fury that he was compelled to fall back after an obstinate resistance. During this combat, two of Hill's brigades, overwhelmed by numbers were compelled to fall back. Gen. Lee ordered Gen. Early to support Gen. Hill. The enemy had already seized a wood which lies in that

part of the field. Furiously assailed by Early, he was compelled to relinquish his prize, and fled pursued by Early
until he came under fire of his batteries. So large was the
force of the enemy at this point, that his right overlapped the
left of Hill, and came opposite to Hood's division, the extreme right of Longstreet's corps. He took possession of a
wood in front of Hood, but was speedily dislodged.

While this battle was going on upon the right of our
line, the enemy were engaged in passing over large bodies
of troops from the Stafford shore, for the purpose of attacking our left under Longstreet. After he had already been
repulsed on our right, he commenced a furious assault upon
our left with the view of getting possession of the heights
which command the town of Fredericksburg. He was repulsed
with great slaughter, only to renew the attempt. On this
part of the line, the destruction of the enemy was fearfully
great. He behaved with great resolution, and repeatedly renewed his efforts, only to be continually driven back with
increased slaughter. Gen. Longstreet had placed a division
in certain stone enclosures used as farm fences, and from
behind these the men shot down the Yankees at their leisure
and in comparative security. The ground was literally piled
up with dead men. The Washington Artillery—as they always
do—distinguished themselves on this part of the field. Having exhausted all their ammunition, they were withdrawn
about night from the spot which they had rendered immortal, and their place was filled by a portion of McLaws'
division, which also highly distinguished itself. All their
attacks upon Longstreet were seconded by the fire of the
enemy's heavy batteries on the Stafford heights. But they
were of no avail against the steady courage and immovable
pertinacity of our troops. By sunset the enemy was hopelessly

beaten at all points, and although he made another assault after dark, upon Longstreet, it was designed only to aid him in drawing off his troops. This he did under cover of the night, leaving his dead and wounded and the field of battle in our possession. A few more hours of daylight would have witnessed the utter destruction of the Yankee army.

Persons in Fredericksburg at the time, who have since come away, assert that the scenes of Saturday night were terrific beyond description. The Yankees had become completely demoralized by their defeat. Their officers were utterly unable to restrain them.— They pillaged every house that had been left. The whole army seemed to be a drunken mob. This frightful scene continued until Monday night, when, under cover of the darkness, Burnside withdrew his whole force to the Northern bank of the Rappahannock.— When our troops re-entered the town they began for the first time to have some idea of the greatness of their victory. Piles of Yankee dead, which they had not had time to bury, (in such alarm were they,) were found lying about in all directions. About 300 wounded and sick had been left behind in their haste. The field of battle presented a horrible spectacle. At least six, some say eight, Yankees were found dead for one Confederate. At one place an officer saw what he supposed to be a regiment lying in ambush in a small enclosure. It proved to be dead Yankees. It is computed, so we learn from a city paper, in official quarters, that the Yankee loss in killed, wounded and prisoners, amounts to at least 18,000 men.— The prisoners were very few. Our own loss in killed, wounded and missing, is over 2,000. The cause of the difference is plain. Our forces were stationed on commanding eminences, and our fire swept the vast plain through which the Yankees approached to attack us. They could do us little injury, while every shot of ours told.

Burnside has disappeared, but whither he is gone, seems not to be known. One account, and that the most probable, is, that he has gone to Acquia Creek, to get on board his fleet. Gen. Lee, it seems, has made him take water; but where next, it is hard to say.

"God Save the South,"
words by George H. Miles,
music by C. T. DeCoëniél,
lithograph by Ernest Crehen,
Richmond, 1863

GENERAL P. G. T. BEAUREGARD

From the frontispiece to the sheet music,
"Gen'l Beauregard's Grande Polka Militaire!"
New Orleans, 1861

1863

The Alabama Versus the Hatteras

HARDLY as large as a modern destroyer, the Confederate cruiser *Alabama* earned a fame all out of proportion to her size. Her record of fifty-seven ships burned and many others boarded and examined brought a glory to a Confederate Navy that had little enough of success. She was the chief of a trio of raiding cruisers built in England for the Confederacy. The *Alabama* and the *Shenandoah* did damage to Federal shipping amounting to more than six million dollars each, and the *Florida* added another three million. Under her gallant and vigorous captain, Commander Raphael Semmes, the *Alabama* sailed more than seventy-five thousand miles— from as far as the China Sea to her doom off the coast of France.

In this unidentified officer's account of her engagement with the *Hatteras* in January, 1863, the *Alabama* is presented in her prime—fresh from her successful sortie from Liverpool and outfitting in the Azores and a victorious maiden cruise in the Atlantic and the Caribbean.

Sunday, 11th.— Fine moderate breeze from the eastward. Read Articles of War. Noon: Eighteen miles from Galveston. As I write this some are discussing the probability of a fight before morning. 2.25 P.M.: Light breeze; sail discovered by the look-out on the bow. Shortly after, three, and at last five, vessels were seen; two of which were reported to be steamers. Every one delighted at the prospect of a fight, no doubt whatever existing as to their being war-vessels—blockaders we supposed. The watch below came on deck, and of their own accord began preparing the guns, &c., for action. Those whose watch it was on deck were engaged in getting the propeller ready for lowering; others were bending a cable to a kedge and putting it over the bow—the engineers firing up for steam, officers looking to their side-arms, &c., and discussing the size of their expected adversary or adversaries. At 2.30 shortened sail and tacked to the southward. 4 P.M.: A steamer reported standing out from the fleet towards us. Backed main-topsail and lowered propeller. 4.50: Everything reported ready for action. Chase bearing N.N.E., distant ten miles. Twilight set in about 5.45. Took in all sail. At 6.20 beat up to quarters, manned the starboard battery, and loaded with fine second shell; turned round, stood for the steamer, having previously made her out to be a two-masted side-wheel, of apparent 1200 tons, though at the distance she was before dark we could not form any correct estimate of her size, &c.

At 6.30 the strange steamer hailed and asked: "What steamer is that?" We replied (in order to be certain who he was), "Her Majesty's ship Petrel! What steamer is that?" Two or three times we asked the question, until we heard, "This is the United States steamer——," not hearing the name. However, United States steamer was sufficient. As no doubt existed as to her character, we said, at 6.35, that this was the "Confederate States steamer, Alabama," accompanying the last syllable of our name with a shell fired over him. The signal being given, the other guns took up the refrain, and a tremendous volley from our whole broadside given to him, every shell striking his side, the shot striking being distinctly heard on board our vessel, and thus found that she was iron.

The enemy replied, and the action became general. A most sharp spirited firing was kept up on both sides, our fellows peppering away as though the action depended on each individual. And so it did. Pistols and rifles were continually pouring from our quarter-deck messengers most deadly, the distance during the hottest of the fight not being more than forty yards! It was a grand, though fearful sight, to see the guns belching forth, in the darkness of the night, sheets of living flame, the deadly missiles striking the enemy with a force that we could *feel*. Then, when the shells struck her side, and especially the percussion ones, her whole side was lit up, and showing rents of five or six feet in length. One shot had just struck our smoke-stack, and wounding one man in the cheek, when the enemy ceased his firing, and fired a lee gun; then a second, and a third. The order was given to "Cease firing." This was at 6.52. A tremendous cheering commenced, and it was not till everybody had cleared his throat to his own satisfaction, that silence could be obtained. We then hailed him, and in reply he stated that he had surrendered, was on fire, and also that he was in a sinking condition. He then sent a boat on board, and surrendered the U. S. gun-boat, Hatteras, nine guns, Lieutenant-Commander Blake, 140 men. Boats were immediately lowered and sent to his assistance, when an alarm was given that another steamer was bearing down for us. The boats were recalled and hoisted up, when it was found to be a false alarm. The order was given, and the boatswain and his mates piped "All hands out boats to save life;" and soon the prisoners were transferred to our ship—the officers under guard on the quarter-deck, and the men in single irons. The boats were then hoisted up, the battery run in and secured, and the main brace spliced. All hands piped down, the enemy's vessel sunk, and we steaming quietly away by 8.30, all having been done in less than two hours. In fact, had it not been for our having the prisoners on board, we would have sworn nothing unusual had taken place—the watch below quietly sleeping in their hammocks. The conduct of our men was truly commendable. No flurry, no noise—all calm and determined. The coolness displayed by them could not be surpassed by any old veterans—our chief boatswain's mate apparently in his glory. "Sponge!" "Load with cartridge!" — "Shell-fire seconds!" — "Run out!" — "Well, down compressors!" — "Left, traverse!" — "Well!" — "Ready!" — "Fire!" — "That's into you!" — "Damn you! that kills your pig!" — "That stops your wind!" &c., &c., was uttered as each shot was heard to strike with a crash that nearly deafened you. The other boatswain's mate seeming equally to enjoy the affair. As he got his gun to bear upon the enemy, he would take aim, and banging away, would plug her, exclaiming, as each shot told — "That's from the scum of England!" — "That's a British pill for you to swallow!" the New York papers having once stated that our men were the "scum of England." All other guns were served with equal precision. We were struck seven times; only one man being hurt during the engagement, and he only receiving a flesh wound in the cheek. One shot struck under the counter, penetrating as far as a timber, then glancing off; a second struck the funnel; a third going through the side, across the berth-deck, and into the opposite side; another raising the deuce in the

lamp-room; the others lodging in the coal-bunkers. Taking
a shell up and examining it, we found it filled with sand
instead of powder. The enemy's fire was directed chiefly
towards our stern, the shots flying pretty quick over the
quarter-deck, near to where our Captain was standing. As
they came whizzing over him, he, with his usual coolness,
would exclaim — "Give it to the rascals!" — "Aim low, men!"
— "Don't be all night sinking that fellow!" when, for all or
anything we knew, she might have been an iron-clad or a
ram.

On Commander Blake surrendering his sword, he said
that "it was with deep regret he did it." Captain Semmes
smacked his lips and invited him down to his cabin. On
Blake giving his rank to Captain Semmes, he gave up his
state-room for Blake's special use, the rest of the officers
being accommodated according to their rank in the ward-
room and steerages, all having previously been paroled, the
crew being placed on the berth-deck, our men sleeping anywhere, so that the prisoners might take their places. Of the
enemy's loss we could obtain no correct accounts, a difference of seventeen being in their number of killed, the Hatteras having on board men she was going to transfer to other
ships. Their acknowledged loss was only two killed and
seven wounded. A boat had been lowered just before the
action to board us; as we anticipated, and learnt afterwards,
it pulled in for the fleet and reached Galveston. From conversation with her First-Lieutenant, I learnt that as soon
as we gave our name and our first broadsides, the whole
after division on board her left the guns, apparently para-
lyzed; it was some time before they recovered themselves.
The conduct of one of her officers was cowardly and disgraceful in the extreme. Some of our shells went completely
through her before exploding, others burst inside her, and

set her on fire in three places. One went through her engines, completely disabling her; another exploding in her steam chest, scalding all within reach. Thus was fought, twenty-eight miles from Galveston, a battle, though small, yet the first yard arm action between two steamers at sea. She was only inferior in weight of metal—her guns being nine in number, viz, four thirty-two pounders, two rifled thirty pounders, carrying 60lb. shot (conical), one rifled twenty pounder, and a couple of small twelve pounders. On account of the conflicting statements made by her officers, we could never arrive at a correct estimate of her crew. Our prisoners numbered seventeen officers, one hundred and one seamen. We further learnt that the Hatteras was one of seven vessels sent to recapture Galveston, it being (although unknown to us) in the possession of our troops. We also found that the flag-ship Brooklyn, twenty-two guns, and the Oneida, nine guns sailed in search of us. By their account of the course they steered they could not fail to have seen us.

The New Richmond Theatre

THE ROLE of a major capital was new to Richmond and bore heavily on her shoulders. Along with the generals and Cabinet members who flocked to the new capital came a horde of hangers-on—charlatans, profiteers, prostitutes, and gamblers. The activities of these members of society were repeatedly deplored by the more responsible citizens. But Richmond was a gayer and more bustling city than she had ever been before. Business was good. The hotels were full to overflowing. The offices were jammed with workers for the mushrooming bureaus of a new government. The saloons and theaters entered an era of unprecedented prosperity. Soldiers on leave as well as the myriad strangers in the city sought public entertainment as never before.

On January 2, 1862, the Richmond Theatre burned. No time was lost in replacing it, first with a company called the Richmond Varieties acting in a converted church building, and then with an entirely new building constructed for the New Richmond Theatre. The opening of the new theater was long heralded in the press. Here are pieces which reflect divergent points of view concerning it.

The first is a sermon by John Lansing Burrows, a prominent Baptist minister, decrying the opening of the theater with its "twenty *gentlemen* for the chorus and the ballet" who might better be in the army. Burrows' complaint is not against the theater as such but against the immorality which seemed to find a home in the theaters of wartime Richmond. His view of the theatrical profession in Richmond was shared by John Hill Hewitt, Confederate poetaster and musician who had briefly managed the old Richmond Theatre. In his manuscript autobiography Hewitt described the difficulties of getting together a company: "How to gather a company was the question. On the breaking out of the war, the best of the profession had fled North, thinking it the safest ground to stand upon—for actors are cosmopolites and claim citizenship no where. I however managed in a short time to collect enough of the *fag-ends* of dismantled companies to open the theatre with a passable exhibition of novelty, if not of talent. . . . The thing took well, and money flowed into the treasury but often had I cause to upbraid myself for having fallen so low in my own estimation, for, I had always considered myself a gentleman, and I found that, in taking the control of this theatre and its vagabond company I had forfeited my claim to a respectable stand in the ranks of Society—with one or two exceptions, the company I had engaged was composed of harlots and 'artful dodgers.' "

Following the extracts from Burrows' sermon is the account of the theater's opening by the drama critic of

The Southern Illustrated News. The account was made memorable by the incorporation into it of Henry Timrod's "Inaugural Poem." Timrod submitted this poem in the competition inspired by manager Richard D'Orsey Ogden's offer of a prize of three hundred dollars for the best such production.

To-morrow night the New Richmond Theatre is to be opened. I deem it fitting, in addition to the notices so liberrally given through the daily press, to give this public notice from the pulpit. With surprising energy, and regardless of cost, in these pinching times of war, a splendid building, with most costly decorations, has been reared from the ashes of the old. Builders, artists, workmen, have devoted themselves with an enterprise and industry that would be praiseworthy, if, in any sense, their work were useful in these pressing times of war. Enough able-bodied men have escaped from the conscription, have, perhaps, purchased the right to keep away from the camp and the battle in order to accomplish this magnificent work, for a consideration. The work is completed; the decorations are finished, and to-morrow night the New Richmond Theatre is to be opened. A strong corps of actors, male and female, have been secured, and, in addition to them, "twenty *gentlemen* for the chorus and the ballet." No cripples from the battle-fields are these—they can sing and dance; they can mimic fighting on the stage. For the serious work of repelling a real enemy they have neither taste nor heart. But they can sing while the country groans, and dance while the cars are bringing, in sad funeral procession, the dead to their very doors, and the dismal ambulance bears the sick and the wounded under the very glare of their lights, and within the sound of their music. They keep themselves out of the war for the noble duty of amusing the populace. Should they not, in these times, be especially encouraged, particularly by those whose own brave sons are in the camp or in the hospital, or whose mangled bodies are mouldering in uncoffined graves? Does it not seem a peculiarly happy time for theatrical amusements? Shall we all go and laugh and clap to the music and the dance, while the grasp of relentless foes is tightening upon the throats of our sons, and the armed heels of trampling hosts are bruising the bosom of our beloved mother land? What fitter time for opening a theatre in the capital of our bleeding country, unless it could have been on the evening of the battle of Malvern Hill or of Fredericksburg? But enterprise and industry could not secure the completion of the building in time for those bloody days, or we should, doubtless, have had the theatre open every night, while the battle raged by day, around the very suburbs of Richmond. "A strong stock company," and "twenty gentlemen for the chorus and the ballet," besides artists, musicians, etc., etc. Men enough, perhaps, to form an effective artillery company, deny themselves the patriotic desire to aid in defending the country against assailing foes, in order that they may devote themselves, fellow citizens, to your amusement. And you, doubtless, in your general liberality, will pay them enough to purchase substitutes, that they may abide in safety, and with these "twenty gentlemen of the chorus and the ballet," minister to your amusement.

I find, in my heart, no sympathy with that austere and morose idea of religion, which forbids a laugh, and prohibits recreation and amusement. I find no pleasure in tracing the wrinkles of seventy upon the brow of seventeen. It is contrary to nature and piety to curb and cramp, perpetually, the cheerful impulses of the young heart, and force it into the unnatural faith that gloom is godliness, and that innocent mirth is but the outburst of depravity. If God had not meant we should laugh, He would not have created the risible nerves and muscles. From the severer duties and struggles of life there may be and there ought to be relaxations and mere pleasures in every family and in every community. Sincere and intelligent piety is always cheerful, and Christians are enjoined in the Word to rejoice and to "rejoice evermore." I am not disposed, therefore, to insist upon any captious or churlish denunciation of the theatre, merely because it is a place of amusement. If there were no graver objections to it than this, you would not be troubled with utterances against it from this desk. Nor is it against the ideal theatre of some pure and poetic minds that I protest. . . . When we hear of a theatre which is not the favorite gathering place of the vicious, where the Gospel of Jesus is preached, or even where a pure and chaste morality is inculcated, where we are not compelled to countenance and mingle with vice in its most odious forms, we shall recommend the place. But the question is not, might not the good visit the theatre if the representations and associations were pure and respectable, but may they do so as it exists? Some talk of the possibility of reforming the theatre and making it reputable. When this is done it will be time to invite the good and the pure within its walls.

Pollock has well said of the theatre,

"It was, from the very first,
"The favorite haunt of sin, though honest men,
"Some very honest, wise and worthy men,

"Maintained it might be turned to good account,
"And so, perhaps, it might, *but never was.*"

"From first to last it was an evil place.
"And now—such things were acted there as made
"The devils blush; and from the neighborhood
"Angels and holy men, trembling, retired."

I would not be understood as denouncing indiscriminately dramatic writings. Shakespeare, and Milton, and Young, and Coleridge, and Sheridan Knowles, and numerous others have written plays that may be profitably read and studied. The dramatic literature is rich in gems. At the same time it cannot be denied that much that assumes the name is rotten and pestiferous, and can scarcely be read even in solitude without polluting the soul. These preliminary remarks will be deemed sufficient to show that I am not, in my views of this subject, ascetical or austerely pietistic . . .

And now, I ask, in all seriousness, is a theatre so conducted, as this New Richmond Theatre is evidently to be, worthy the patronage and presence of reputable people? That there will be crowds nightly gathered within its walls is very probable. There are, alas! in our community enough of the vile, the unprincipled, and the mere pleasure loving to support such an institution liberally. There are also many very respectable people who will seek for amusement without regard to the influence of their example upon others. It may be that some very decent fathers and mothers will take their sons and even their daughters to a place, a portion of which they know is set apart for vilest assignations, where libertines parade their shameless profligacy, where the infamous wait for the vicious.

None of this congregation shall do this without honest and faithful warning; without an exposure of the influences to which they choose to subject themselves and their children.

I am not morose or puritanic. My religion is not of the gloomy type. God has made men to be cheerful and happy. The ringing laugh of innocent enjoyment I love to hear. I am no enemy to pleasure. I take delight in witnessing the sports of childhood and youth. I strive to cultivate and exhibit a cheerful, joyous spirit. But life has its stern, grave duties, and whatever unfits the mind and heart for these; whatever creates a distaste for their earnest fulfilment; whatever sullies the innocency of the heart, or perverts and distorts the nobler faculties of the soul; whatever ministers to the development of a prurient imagination, at the expense of the more practicable and serviceable powers of the mind, is injury to the individual and a mischief to society. All this, and more than this, I believe to be the influence of the stage in its best aspects, and even without the infamous associations to which I have alluded. You cannot visit the theatre and love it and remain innocent and pure.

❂   ❂   ❂   ❂

THE OPENING OF THE NEW RICHMOND THEATRE

According to announcement the New Richmond Theatre was opened on Monday night last. Glowing descriptions of the magnificence of the building, and the lengthy announcements in all the Richmond papers of the opening by the manager, had raised public expectation to its very highest pitch. The old man who had not crossed the portals of a hall of amusement since his hair had become tinged with gray—the young cavalier who had read, seen or heard of nothing but "wars and rumors of wars," since the vandal horde had invaded our land—the gay-hearted maiden, with sweet and ruby lips—the politician or man of office, with care-worn look, as if great matters of State still weighed heavily upon his heart—all Monday night, quietly wending their way to the new and gorgeous temple of Thespis. Through the courtesy of the manager, we, in company with several other members of the press, were *"undeservedly"* shown through a private entrance to a box (thus saving ourselves the necessity of elbowing through the crowd).

At half-past seven a full head of gas is turned on—the interior of the building is brilliantly illuminated—the dress circle is lined with a bevy of handsome and bright faces—some with that beautiful rosy tinge upon the cheeks and lips which nature alone gives, while others appear fresh from the artist's hand, the superfluous *rouge* not yet brushed away —the soldier with his immense circular-saw spurs, jingling like so many sleigh bells—the gay gambler, with his flash apparel, and magnificent diamonds dazzling the eye as the soft lambent light falls upon them, while he saunters to and fro with a *nonchalant* air, and seemingly wondering if the whole audience is not gazing admiringly upon him—the quiet observer commanding the beautiful Arabesque, and pointing out the failures of the artists in their attempts at Figures—all rise involuntarily and gaze in wonder and admiration. At quarter to eight the door in the Orchestra box opens—the members of the Orchestra singly appear and take their respective seats—Prof. Loebman nods his head and the members join in one grand "concord of sweet sounds."

The strains of the music had scarcely died away, when Mr. Keeble entered from the door under the private box and delivered the following

INAUGURAL POEM,

By Harry Timrod.

A fairy ring
Drawn in the crimson of a battle plain,—
From whose weird cricle every loathsome thing
    And sight and sound of pain
Are banished, while about in the air,
And from the ground and from the low-hung skies,
    Throng in a vision fair
As ever lit a prophet's dying eyes,
    Gleams of that unseen world
That lies about us, rainbow-tinted shapes
    With starry wings unfurled,
Poised for a moment on such airy capes
    As pierce the golden foam
Not on themselves, but on some outstretched hand,
That once a single mind suffice to quell
The malice of a tyrant; let them know
That each may crowd in every well-aimed blow,
Not the poor strength alone of arm and brand,
But the whole spirit of a mighty land!

Bid Liberty rejoice! Aye, though its day
Be far or near, these clouds shall yet be red
With the large promise of the coming ray.
Meanwhile, with that calm courage which can smile

Amid the terrors of the wildest fray,
Let us among the charms of Art awhile
    Fleet the deep gloom away;
Nor yet forget that on each hand and head
Rest the dear rights for which we fight and pray.

The reading of the Poem was followed by the singing of
the "Marseillaise," by Mr. Chas. Morton, aided by a full
chorus. The group which surrounded the gentleman during
the singing of the Hymn presented a picture which an artist
would not fail to gaze admiringly on. There stood the maiden
of "sweet sixteen," blushing and laughing—the "lambs of
many summers" with the pristine smile yet hanging upon
their lips—and towering head and shoulders above them all,
in theatrical knowledge, stood the Queen of all the party,
Mrs. DeBar—all joining in the chorus with a hearty good
will. The singing was succeeded by a tableau representing
the Virginia coat of arms.

Then came the play—Shakespeare's "As You Like It," but
not as *we like it*. . . .

We are glad to announce that the audience evinced a disposition at once to stop all rowdyism. When the "call boy"
appeared in front of the curtain, for the purpose of fastening
down the carpet some ill-bred persons commenced to yell
"Soup, Soup," which was promptly hushed by the audience.
Another marked alteration was the ignoring of the rapturous,
boisterous manner of applauding, so much in vogue of late
years. The clapping of hands was the loudest manifestations
of applause evinced during the night.

Thus was our new Richmond Theatre dedicated. We trust
it will ever continue a place of amusement, where all may
be able to enjoy themselves in a rational manner, without
fear of having the blush brought to their cheeks by the im-

prudence of jack-plane actors, who have no ambition above that of making the unwashed laugh, stamp their feet, and yell in an uncouth and demi-savage style—that it may prove a temple where the wife, the mother, the sister and the sweetheart may pass some of their leisure hours pleasantly, in defiance of the sickly sentimentality and hypocrisy of the present day is the desire of all lovers of the legitimate drama.

Mosby Makes a Night Raid

IN MAJOR JOHN SINGLETON MOSBY Confederates found a hero almost equal to his commanding general, Jeb Stuart. Here is the commendatory general order published by Stuart to announce to the army Mosby's brilliant capture of Yankee General E. H. Stoughton. Following Stuart's order is the sketch of Mosby published in *The War and Its Heroes*. Much of this sketch was drawn from an article written for *The Southern Illustrated News* in the spring of 1863 by John Esten Cooke.

HEADQUARTERS CAVALRY DIVISION,⎰
ARMY OF N. VA., March 12, 1863.   ⎱

General Orders,⎱
    No. —— ⎰

Captain JOHN S. MOSBY has for a long time attracted the attention of his Generals by his boldness, skill and success, so signally displayed in his numerous forays upon the invaders of his native State.

None know his daring enterprise and dashing heroism, better than those foul invaders, though strangers themselves to such noble traits.

His late brilliant exploit—the capture of Brig. Gen. STOUGHTON, U. S. A., two Captains, thirty other prisoners, together with their arms, equipments and fifty-eight horses— justifies this recognition in General Orders.

This feat, unparalleled in the war, was performed in the midst of the enemy's troops, at Fairfax C. H., without loss or injury.

The gallant band of Capt. Mosby share the glory, as they did the danger of this enterprise, and are worthy of such a leader.

J. E. B. Stuart,
Major General Commanding.

MAJOR JOHN SINGLETON MOSBY

Among the daring partisans of the present war, few have rendered such valuable services to the cause as Major John S. Mosby.

John Singleton Mosby is the son of Alfred D. Mosby formerly of Albemarle county, Va., but now residing in the vicinity of Lynchburg. He is the maternal grandson of Mr. James McLaurine, Sr., late of Powhatan county, Virginia. His mother was Miss Virginia J. McLaurine.

The subject of our sketch was born in Powhatan county, Va., on the 6th of December, 1833, and was educated at the University of Virginia. When quite a young man he was married to the daughter of the Hon. Beverly Clarke, late United States minister to Central America.

At the commencement of hostilities between the North and South, Mosby resided at Bristol, Washington county,

Va., where he was successfully engaged in the practice of law. He immediately gave up his profession, and entered the army as a private, becoming a member of a company raised in Washington county, and commanded by Captain Jones—now General Jones—in which position he served for twelve months. Upon the promotion of Captain Jones to the colonelcy of the 1st Virginia Cavalry, Mosby was chosen as adjutant.

He continued in this position but a short time, for upon the re-organization of the regiment, from some cause the colonel was thrown out, and consequently his adjutant relieved of duty. Mosby was then chosen by General J. E. B. Stuart as a sort of independent scout.

He first attracted public attention when General Joseph E. Johnston, then in command of the Army of the Potomac, fell back from Manassas. On this occasion, desiring to ascertain whether the movement of McClellan was a feint, or if he really intended to march his army to the Peninsula, General Johnston despatched Mosby to gain the desired information. Taking five men with him. Mosby went in the rear of McClellan's army, where he remained some days, spending his time in converse with the Yankee soldiers, from whom he gained all necessary information, and then made his way safely back to General Johnston's headquarters.

During the summer of 1862, Major Mosby was sent from Hanover Courthouse on a mission to General Jackson, who was then on the upper Rapidan. He was the bearer of an oral communication, and as the route was dangerous, had no papers about him except a brief note to serve as a voucher of his identity and reliability. With this note the major proceeded on his journey, and stopping at Beaver Dam station, on the Virginia Central Railroad, to rest and feed his horse, was, while quietly sitting on the platform at the depot, surprised and bagged by a detachment of the enemy's cavalry.

Now, to be caught thus napping, in an unguarded moment, was gall and wormwood to the brave major. He had deceived and outwitted the enemy so often, had escaped from their clutches so regularly up to that time, that to find himself surprised thus, filled him with internal rage. From that moment his sentiments toward the enemy increased in intensity. They had been all along decidedly unfriendly— they were now bitter. They took him away with them, searched him, and filched his credentials, and published them as an item of interest in the Northern papers, and immured the partisan in the Old Capitol.

In due course of time he was exchanged. He returned with a handsome new satchel and an increased affection for the Yankees. He laughed at his misfortunes, but set down the account to the credit of the enemy, to be settled at a more convenient opportunity.

One of the most daring exploits of this gallant partisan is thus graphically described by the army correspondent of the "Illustrated News:"

Previous to the 8th of March, Major Mosby had put himself to much trouble to discover the strength and positions of the enemy in Fairfax county, with the design of making a raid in that direction, if circumstances permitted. The information brought to him was as follows: On the Little River turnpike, at Germantown, a mile or two distant from Fairfax, were three regiments of the enemy's cavalry, commanded by Colonel Wyndham, acting brigadier-general, with his headquarters at the court-house. Within a few hundred yards of the town were two infantry regiments. In the vicinity of Fairfax station, about two miles off, an infantry brigade was encamped. And at Centreville there was another infantry brigade, with cavalry and artillery.

Thus the way to Fairfax Court-house, the point which the major desired to reach, seemed completely blocked up with troops of all arms—infantry, artillery and cavalry. If he attempted to approach by the Little River turnpike, Colonel Wyndham's troopers would meet him full in front. If he tried the route by the Warrenton turnpike, a brigade of infantry, with cavalry to pursue and artillery to thunder at him, was first to be defeated. If he glided in along the railroad, the brigade at Fairfax station was in his track.

The "situation" would have appeared desperate to almost any one, however adventurous, but danger and adventure had attractions for Major Mosby. If the peril was great and the probability of success slender, all the greater would be the glory if he succeeded. And the temptation was great. At Fairfax Court-house, the general headquarters of that portion of the army, Brigadier-General Stoughton and other officers of high rank were there known to be, and if these could be captured, great would be his triumph, and horrible the consequent gnashing of teeth among the enemy.

In spite of the enormous obstacles which presented themselves in his path, Major Mosby determined to undertake no less an enterprise than entering the town, seizing the officers in their beds, destroying the huge quantities of public stores, and bearing off his prisoners in triumph.

The night of Sunday, March 8th, was chosen as favorable to the expedition. The weather was infamous, the night as dark as pitch, and it was raining steadily. With a detachment of twenty-nine men, Major Mosby set out on his raid.

He made his approach from the direction of Aldie. Proceeding down the Little River turnpike, the main route from the court-house to the mountains, he reached a point within about three miles of Chantilly. Here, turning to the right, he crossed the Frying Pan road, about half-way between Centreville and the turnpike, keeping in the woods, and leaving Centreville well to the right. He was now advancing in the triangle which is made by the Little River and Warrenton turnpikes and the Frying Pan road. Those who are familiar with the country there will easily understand the object of this proceeding. By thus cutting through the triangle, Major Mosby avoided all pickets, scouting parties, and the enemy generally, who would only keep a look out for intruders on the main roads.

Advancing in this manner through the woods, pierced with devious and uncertain paths only, which the dense darkness scarcely enabled them to follow, the partisan and his little band finally struck into the Warrenton road, between Centreville and Fairfax, at a point about mid-way between the two places. One danger had thus been successfully avoided— a challenge from parties of cavalry on the Little River road, or discovery by the force posted at Centreville. That place was now in their rear; they had "snaked" around it and its warders; but the perils of the enterprise had scarcely commenced. Fairfax Court-house was still about four miles distant, and it was girdled with cavalry and infantry. Every approach was guarded, and the attempt to enter the place seemed desperate, but the major determined to essay it.

Advancing resolutely, he came within a mile and a half of the place, when he found the way barred by a heavy force. Directly in his path were the infantry camps, of which he had been notified, and all advance was checked in that direction. The major did not waver in his purpose, however. Making a detour to the right, and leaving the enemy's camps far to his left, he struck into the road leading from Fairfax southward to the railroad.

This avenue was guarded like the rest, but by a picket only; and Mosby knew thoroughly how to deal with pickets. Before the sleepy and unsuspicious Yankees were aware of their danger, they found pistols presented at their heads, with the option of surrender or death presented to them. They surrendered immediately, were taken in charge, and, without further ceremony, Major Mosby and his band entered the town.

From that moment the utmost silence, energy and rapidity of action were requisite. The Major had designed reaching the court-house at midnight, but had been delayed two hours by mistaking the road in the pitch darkness. It was now two o'clock in the morning, and an hour and a half, at the very utmost, was left him to finish his business and escape before daylight. If morning found him anywhere in that vicinity, he knew that his retreat would be cut off, and the whole party killed or captured, and this would have spoiled the whole fun of the affair. He accordingly made his dispositions rapidly, enjoined complete silence, and set to work in earnest. The small band was divided into detachments, with special duties assigned to each. Two or three of these detachments were sent to the public stables where the fine horses of the general and his staff officers occupied, with instructions to carry them off without noise. Another party was sent to Colonel Wyndham's headquarters to take him prisoner. Another to Colonel Johnson's, with similar orders.

Taking six men with him, Major Mosby, who proceeded upon sure information, went straight to the headquarters of Brigadier-General Stoughton. This worthy was a Vermonter, and a terrific son of Mars; a graduate of West Point, and a suppress-the-rebellion-in-ninety-days man. He had just been assigned to the command of the post, and much was expected from a brigadier of such ardor and zeal in the service.

Alas! how little control have we over our own fates—a moral observation which the present narrative powerfully enforces:

> " 'Twas midnight, in his guarded tent
> The Turk was dreaming of the hour
> When Greece, her knee in suppliance bent,
> Should tremble at his power."

And, lo! the brigadier was even then in the power of that Marco Bozzaris, Major Mosby. "Stoughton's Bitters" came in the shape of a Confederate partisan!

The major entered his chamber without much ceremony, and found him reposing in all the dignity and grandeur of a brigadier-general commanding, whose person and slumbers are sacred. Making his way toward the bed, in the dark, the partisan shook him suddenly by the shoulder.

"Who is that?" growled the sleepy brigadier.

"Get up quick, I want you," responded the major.

"Do you know who I am," cried the brigadier, sitting up in bed, with a scowl. "I will have you arrested, sir."

"Do you know who *I* am?" retorted the major, shortly.

"Who are you?"

"Did you ever hear of Mosby?"

"Yes! Tell me, have you caught the —— rascal!"

"No; but he has caught you!" And the major chuckled.

"What does all this mean, sir?" cried the furious brigadier.

"It means, sir," the major replied, very coolly, "that Stuart's cavalry are in possession of this place, and you are my prisoner. Get up and come along, or you are a dead man!"

The brigadier groaned in anguish of soul, but was compelled to obey, and the partisan mounted, and placed him under guard. His staff and escort were captured without difficulty, but two of the former, owing to the darkness and confusion, subsequently made their escape.

Meanwhile the other detachments were at work. They entered the stables, and led out fifty-eight horses, with their accoutrements, all belonging to officers, and took a number of prisoners. Hundreds of horses were left, for fear of encumbering the retreat.

The other parties were less successful. Colonel Wyndham had gone to Washington on the preceding day; but his acting adjutant-general and aide-de-camp were made prisoners. Colonel Johnson, having received notice of the presence of the party, succeeded in making his escape.

It was now about half-past three in the morning, and it behooved Major Mosby, unless he relished being killed or captured, to effect his retreat. Time was barely left him to get out of the lines of the enemy before daylight, and none was to be lost.

He had intended to destroy the valuable quartermaster, commissary and sutler's stores in the place, but these were found to be in the houses which it would have been necessary to burn; and, even had the proceeding been advisable, time was wanting. The band was encumbered by three times as many horses and prisoners as it numbered men, and day was approaching. The major accordingly made his dispositions rapidly for retiring.

The prisoners, thirty-five in number, were as follows: Brigadier-General E. H. Stoughton; Baron R. Wordener, an Austrian, aide-de-camp to Colonel Wyndham; Captain A. Barker, 5th New York Cavalry; Colonel Wyndham's acting adjutant-general; thirty prisoners, chiefly of the 18th Pennsylvania and 1st Ohio Cavalry, and the telegraph operator at the place. These were placed upon the captured horses, and the band set out in silence on their return.

Major Mosby took the same road which had conducted him into the court-house—that which led to Fairfax station. But this was only to deceive the enemy as to his line of retreat, if they attempted pursuit. He soon turned off, and pursued the same road which he had followed in advancing, coming out on the Warrenton turnpike, about a mile and a half from the town. This time, finding no guards on the main road, he continued to follow the turnpike until he came to the belt of woods, which crosses the road, about half a mile from Centreville. At this point of the march, one of the prisoners, Captain Barker, no doubt counting on aid from the garrison, made a desperate effort to effect his escape. He broke from the guards, dashed out of the ranks, and tried hard to reach the fort. He was stopped, however, by a shot from one of the party, which came so near him that he thought it advisable not to risk a repetition of it. He accordingly came back and gave himself up again to his enemies.

Again turning to the right, the major proceeded on his way, passing directly beneath the frowning fortifications. He passed so near them that he distinctly saw the bristling muzzles of the cannon in the embrazures, and was challenged by the sentinel on the redoubt. Making no reply, he pushed on rapidly—for the day was dawning and no time was to be lost—passed within a hundred yards of the infantry pickets without molestation, swam Cub Run, and again came out on the Warrenton turnpike at Groveton. He had passed through all his enemies, flanked Centreville, was on the open road to the South; he was safe! He had penetrated to the very heart of the enemy's position; glided through their camps; captured their pickets; seized their officers in bed; borne off their horses; laughed at, and befooled, and outwitted them completely; and had not lost a man in the enterprise!

The exploits of Major Mosby would furnish material for a volume which would resemble rather a romance than a true statement of actual occurrences. He has been the chief actor in so many raids, encounters and adventures, that his memoirs, if he committed them to paper, would be regarded as the efforts of his fancy.

The same correspondent gives the annexed pen-and-ink sketch of the gallant major: His figure is slight, muscular, supple and vigorous; his eye is keen, penetrating, ever on the alert; he wears his sabre and pistol with the air of a man who sleeps with them buckled around his waist, and handles them habitually, almost unconsciously. The major is a determined man in a charge, dangerous on a scout, hard to outwit, and prone to "turn up" suddenly where he is least expected, and bang away with pistol and carbine.

A Journey across Texas

A N INTERESTED and acute observer was Sir Arthur James Lyon Fremantle. An officer of the venerable and elite Coldstream Guards, he had a strong curiosity about the war in America. Pro-Union at first, his sympathies shifted toward the Confederacy, and after meeting Commander Raphael Semmes at Gibraltar he determined to visit the scene of the great conflict on his next leave. Entering the Confederacy at Brownsville, Texas, in the spring of 1863, Colonel Fremantle made his way across the breadth of the South and ended his trip as the guest of General James Longstreet and his staff at the Battle of Gettysburg.

Fremantle returned to England and wrote an account of his travels that was admittedly pro-Confederate, but dignified and restrained. A copy of his book was sent by diplomatic courier to President Davis, and other copies soon found their way into the South. In 1864 *Three Months in the Southern States* was republished in a Confederate edition by S. H. Goetzel of Mobile—bound in wallpaper because of the shortage of proper binding materials.

This is Fremantle's account of a part of his journey across Texas.

30th April (Thursday).—I have to-day acquired my first experience of Texan railroads.

In this country, where every white man is as good as another (by theory), and every white female is by courtesy a lady, there is only one class. The train from Alleyton consisted of two long cars, each holding about fifty persons. Their interior is like the aisle of a church, twelve seats on either side, each for two persons. The seats are comfortably stuffed, and seemed luxurious after the stage.

Before starting, the engine gives two preliminary snorts, which, with a yell from the official of *"all aboard,"* warn the passengers to hold on; for they are closely followed by a tremendous jerk, which sets the cars in motion.

Every passenger is allowed to use his own discretion about breaking his arm, neck, or leg, without interference by the railway officials.

People are continually jumping on and off whilst the train is in motion, and larking from one car to the other. There is no sort of fence or other obstacle to prevent "humans" or cattle from getting on the line.

We left Alleyton at 8 A. M., and got a miserable meal at Richmond at 12.30. At this little town I was introduced to a seedy-looking man, in rusty black clothes and a broken-down "stove-pipe" hat. This was Judge Stockdale, who will probably be the next governor of Texas. He is an agreeable man, and his conversation is far superior to his clothing. The rival candidate is General Chambers (I think), who has become very popular by the following sentence in his manifesto:— "I am of opinion that married soldiers should be given the opportunity of embracing their families at least once a year, their places in the ranks being taken by unmarried men. The population must not be allowed to suffer."

Richmond is on the Brazos river, which is crossed in a peculiar manner. A steep inclined plane leads to a low, rickety, trestle bridge, and a similar inclined plane is cut in the opposite bank. The engine cracks on all steam, and gets sufficient impetus in going down the first incline to shoot across the bridge and up the second incline. But even in Texas this method of crossing a river is considered rather unsafe.

After crossing the river in this manner, the rail traverses some very fertile land, part of which forms the estate of the late Colonel Terry. There are more than two hundred negroes on the plantation. Some of the fields were planted with cotton and Indian corn mixed, three rows of the former between two of the latter. I saw also fields of cotton and sugar mixed.

We changed carriages at Harrisburg, and I completed my journey to Houston on a cotton truck.

The country near Houston is very pretty, and is studded with white wooden villas, which are raised off the ground on blocks like haystacks. I reached Houston at 4.30 P. M., and drove to the Fannin House hotel.

Houston is a much better place than I expected. The main street can boast of many well-built brick and iron houses. It was very full, as it now contained all the refugees from the deserted town of Galveston.

After an extremely mild supper, I was introduced to Lieutenant Lee, a wounded hero, who lost his leg at Shiloh, also to Colonel Pyron, a distinguished officer, who commands the regiment named after him.

The fat German, Mr. Lee, and myself, went to the theatre afterwards.

As a great favor, my British prejudices were respected, and I was allowed a bed to myself; but the four other beds in the room had two occupants each. A captain, whose acquaintance I had made in the cars, slept in the next bed to me. Directly after we had got into bed a negro came in, who, squatting down between our beds, began to clean our boots. The Southerner pointed at the slave, and thus held forth:—"Well, Kernel, I reckon you've got servants in your country, but not of that color. Now, sir, this is a real genuine African. He's as happy as the day's long; and if he was on a sugar plantation he'd be dancing half the night; but if you was to collect a thousand of them together, and fire one bomb in amongst them, they'd all run like hell." The negro grinned, and seemed quite flattered.

1st May (Friday).—I called on General Scurry, and found him suffering from severe ophthalmia. When I presented General Magruder's letter, he insisted that I should come and live with him so long as I remained here. He also telegraphed to Galveston for a steamer to take me there and back.

We dined at 4 P. M.: the party consisted of Colonel and Judge Terrill (a clever and agreeable man), Colonel Pyron, Captain Wharton, quartermaster-general, Major Watkins (a handsome fellow, and hero of the Sabine Pass affair), and Colonel Cook, commanding the artillery at Galveston (late of the U. S. navy, who enjoys the reputation of being a zealous Methodist preacher and a daring officer). The latter told me he could hardly understand how I could be an Englishman, as I pronounced my h's all right. General Scurry himself is very amusing, and is an admirable mimic. His numerous anecdotes of the war were very interesting. In peace times he is a lawyer. He was a volunteer major in the Mexican war, and distinguished himself very much in the late campaigns in New Mexico and Arizona, and at the recapture of Galveston.

After dinner, the Queen's health was proposed; and the party expressed the greatest admiration for Her Majesty, and respect for the British Constitution. They all said that universal suffrage did not produce such deplorable results in the South as in the North; because the population in the South is so very scattered, and the whites being the superior race, they form a sort of aristocracy.

They all wanted me to put off going to Galveston till Monday, in order that some ladies might go; but I was inexorable, as it must now be my object to cross the Mississippi without delay. All these officers despised sabres, and considered double-barrelled shot-guns and revolvers the best arms for cavalry.

2nd May (Saturday).—As the steamer had not arrived in the morning, I left by railroad for Galveston. General Scurry insisted upon sending his servant to wait upon me, in order that I might become acquainted with "an aristocratic negro." "John" was a very smart fellow, and at first sight nearly as white as myself.

In the cars I was introduced to General Samuel Houston, the founder of Texan independence. He told me he was born in Virginia seventy years ago, that he was United States senator at thirty, and governor of Tennessee at thirty-six. He emigrated into Texas in 1832; headed the revolt of Texas, and defeated the Mexicans at San Jacinto in 1836. He then became President of the Republic of Texas, which he annexed to the United States in 1845. As Governor of the State in 1860, he had opposed the secession movement, and was *deposed*. Though evidently a remarkable and clever man, he is extremely egotistical and vain, and much disappointed at having to subside from his former grandeur. The town of Houston is named after him. In appearance he is a tall, handsome old man, much given to chewing tobacco, and blowing his nose with his fingers.*

I was also introduced to another "character," Capt. Chubb, who told me he was a Yankee by birth, and served as coxswain to the United States ship Java in 1827. He was afterwards imprisoned at Boston on suspicion of being engaged in the slave trade; but he escaped. At the beginning of this war he was captured by the Yankees, when he was in command of the Confederate States steamer Royal Yacht, and taken to New York in chains, where he was condemned to be hung as a pirate; but he was eventually exchanged. I was afterwards told that the slave-trading escapade of which he was accused consisted in his having hired a colored crew at Boston, and then coolly *selling* them at Galveston.

At 1 P. M., we arrived at Virginia Point, a *tête-de-pont* at the extremity of the mainland. Here Bates's battalion was encamped—called also the "swamp angels," on account of the marshy nature of their quarters, and of their predatory and irregular habits.

The railroad then traverses a shallow lagoon (called Galveston Bay) on a trestle-bridge two miles long; this leads to another *tête-de-pont* on Galveston island, and in a few minutes the city is reached.

In the train I had received the following message by tele-

* He is reported to have died in August, 1863.

graph from Colonel Debray, who commands at Galveston: "Will Col. Fremantle sleep to-night at the house of a block-aded rebel?" I answered:—"Delighted;" and was received at the terminus by Capt. Foster of the Staff, who conducted me in an ambulance to headquarters, which were at the house of the Roman Catholic bishop. I was received there by Colonel Debray and two very gentlemanlike French priests.

We sat down to dinner at 2 P. M., but were soon inter-rupted by an indignant drayman, who came to complain of a military outrage. It appeared that immediately after I had left the cars, a semi-drunken Texan of Pyron's regiment had desired this drayman to stop, and upon the latter declining to do so, the Texan fired five shots at him from his "six-shooter," and the last shot killed the drayman's horse. Captain Foster (who is a Louisianian, and very sarcastic about Texas) said that the regiment would probably hang the soldier for being such a *disgraceful bad shot.*

After dinner Colonel Debray took me into the observatory, which commands a good view of the city, bay, and gulf.

Galveston is situated near the eastern end of an island thirty miles long by three and a half wide. Its houses are well built; its streets are long, straight, and shaded with trees; but the city was now desolate, blockaded, and under military law. Most of the houses were empty, and bore many marks of the ill-directed fire of the Federal ships during the night of the 1st of January last.

The whole of Galveston Bay is very shallow, except a nar-row channel of about one hundred yards immediately in front of the now deserted wharves. The entrance to this channel is at the northeastern extremity of the island, and is defended by the new works which are now in progress there. It is also blocked up with piles, torpedoes, and other obstacles.

The blockaders were plainly visible about four miles from land; they consisted of three gunboats and an ugly paddle steamer, also two supply vessels.

The wreck of the Confederate cotton-steamer Neptune (destroyed in her attack on the Harriet Lane), was close off one of the wharves. That of the Westfield (blown up by the Yankee Commodore), was off Pelican Island.

In the night of the 1st January, General Magruder suddenly entered Galveston, placed his field-pieces along the line of wharves, and unexpectedly opened fire in the dark upon the Yankee war vessels at a range of about one hundred yards; but so heavy (though badly directed) was the reply from the ships, that the field-pieces had to be withdrawn. The attack by Colonel Cook upon a Massachusetts regiment fortified at the end of a wharf, also failed, and the Confederates thought themselves "badly whipped." But after daylight the fortunate surrender of the Harriet Lane to the cotton-boat Bayou City, and the extraordinary conduct of Commodore Renshaw, converted a Confederate disaster into the recapture of Galveston. General Magruder certainly deserves immense credit for his boldness in attacking a heavily armed naval squadron with a few field-pieces and two river steamers protected with cotton bales and manned with Texan cavalry soldiers.

I rode with Colonel Debray to examine Forts Scurry, Magruder, Bankhead, and Point. These works have been ingeniously designed by Colonel Sulokowski (formerly in the Austrian army), and they were being very well constructed by one hundred and fifty whites and six hundred blacks under that officer's superintendence, the blacks being lent by the neighboring planters.

Although the blockaders can easily approach to within three miles of the works, and although one shell will always "stampede" the negroes, yet they have not thrown any for a long time.*

Colonel Debray is a broad-shouldered Frenchman, and is a very good fellow. He told me that he emigrated to America in 1848; he raised a company in 1861, in which he was only a private; he was next appointed aide-de-camp to the governor of Texas, with the rank of brigadier-general; he then descended to a major of infantry, afterwards rose to a lieutenant-colonel of cavalry, and is now colonel.

Captain Foster is properly on Magruder's Staff, and is very good company. His property at New Orleans had been destroyed by the Yankees.

In the evening we went to a dance given by Colonel Manly, which was great fun. I danced an American cotillion with Mrs. Manly; it was very violent exercise, and not the least like any thing I had seen before. A gentleman stands by shouting out the different figures to be performed, and every one obeys his orders with much gravity and energy. Colonel Manly is a very gentlemanlike Carolinian; the ladies were pretty, and, considering the blockade, they were very well dressed. Six deserters from Banks' army arrived here to-day. Banks seems to be advancing steadily, and overcoming the opposition offered by the handful of Confederates in the Teche country.

Banks himself is much despised as a soldier, and is always called by the Confederates Mr. Commissary Banks, on account of the efficient manner in which he performed the

* Such a stampede did occur when the blockaders threw two or three shells. All the negroes ran, showing every sign of great dismay, and two of them, in their terror, ran into the sea, and were unfortunately drowned. It is now, however, too late for the ships to try this experiment, as some heavy guns are in position. A description of the different works is of course omitted here.

duties of that office for "Stonewall" Jackson in Virginia. The officer who is supposed *really* to command the advancing Federals, is Weitzel; and he is acknowledged by all here to be an able man, a good soldier, and well acquainted with the country in which he is manœuvring.

3d May (Sunday).—I paid a long visit this morning to Mr. Lynn the British Consul, who told me that he had great difficulty in communicating with the outer world, and had seen no British man-of-war since the Immortalité.

At 1.30 I saw Pyron's regiment embark for Niblitt's Bluff to meet Banks. This corps is now dismounted cavalry, and the procession was a droll one. First came eight or ten instruments braying discordantly, then an enormous Confederate flag, followed by about four hundred men moving by fours— dressed in every variety of costume, and armed with every variety of weapon; about sixty had Enfield rifles; the remainder carried shot-guns (fowling-pieces), carbines, or long rifles of a peculiar and antiquated manufacture. None had swords or bayonets—all had six-shooters and bowie-knives. The men were a fine, determined-looking lot; and I saw among them a short stout boy of fourteen, who had served through the Arizona campaign. I saw many of the soldiers take off their hats to the French priests, who seemed much respected in Galveston. This regiment is considered down here to be a very good one, and its colonel is spoken as one of the bravest officers in the army. The regiment was to be harangued by Old Houston before it embarked.*

In getting into the cars to return to Houston, I was nearly forced to step over the dead body of the horse shot by the

---

* At the outbreak of the war it was found very difficult to raise infantry in Texas, as no Texan walks a yard if he can help it. Many mounted regiments were therefore organized, and afterwards dismounted.

soldier yesterday, and which the authorities had not thought necessary to remove.

I got back to General Scurry's house at Houston at 4.30 P. M. The general took me out for a drive in his ambulance, and I saw innumerable negroes and negresses parading about the streets in the most outrageously grand costumes—silks, satins, crinolines, hats with feathers, lace mantles, &c., forming an absurd contrast to the simple dresses of their mistresses. Many were driving about in their master's carriages, or riding on horses which are often lent to them on Sunday afternoons; all seemed intensely happy and satisfied with themselves.

—— told me that old Sam Houston lived for several years amongst the Cherokee Indians, who used to call him "the Raven" or the "Big Drunk." He married an Indian squaw when he was with them.

The South Mourns Jackson

IN THE INDOMITABLE WILL of "Stonewall" Jackson was exemplified the strength and the ambition of the Confederacy. His death after the Battle of Chancellorsville, where he was accidentally shot by his own troops, was, in effect, the spiritual climax of the Confederacy. Never again would the tides of Confederate hopes and Confederate victories rise as high as they had at the news of Jackson's successes in the Valley of Virginia, at second Manassas, and at Fredericksburg.

This obituary tribute from *The Southern Illustrated News* is indicative of the grief which swept the South at the news of Jackson's death.

THE ILLUSTRIOUS DEAD

Day before yesterday, at Lexington, in the very heart of Virginia, there was committed to the earth the inanimate remains of one of the most remarkable men of his time. Many beautiful and affecting tributes have been rendered to his lofty character and his immeasurable services, which are yet but a most inadequate expression of the public grief; and we might well hesitate, when the pens of ready writers have failed to set forth the genius and worth of the hero and the love and sorrow which followed him to the tomb, to write one line upon an event at once so august and so appalling as that single death. But we can write of nothing else. The wailing music of the funeral dirge is still sounding in our ears; we still see the ghastly plumes nodding above the bier; and when we endeavor to direct our thoughts to subjects such as ordinarily engage us in these columns, the mournful calamity, in all its weight of woe, rushes back upon us, and excludes every other consideration.

It were unwise, perhaps immodest, in us, all unlearned in the science of war, to attempt a characterization of THOMAS JONATHAN JACKSON as a military man. But we do not hesitate to say that he appears to us to belong to that little family of inspired conquerors who, in the march of the centuries, have seemed to lure Victory to their standards as her own proper perch, and who have made all the difficulties and dangers that stood in their way subservient to their imperial will and auxiliary to their further progress. They are but a small band, indeed, these Makers of Destiny and Masters of War, not enough to form a company, far less a regiment, in Hades—Alexander, Hannibal, Cæsar, Frederick, Napoleon—and others of less shining note, whose path of conquest we trace across the Bosphorus and over the Alps, through Russian snows and under Syrian suns, and to whose career no lapse of time can make the world indifferent, from whose wonderful achievements no physical changes of the earth's surface, no shiftings of empire from East to West, can ever withdraw the attention of mankind. Among these heroes JACKSON will take his place when the Plutarch of the future shall chronicle the Lives of this Nineteenth Century. His military

life was short, as compared with that of any one of them.
Two years (for we cannot properly include his service in the
war with Mexico, distinguished as it was, in the estimate,)
comprise all that he did in the eyes of the world. Nor were
the results of his astonishing labors comparable with those
which attended the long campaigns of the warriors of history. Yet when we place in effective contrast *what he did*
with the means at his command to do it; when we consider
how he went on from victory to victory, despite every drawback and discouragement, cleaving down the masses of men
that opposed him with his irresistible arm, making the little
body of troops which he could neither clothe nor feed more
than equal to twice their numbers; when we remember that
he fought always in a subordinate position, in which his
plans were liable at any moment to be overruled, and that
he never, indeed, had the theatre and the opportunity for
the full exhibition of his genius, we are confirmed in the
belief that the common verdict of his contemporaries, which
assigns him the first rank in warfare, will not hereafter be set
aside.

But if JACKSON achieved less than the great Captains of
ancient or modern times, (though it may be doubted if the
campaign in the Valley of Virginia in the summer of 1862
has ever been surpassed,) he rises immeasurably above them
in contemplation of the motive which impelled him to action.
He followed no star, he sought no throne, he asked no earthly
guerdon, was guided by no selfish consideration, and lured
by no vulgar ambition. Duty, and duty alone, was the principle of his conduct. He recognized a call to fight for Virginia
in her hour of agony, and he obeyed it. He felt within him
the mastery of the occasion, and he exerted it. Otherwise the
world had not heard of JACKSON. But for this diabolical

war, the modest Professor would have gone on lecturing to the class of Natural Philosophy at the Military Institute, with less *éclat* than Mr. Faraday across the water; the "Blue Light Elder" might have run his obscure round of serving God in the village where the war found him, until he was called to the Congregation of the Saints above.— Such was the simple, earnest moral of his life. What a record it is! How bright, how clear, how complete! May we not say, in the language which Clarendon employs in lamenting the death of Lucius Carey, Lord Falkland, that "if there were no other brand upon this odious and accursed civil war, than that single loss, it must be most infamous and execrable to all posterity"?

After all, perhaps, grateful for the services which this illustrious man rendered Virginia in her time of sorest need, and sorrowing over his fall in utter desolation of heart, we may see the greatest good of JACKSON'S life in the example he bequeathes to those who are to come after us. As the images on the friezes of the Parthenon follow one another in one continuous succession of noble and majestic forms, each a hero or a god, so is the long line of the worthies of the Ancient Commonwealth and Dominion of Virginia perpetuated in the lofty figures that move before men in this second age of Greatness and Virtue; and among them none shall more certainly wear the antique cast of heroism, none shall appear worthier of the better, earlier days of the Republic, than the tall, stern effigy of STONEWALL JACKSON. And if the lives of the great and good are the most precious heritage that one generation can hand down to another, the age in which we live, in the story of this one life, shall transmit to its successor an incomputable wealth.

The literature of the future will be rich with the inspiration of his career. Poets will sing of him, and romanticists will

ORDER OF THE PROCESSION
AT THE FUNERAL OF
LIEUT. GEN. T. J. JACKSON.

1st. Military
2d. Pall Bearers. }BODY.{ Pall Bearers.
3d. Family of the deceased.
4th. Faculty of the Va. Military Institute.
Officers " " " " "
Members of the Quartermaster Dep't.
" " " Subsistence "
Servants of the Va. Military Institute.
5th. Elders of the Lex'n. Presbyterian Church.
6th. Deacons of the Lexington Pres. Church.
7th. Reverend Clergy.
8th. Trustees, Professors and Students of Washington College.
9th. Franklin Society.
10th. Town Council.
11th. County Magistrates.
12th. Members of the Bar and Medical Profession.
13th. Officers and Soldiers of the Confederate Army.
14th. Bible Society.
15th. Sabbath Schools.
16th. Citizens.

The Procession will be formed at the V. M. I. at 10 o'clock, A. M., on Saturday, the 16th inst.

The body will lie in state at the V. M. I. during Friday.　　　FRANCIS H. SMITH,
V. M. I., May 10th, 1863.　　Superintendent.

192

weave his deeds into the warp and woof of fiction. The beautiful region of the Shenandoah will be classic ground as associated with his memory, and the cottages of the Valley will long preserve traditions of his less familiar traits. "Tell us of JACKSON," shall the children cry around the fireside, as Béranger says the idle villagers of France call upon the old women for stories of Napoleon—

> "Parlez nous de lui, grandmère,
> Parlez nous de lui!"

Of the sweet, sad incidents that attended his last illness and death, of his affecting serenity of mind, and humble submission to the will of God, of the general outburst of sorrow all over the land when he was taken from us, of his obsequies here in Richmond, and the consecration of the new flag of the Republic, in its having been first used as his pall—we need not speak, for these are yet too fresh in the hearts of all. "Beautiful! What we might call a classic, sacred death; if it were not rather an Elijah-translation,—in a chariot, not of fire and terror, but of hope and soft vernal sun-beams!"

And here we say farewell to STONEWALL JACKSON. We lay our little wreath upon his coffin, fragrant with lilies deposited by soft white hands, wet with tears rained from bright eyes, and turn sorrowfully away—

> Ashes to ashes, dust to dust;
> He is gone who seem'd so great.
> Gone; but nothing can bereave him
> Of the force he made his own
> Being here, and we believe him
> Something far advanced in state,
> And that he wears a truer crown
> Than any wreath that man can weave him.

But speak no more of his renown,
Lay your earthly fancies down,
And in earth's embraces leave him:
God accept him, Christ receive him.

Defeat at Vicksburg

Having successfully repelled the invader throughout one summer, Vicksburg confidently settled down for another long siege in the late spring of 1863. But the Yankees were throwing new and stronger forces at the little city. After a siege of forty-seven days, the Confederates fell before the soldiers of General U. S. Grant. Notwithstanding an unprecedented artillery bombardment and equally heavy hardship caused by the lack of food within the Confederate lines, many Confederates felt bitterly that the siege should have been longer resisted and that General Pemberton had not performed his full duty in relinquishing the city. Pemberton, however, had directed a gallant fight, and the failure of Confederate troops under General Joseph E. Johnston to reach him in time left him no choice but surrender.

Among the Confederates in the besieged city was Alexander St. Clair Abrams. Abrams had served through the siege of 1862, been wounded, and released from the army. In September, 1862, he had resumed his old occupation as a newspaperman in a place on the staff of the Vicksburg *Whig*. After the capture of Vicksburg he was paroled as a prisoner and moved first to Mobile and then to Atlanta, where he published, later in 1863, his account of what had happened. "By the middle of June," he wrote, "Vicksburg was in a deplorable condition. There was scarcely a building but what had been struck by the enemy's shells, while many of them were entirely demolished. The city had the appearance of a half-ruined pile of buildings, and on every street unmistakable signs of the fearful bombardment it had undergone, presented themselves to the observer."

The following passage is Abrams' account of the Confederate surrender.

At about three o'clock in the afternoon of the third of July, Lieutenant General Pemberton, accompanied by Major General Bowen, left our lines and proceeded to the neutral ground, previously designated, and had an interview with General Grant. . . . After an absence of about two hours' duration, Lieutenant General Pemberton and Major General Bowen returned into our lines. As an armistice had been declared until ten o'clock that evening, the firing ceased, and the shades of night descended upon the two opposing armies in quietude, unbroken, save by the voices of the soldiers in low but angry and indignant conversation, at what they deemed a disgrace upon their country in surrendering the city they had so long and nobly fought, and endured the pangs of hunger to defend.

At dark, on the evening of this day, a council of all the Generals was held at General Pemberton's headquarters, which lasted for several hours. Although we could not learn what transpired in an official way, we received information, from good authority, that it was decided, by a majority of the general officers, that the troops were entirely too weak from the want of food to cut their way through, and that if the position had to be yielded, it was useless to sacrifice the lives of the men in a fruitless endeavor; so that the only course left was to surrender the garrison on General Grant's terms of capitulation. Of the Major Generals present, we understand that Major General M. L. Smith was the only one who absolutely opposed surrendering on any condition, preferring to remain behind the breastworks and starve rather than give up the city. A majority of the council, being of a contrary opinion, however, he was, of course, necessitated to abide by their decision, and about three o'clock a messenger was sent into General Grant's lines with dispatches from Lieutenant General Pemberton.

On Saturday morning, a circular was issued from headquarters, announcing the surrender of Vicksburg and garrison, and stating the terms of capitulation to be as follows:

1st. The entire garrison of Confederate troops was to be surrendered to Major General Grant, commanding the United States forces.

2d. The prisoners of war to be paroled and sent out of the city as soon as blank paroles were printed.

3d. All mounted officers to have the privilege of retaining their horses.

4th. All officers of every grade and rank were to retain their side arms, &c.

5th. All citizens desiring to leave the city with the Confederate forces, could do so on being paroled.

6th. All ammunition, stores, field artillery and siege guns, were to be surrendered to the United States forces, as also all small arms in our possession.

These are about the substance of the terms of capitulation. Although we made no copy of Lieutenant General Pemberton's circular, this will be found as correct a statement as could be desired.

When it was officially announced to our men that Vicksburg was surrendered to the enemy, their indignation knew no bounds. Having been among the troops, we can truthfully speak what we heard and saw of the expressions of sentiment on their part relative to the surrender. With almost an unanimous voice the soldiers declared that General Pemberton had yielded the city without their will, and against any desire on their part. All expressed a determination never to serve under him again, many stating that, rather than be under the command of such a man, they would desert from the army, if they were afterwards shot for it. It is not to be denied that the feeling among the men amounted almost to a mutinous one—to such a degree, indeed, was it, that many threats were made, which only the argument and supplication of the officers prevented the men from putting into execution. . . .

On Saturday morning, the fourth of July, and the anniversary of American Independence, the troops composing the army of Lieutenant General Pemberton marched from the line of intrenchments they had defended and held for nearly two months, amid hardships and privations unsurpassed in the annals of modern warfare, and after stacking the arms they had so well and nobly used, and lowering the standards which had proudly floated on many a bloody battle-field, returned inside the works, prisoners of war to their bitterest foe.

On Saturday, at twelve o'clock, M., Logan's division of McPherson's corps, of the Federal army, commenced entering the city, and in a quarter of an hour Vicksburg was crammed with them. Their first act was to take possession of the court house, on the spire of which they hoisted the United States flag, amid the exultant shouts of their comrades, and a deep feeling of humiliation on the part of the Confederate soldiers who witnessed the hauling up of the flag which they had hoped never to see floating over the city they had so long and proudly boasted impregnable, and never to be taken by the enemy of the South.

After the enemy's forces had stacked their arms, they scattered over the city, and then commenced a scene of pillage and destruction which beggars all description. Houses and stores were broken open, and their contents appropriated by the plunderers. The amount of money and property stolen in this way was enormous, and the Yankee soldiers appeared to glory in their vandalism. One merchant, by the name of G. C. Kress, had his safe broken open, and twenty thousand dollars in money, with a large supply of clothing, taken away. Another merchant, and well-known citizen of Mississippi, by the name of W. H. Stephens, had his store broken open and nearly all the contents taken away. In fact, every place that they could possibly enter without fear of resistance, was broken open and robbed of what was contained in them. The enemy appeared to glory in their course, and on one occasion, in reply to a remonstrance on the part of a gentleman whose residence they had broken open, they said, "we have fought hard enough to capture Vicksburg, and now we have got it, we intend to plunder every house in the d——d rebel city." . . .

With that enterprise and greed for gain which characterizes the universal Yankee nation, on the same day that the Federal army entered Vicksburg, several places of business were opened, and signs informing the public that metallic coffins were on hand to remove the dead bodies of friends, and that express offices, book and fruit stores were "within," were to be seen upon several establishments on Washington street.

Soon after the enemy entered the city, Mr. William Lunn, a well-known citizen of Vicksburg, took the oath of allegiance, and General Grant made his headquarters at the residence of this gentleman. The Jewish portion of the population, composed principally of Germans, with but one honorable exception, went forward and received the oath of allegiance to the United States. The one honorable exception sacrificed a store of goods, which cost him between thirty-five and forty thousand dollars, rather than remain under the control of the enemy.

The conduct of the negroes, after the entrance of their "liberators," was beyond all expression. While the Yankee army was marching through the streets, crowds of them congregated on the sidewalks, with a broad grin of satisfaction on their ebony countenances. The next day, which was Sunday, witnessed a sight, which would have been ludicrous had it not galled our soldiers by the reflection that they were compelled to submit to it. There was a great turn out of the "contrabands," dressed up in the most extravagant style imaginable, promenading through the streets, as if Vicksburg had been confiscated and turned over [to] them. In familiar conversation with the negro wenches, the soldiers of the Federal army were seen, arm-in-arm, marching through the streets, while the "bucks" congregated on the corners and discussed the happy event that had brought them freedom.

So arrogant did the negroes become after the entrance of the Federal forces, that no white Confederate citizen or soldier dared to speak to them, for fear of being called a rebel, or some other abusive epithet. One of the Confederate soldiers, happening to enter the garden of the house that the author of this work resided in, for the purpose of picking a peach, a negro, belonging to a gentleman of Vicksburg, who had charge of the garden, brought out a gun, and, taking deliberate aim at the soldier, was about to fire. We immediately threw up the gun, and, drawing a knife, threatened the negro if he fired at the man; no sooner was the threat made, than the negro, with an oath, levelled the gun at us and drew the trigger; luckily the cap snapped without exploding, and we succeeded in getting the gun away and discharging it.

While making these observations about the negroes, we would say that it was confined to the city negroes alone. The slaves brought in by planters, and servants of soldiers and officers, did not appear the least gratified at their freedom. The majority of those connected with our army were very desirous of leaving with their masters, and General Grant at first consented that those who desired it should leave; but as soon as a few passes were made out, he revoked the order, and compelled the balance to remain. These differences in the conduct of city and country negroes, should not be a matter of surprise, when we consider the privileges given to the negroes in the cities of the South, and demands a change of policy on the part of slaveowners residing in densely populated places. Many of the negroes, who were compelled to remain in Vicksburg, when their masters in the army left, afterwards made their escape, and returned to the Confederate lines.

The loss of the Confederate forces during the siege, is estimated by good judges at a number not exceeding 4,000 in killed and wounded. A number of our casualties resulted from the indiscretion of the soldiers in exposing themselves

to the enemy's sharpshooters. The loss of the enemy we
would estimate as follows:

Attack on Shoup's line, 19th
　　of May ....   600 killed and wounded
General assault on the 22d May 9,000　　"　　　　"
Attack on Hebert's line, 25th
　　June ....   600　　"　　　　"
Prisoners captured 500
Other casualties during the
　　siege 2,000
Making a total of 12,700

This estimate we believe to be much beneath what it really
was, as in our opinion the enemy lost nearly as much as the
total, on the twenty-second of May, for, taking the ratio of
six men wounded for one killed, we find that as many as two
thousand bodies were buried by the enemy on the Monday
following. This would make their loss on the day alone 14,000,
or more than the grand total we give above. The assertion
of Grant, in his official report, that he lost only 8,000 men
during the campaign, is a glaring falsehood, as we feel certain that on the day mentioned above he lost more than he
states his casualties to be from the landing at Bruinsburg to
the surrender of the city.

The total amount of prisoners captured at Vicksburg by
the enemy did not exceed twenty-four thousand, of which,
nearly six thousand were either sick or wounded. The following general officers were captured. Lieutenant General Pemberton; Major Generals M. L. Smith, J. H. Forney, J. Bowen,
and C. L. Stephenson. The names of the Brigadier Generals
captured were: Hebert, Moore, Barton, Lee, Buford, Shoup,
Baldwin, Vaughn and Taylor, the latter being Inspector
General of the army.

Our loss in small arms and artillery was about as follow:

Small Arms 35,000
Siege Guns 27
Field Artillery 70

A great many pieces of the artillery were unfit for use, and could have been of no use to the enemy.

The amount of ammunition delivered over to the Yankee officers was large, and as near as we could find out, was as follows:

Musket Cartridges .... 600,000 rounds
Field Artillery Cartridges ...... 15,000 "
Heavy Artillery Cartridges .... 15,000 "
Percussion caps .... 350,000 "

This estimate we believe very moderate, as it only gives for each man thirty-five rounds of musket cartridges, and about twenty percussion caps each. We are quite certain that a considerably larger amount of ammunition was surrendered to the enemy. This estimate, however, is made to avoid all charges of exaggeration.

Our line of works was pronounced by the enemy's engineer officers to be the most contemptible they had seen erected during the war. All expressed great astonishment that, with fifteen months of time before us, we had not converted Vicksburg into an impregnable fortress. They expressed themselves very much deceived in the strength of our works, as the representations of the Northern press, and our own boasting, had made them believe that Vicksburg was defended by well-made works, and had between two and three hundred guns mounted.

Our works were, indeed, the most outrageous ever made during the war. The supervisors of their construction could have known no more about erecting fortifications than we do; in fact, there was not one engineer in the army of Vicks-who understood his profession thoroughly—they existed but in name, and in the position they held in the Confederate service. The ground on which the works were erected was naturally a strong one, and to that advantage alone were we enabled to hold the city for so long a time, otherwise they would have offered but little or no impediment to the overwhelming numbers of the enemy which were thrown on the line in their attack on the twenty-second of May.

After the enemy had taken possession of Vicksburg, Major General McPherson rode over the entire line, and was so impressed with the defective manner in which they were constructed, that he is reported to have exclaimed: "Good Heavens! are these the long-boasted fortifications of Vicksburg? It was the rebels, and not their works, that kept us out of the city." While this was a great compliment to the valor of the "rebels," it certainly expressed the greatest contempt possible for the fortifications surrounding Vicksburg.

The Federal officers candidly gave the Confederate garrison the credit of being as brave troops as they ever saw, and more than one compliment to the heroism of our soldiers was paid, coupled with a regret on the part of the officers of rank, that such men should be in arms against the United States. Not a word was said by the Yankees claiming superiority in fighting qualities; they all acknowledged that starvation had conquered us, and not the prowess of their arms, and during the stay of the garrison in Vicksburg, the greatest courtesy and consideration was shown to our soldiers by the Federal officers; their privates alone manifesting any desire to gloat over our reverse.

The Confederate army remained in Vicksburg, as prisoners of war, for one week after the surrender, that time being taken to prepare the rolls of the different commands, and parole the men. During this period many severe street fights took place between the Federal and Confederate soldiers, in consequence of the taunts and abuse of the victorious army. Several of the Federal soldiers were severely beaten, and one or two killed. In one of these street brawls, a young man, a citizen of Vicksburg, and volunteer aid on Gen. Baldwin's staff, shot a Federal soldier dead for using insulting language. He was taken to General Grant's headquarters, and after a hearing released.

During the week spent in the enemy's lines, we had several opportunities of hearing the sentiments of both the officers and soldiers of the Federal army. Among the officers, it was the same everlasting cant about the Union, and their determination that it should be restored; but among the privates the greed for gain, and the object with which they fight was not concealed in the slightest degree. They spoke in raptures of the capacity of Mississippi's soil for white labor, and declared their intention to get a grant of land from the United States and settle there after the war is over. This unblushing declaration was accompanied by the assertion that, as the South had rebelled against their government, it was only just that the property of the people be divided among their troops. Such remarks were the principal cause of the street fights between the two armies, as the spirit of our soldiers could ill brook this style of apportioning their homes and property by the enemy.

By Friday, the 10th of July, the prisoners having been paroled, the Confederate soldiers took up their line of march. It was a mournful and harrowing sight. The soldiers felt their disgrace, and there was not one gallant heart in the mass of men, that did not feel half bursting with sorrow and humiliation at being compelled to march through the enemy's guards who were stationed on both sides of the road to some distance beyond the entrenchments. But nothing could avert the degradation; so with downcast looks, and countenances on which a knowledge of the bitterness of their defeat could be seen plainly stamped, they filed past the enemy, who gathered in large number to witness their departure.

It was a day never to be forgotten by those who assisted in the defense of Vicksburg. So filled with emotion were many of our men, that large tear drops could be seen on their weather-beaten countenances, and ever and anon they would pause in their march, and, turning back, take one last sad look at the city they had fought and bled for. All felt that, serious as the disaster was to the Confederate cause, it was nothing to their humiliation. Amid the storm of shot and shell that poured upon them, they had remained cheerful and confident; but at this moment their hopefulness had departed; the yell of defiance that had so often struck terror in the hearts of their foe, was not to be heard; their willing hands no longer grasped the weapons of a good cause; their standards trailed in the dust, and they were prisoners of war. Silently and sadly they marched on, and in a few minutes Vicksburg was lost to their view.

Thus fell the city of Vicksburg after a defense of over twelve months, and a siege which lasted for forty-seven days, forty-two of which a garrison of not more than twenty-five thousand effective men had subsisted on less than one-quarter rations. The Confederate army fought with a valor that not even the defenders of Saragossa and Mantua ever surpassed. Subject to a bombardment of a nature so terrific that its equal has never been known in civilized warfare; through rain and sunshine, storm and calm, writhing under the pangs of starvation, these gallant Southern troops, whose deeds will form one of history's brightest pages when the annals of this siege shall become known, stood up to their post, and, with almost superhuman valor, repulsed every attack made by their enemy, and inflicting tremendous loss on him, until surrendered by the General whose want of ability and confidence in himself had entailed these sufferings and hardships on them.

It is estimated that the number of missiles thrown in the entrenchments, exceeded thirty thousand daily; and by the official report of General Grant's Chief of Artillery, it would appear that twenty million three hundred and seventy thousand one hundred and twenty-two missiles of all kinds were thrown in the works, which would make it, by calculation, over four hundred thousand missiles, including small arms ammunition, daily thrown. This, however, must be an exaggeration, unless Grant's Chief of Artillery included the number of rounds of small arms used in the different battles prior to the investment of Vicksburg, which lasted only forty-seven days. He, however, gives the number as having been fired *into the city*, which, if correct, would only show the gigantic nature of the bombardment. . . .

We cannot close this chapter without passing a just compliment to the Surgeons attached to the garrison at Vicksburg. Although they were from morning to night engaged in their duties to the soldiers, they were always found administering to the sick and wounded non-combatants of the city. Among the many, we must mention Dr. E. McD. Coffey, Chief Surgeon of Bowen's division, who was unremitting in his attention to this class of sufferers, and always had several sick and wounded women and children under his charge. To this gentleman we were indebted for an introduction to Major General McPherson, who is, without doubt, the only real gentleman among the Federal Generals to whom we were introduced. He was very polite, never using the epithet "rebel" in the presence of our officers or soldiers, and avoided, as much as possible, any expression of exultation at the fall of Vicksburg when in our company.

Before bringing this chapter to a close, we would endeavor to remove the false idea among our people, that Vicksburg was surrendered after a feeble defense. The city was defended as desperately as could be required. The only thing to be said is, that had proper generalship been displayed, there would have been no necessity to use the works surrounding Vicksburg. *After* we were invested, the defense of Vicksburg *commenced*, and though the city is now in the hands of the enemy, it has brought him no honor in its capture, nor added a single laurel to his wreath of victory. *Starvation* succeeded in doing what the prowess of their arms could never have performed. The result was a reverse to the Confederate arms; but when future generations shall speak of this war, the deeds of the gallant men who defended the city, will be extolled among the most heroic feats of the war, and the descendants of those who fought behind the entrenchments of Vicksburg, will be proud of the knowledge that their fathers aided in its defense. All honor to these unswerving patriots! Nobly did they sustain the honor of their country, and the glory of their past deeds; and, falling as they did, the historian of this war will declare that, in their fall as much honor was gained as if they had triumphed in their defense.

Mule Meat at the Hotel de Vicksburg

AFTER THE SURRENDER of Vicksburg Northern newspapers published as an amusing tidbit the "Bill of
Fare" said to have been found in one of the Confederate
Army camps. If authentic, it is the work of a Confederate
who had not lost his sense of humor amid almost un-
endurable hardship. If the work of a Yankee prankster,
it was written by one familiar with conditions behind the
Confederate lines.

Reporter Alexander St. Clair Abrams confirms the basis
of such a menu in his description of conditions at Vicksburg in the weeks before the surrender: "Many families of
wealth had eaten the last mouthful of food in their possession, and the poor class of non-combatants were on the
verge of starvation. . . . Starvation, in its worst forms,
now confronted the inhabitants, and, had the siege lasted
two weeks longer, the consequences would have been
terrible. All the beef in the city was exhausted by this
time, and mules were soon brought in requisition, and
their meat sold readily at one dollar per pound, the citizens being as anxious to get it as they were before the
investment to purchase the delicacies of the season. It
was also distributed among the soldiers, to those who

desired it, although it was not given out under the name of rations. A great many of them, however, accepted it in preference to doing without any meat, and the flesh of the mules was found equal to the best venison. The author of this work partook of mule meat for three or four days, and found the flesh tender and nutritious, and, under the *peculiar circumstances*, a most desirable description of food."

Southern Punch copied the "Bill of Fare" from the Chicago *Tribune* so that all Confederates might read it.

The Chicago Tribune publishes the following bill of fare found in one of the camps at Vicksburg. It is surrounded by an engraving of a mule's head, behind which is a hand brandishing what may be a bowie, or may be a carving knife. The Tribune thinks it is a melancholy burlesque. The most melancholy thing about it is the reflection which it must suggest to a thoughtful Yankee—if there be such an animal—on the prospect of conquering the men who can live and jest on such fare:

HOTEL DE VICKSBURG

Bill of Fare for July, 1863.

SOUP.

Mule Tail.

BOILED.

Mule bacon with poke greens.
Mule ham canvassed.

ROAST.

Mule sirloin.
Mule rump stuffed with rice.

VEGETABLES.

Peas and Rice.

ENTREES.

Mule head stuffed a-la-Mode.
Mule beef jerked a-la-Mexicana.
Mule ears fricasseed a-la-gotch.
Mule side stewed, new style, hair on.
Mule spare ribs plain.
Mule liver, hashed.

SIDE DISHES.

Mule salad.
Mule hoof soused.
Mule brains a-la-omelette.
Mule kidney stuffed with peas.
Mule tripe fried in pea meal batter.
Mule tongue cold a-la-Bray.

JELLIES.

Mule foot.

PASTRY.

Pea meal pudding, blackberry sauce.
Cotton-wood berry pies
China berry tart.

DES[S]ERT.

White-oak acorns.
Beech nuts.
Blackberry leaf tea.
Genuine Confederate Coffee.

LIQUORS.

Mississippi Water, vintage of 1498, superior, $3.00.
Limestone Water, late importation, very fine, $2.75.
Spring Water, Vicksburg brand, $1.50.

Meals at all hours. Gentlemen to wait upon themselves. Any inattention on the part of servants will be promptly reported at the office.

JEFF. DAVIS & CO., Proprietors.

CARD.—The proprietors of the justly celebrated Hotel are now prepared to accommodate all who may favor them with a call. Parties arriving by the river, or Grant's inland route, will find Grape, Canister, & Co's., carriages at the landing, or any depot on the line of intrenchments. Buck, Ball & Co., take charge of all baggage. No effort will be spared to make the visit of all as interesting as possible.

Gettysburg

A TWIN with the surrender at Vicksburg was the Confederate failure at Gettysburg. Hailed at the time as a victory by both sides, Gettysburg was in reality a turning point of the war and a far-reaching defeat for the Confederacy. Though Lee had achieved a measure of success on the battlefield, it was a success which left him unable to follow through the advantage gained. His retreat across the Potomac ended the Confederacy's last great thrust into the territory of the enemy, and the campaign upon which the hopes of the South had been banked had amounted to no gain.

Here is *The Southern Illustrated News* account of the blows at Gettysburg and Vicksburg from its fortnightly summary of war news.

On Wednesday, Thursday and Friday, (1st, 2d and 3d of July,) was fought the great battle of Gettysburg, in Pennsylvania, between the forces of Gen. Lee and the Yankee army under the command of Gen. Meade, who succeeds Hooker,

MASTER ABRAHAM LINCOLN GETS A NEW TOY.

superseded for incompetency. This was probably the most obstinate battle of the war. For the first two days our troops drove those of the enemy before them, and captured 4,000 prisoners, who were paroled through the enemy's lines. The Yankee General, taking advantage of the late Washington decision, refused to acknowledge their parole, and ordered the men back into the ranks. On Friday Gen. Lee renewed the attack on the enemy, and drove him to some strong entrenchments which he had on high ground. These entrenchments were stormed after severe fighting, and the victory remained with us. But Gen. Lee, perceiving that they were commanded by entrenchments still higher up the mountains, after holding the works for twelve hours, fell slowly back. He had taken a large number of prisoners, and to secure them he fell back to Hagerstown. The Yankees had already retreated before he did, but he was not aware of the fact. Had he been so, we might have pressed them, in all probability, until they had become entirely demoralized. As it was, finding that *he* also had begun to fall back, the Yankees returned to the field and raised a shout of victory. The most astounding lies were telegraphed to the cities, and spread over the country by means of the press. Lee's army, according to them, had been completely routed and disorganized. Thousands of prisoners and acres of cannon had been taken. The terrible Yankee cavalry were in pursuit, Couch was interposing between Lee and the Potomac, and the death or capture of the whole army was certain. In the meantime, a telegram announcing a great victory and the capture of 40,000 Yankees, had been received in Richmond, and the people were jubilant. Suddenly their joy was cut short by the arrival of the flag of truce boat with the Yankee papers. Something very like a panic succeeded. The people seemed to take the Yankee lies for gospel; and when news arrived of the surrender of Pemberton at Vicksburg, the public pulse ebbed lower than we have ever known it. Before the end of the week, the truth with regard to Lee began to come out. He had gained a great victory, and captured thousands of prisoners. He had fallen back to Hagerstown at his leisure, and in the most perfect order. The Yankees had not dared to pursue him, and he held at the last dates a strong position, with an army in fine condition and eager to renew the trial of strength. The operations of Gen. Stuart, in the meantime, had been eminently successful. He had captured fifteen miles of wagons, and they are believed to be secure on this side of the river.

During the early part of the present week the greatest anxiety was felt by the public in regard to the situation of affairs. This uneasiness, however, was relieved on Thursday evening, by the reception of a despatch from Gen. Lee, announcing that he had re-crossed the Potomac with his army in good condition.— What necessitated this movement on the part of Gen. Lee is, of course, a matter of conjecture. Be the cause what it may, our people repose the utmost confidence in the skill and judgement of the great commander.

Vicksburg capitulated on the 4th, compelled by the presence of absolute famine. This blow was harder on our citizens, even, than the reported repulse of Lee.

All-Out War

THE HARDEST THING of all for the Confederates to learn was that this was a new kind of war, not at all like the battles they had read about in books of ancient history and the romances of Walter Scott. This was a war brought home to the people. But the Confederates forgot that all is fair in war and sometimes acted as if they were still fighting a tournament of sportsmen.

There were atrocities, of course. There are atrocities in all wars. War itself is an atrocity. But the atrocities were not all on the part of the Yankees. Both sides attempted to make propagandistic point of the worst acts of the other, but the Confederates were far behind the Yankees in realizing that war is war and that, to win, there must be no quarter given.

In the following selection the Rev. Joseph Cross cites how Union troops carried the war home to the people of the South. It is a chapter from his *Camp and Field*, there sarcastically titled "Civilized Warfare."

O that Mr. Lincoln could see himself as others see him! Here is an excerpt from an Irish paper, the Belfast News Letter, which is earnestly commended to his perusal. Let it be borne in mind that this voice comes from a country whose sympathies are all against slavery:

"If Mr. Lincoln were a Brahmin we could understand him, for the religion of the Brahmin teaches him that his sins and shortcomings are not to be regarded as those of common men. The law promulgated by Mr. Lincoln is like that of Menu, which declares that the Brahmin is entitled to all that exists in the universe by his primogeniture and eminence of birth. This eminent Yankee claims sovereign sway from Staten island to the Rocky mountains. He can not bring his mind to the contemplation of the indisputable fact that he is a very humble person after all, and that, in all human probability, he will return to his native obscurity in a few short months, and leave behind him nothing but a name infamous for all time.

"His Emancipation proclamation is nothing more nor less than a premium for murdering men and outraging women. It is the most odious and atrocious outburst of brutal and cowardly vindictiveness that ever emanated from a pagan or 'christian' tyrant. The author of it, and the 'christian' people who approve it, are more debased than the besotted savages of the Feejee islands; and, if the great powers of Europe do not step in to prevent it, they will deserve, as assuredly they will incur, the execration of posterity. Heretofore the patriots of the South have scorned to avail themselves of servile defenders. The last and foulest crime just perpetrated by the Lincoln administration will, however, justify any use to which they may now convert the enormous and undeveloped power within their hands.

"Another feature in this cruel and most unnatural war,

which appears to have escaped the attention it deserves, is the fact that the people of the Confederate States have imposed upon themselves burdens and taxes without a precedent in the history of the world. What would be said in the United Kingdom of such sacrifices? Yet this sacrifice has been voluntarily made by this heroic people, who will perish to a man before they will consent to the hateful yoke of the detested Yankees."

The London Times speaks of the war waged against the South by the North as disclosing "a cruelty and ferocity far surpassing all that is recorded of the wickedness and barbarity of men in former wars," and affirms that though men may wrangle and dispute about the causes, the rights and wrongs of this great quarrel, yet as to the measures employed by our enemies "posterity can have but one verdict to pronounce—a verdict of horror and execration." The editor finds it difficult to express the abhorrence inspired in the British mind by "acts so wanton and ferocious as that of letting loose the waters of the Mississippi over the plantations of the South, and overwhelming with the waves that which they found it impossible to subdue." From a long article, in which he animadverts with just severity upon this most diabolical deed, I copy a few sentences:

"Not satisfied with all the destruction which modern science has enabled mankind to wreak upon each other, the North has called to its aid the mighty agencies of nature, and seeks to ruin and mutilate half a continent in the vain hope to overthrow or intimidate its inhabitants. It is calculated that, by the action of the Federals in cutting the levees, or dams, which keep the Mississippi in its course as it runs through the level land toward the sea, a district as large as Scotland has been drowned in the State of Mississippi, and five thousand square miles in the State of Louisiana.

"Had some enormous strategical advantage been obtainable by this proceeding, mankind must have deplored the harsh and dreadful necessity which, in a continent of which so small a portion has as yet been reclaimed for the use of civilized man, drove the Federals to lay waste and devastate so considerable a portion of its surface. But there is no reason to suppose that any advantage in the least degree commensurate with the amount of wanton and cruel destruction which has been perpetrated, could anyhow have obtained. Most certainly no such advantage has been gained. The expedition from Yazoo Pass, so far from reaching its destined point near Vicksburg, has been encountered and defeated by Confederate batteries, and driven to take refuge in another river to avoid further injuries. The act, therefore, stands out in all its naked deformity. Those who have called the mighty Mississippi to their aid have proved themselves unworthy of their potent ally, and, powerful only for mischief, have been singularly discomfited in the endeavor to profit by that new and singular enterprise.

"At the beginning of the war the North went forth to battle in all the presumption of overweening strength and numbers. Their notions of success were thoroughly Oriental. They had the largest number of men under arms, and doubted not of victory, especially as they had the largest resources to feed, arm, and recruit them. Received in the field by troops far less numerous than their own, they found to their astonishment how little the leaders of the South had to dread from them in the open field. From that time the whole aspect of the war has entirely changed. In proportion as success has become more difficult, the means employed for its attainment have been more odious and cruel. Every effort has been made to light the torch of servile insurrection, and, as if this was not dreadful enough, water has been called in to supplement the tardy vengeance of that fire which, kindled by the hands of slaves, would, if the pious and decorous North could have had their will, wrap in one mighty conflagration the labors of a hundred years. Men may wrangle and dispute about the causes, the rights and wrongs of this great quarrel, but as to these measures posterity will have but one verdict to pronounce—a verdict of horror and execration.

"It is difficult to say what time—what interest may not effect. Nations have shed each other's blood like water on fields of battle. They have covered the ocean with the wrecks of their naval engagements and the bodies of their seamen. These things may be expiated, may be forgiven, may at last be forgotten; but deeds like those by which the Northern States are making their present war with the South singular and execrable among the worst and bloodiest annals of mankind, can never be forgiven or forgotten. The moment any idea of reconciliation is entertained, these dreadful memories will rise up like a spectre between the two parties, and forbid every attempt at reconciliation.

"No one can presume to say what are the reverses and vicissitudes which fortune, not yet satisfied with the sufferings of the American people, has in store for either party. But the information which has just reached us makes it abundantly evident, if it were not so before, that the choice henceforth for the South is between victory and extermination, for the North between peace and ruin—ruin certain if the war is protracted, as it easily may be, to a point which will leave the President without a revenue and without an army—ruin still more certain and complete if the wicked aspirations of fanatical hate be accomplished, and the central government, already triumphant over the liberties of the North, shall obtain, as the price of success, the unenviable duty of holding down, under the heel of military despotism, the struggling and palpitating remains of what were once the Southern States."

A Prayer by General Lee

THE FREQUENT DAYS of prayer appointed by President Davis were days of self-examining sermons by the clergy of the Confederate States and of formal addresses to the troops in armies not occupied by sterner duties. As the tide of war went against the South in the summer of 1863, a day of "fasting, humiliation and prayer" was appointed by the President for August 13.

In the second paragraph of his General Order directing observance of this day General Lee wrote a sincere prayer beseeching the eventual success of Confederate arms on a foundation of national rectitude.

HEAD QRS. ARMY NORTHERN VA.
August 13, 1863.

GENERAL ORDERS,⎱
    No. 83. ⎰

The President of the Confederate States has, in the name of the people, appointed the 21st day of August as a day of fasting, humiliation and prayer. A strict observance of the day is enjoined upon the officers and soldiers of this army. All military duties, except such as are absolutely necessary, will be suspended. The commanding officers of brigades and regiments are requested to cause divine services, suitable to the occasion, to be performed in their respective commands.

Soldiers! we have sinned against Almighty God. We have forgotten his signal mercies, and have cultivated a revengeful, haughty and boastful spirit. We have not remembered that the defenders of a just cause should be pure in his eyes; that "our times are in his hand"—and we have relied too much on our own arms for the achievement of our independence. God is our only refuge and our strength. Let us humble ourselves before him. Let us confess our many sins, and beseech him to give us a higher courage, a purer patriotism and more determined will: that he will convert the hearts of our enemies: that he will hasten the time when war, with its sorrows and sufferings, shall cease, and that he will give us a name and place among the nations of the earth.

R. E. Lee,
General.

In Camp near Chickamauga

Like Colonel Fremantle, Captain Fitzgerald Ross was an observer at the Battle of Gettysburg. Ross was an officer of hussars in the Imperial Austrian Army. Unlike Fremantle, Ross could not sit calmly in a tree and watch a battle, but succumbed to the temptation to pick up a rifle and join in the fight. For him Gettysburg was the first stop, not the last, on a tour of Confederate camps, battle-fields, and cities, and he went on from Gettysburg to visit Richmond and the lower South.

In the following excerpt he describes his visit to the Confederate camp near Chickamauga, where the Confederates had shortly before gained a considerable victory.

After a few sunshiny days we had some pouring wet ones; it was found that our camp was on too low ground to be comfortable, and we removed some distance to the rear.

By this time Dr. Cullen had arrived from Richmond, and with him came [Francis] L[awley]; and as Dr. Cullen had

—besides his own tent and those of the other staff doctors who had not yet arrived—a large hospital tent, large enough to accommodate twenty people, I thought I had crowded my friends long enough, and accepted his kind invitation to move over and take up my old quarters again with him.

Old Jeff, the cook, was rather in a grumbling mood. "This is not like old Virginy, sir; I shall find it very hard to keep up my dignity here, sir;" his dignity consisting in providing us good breakfasts and dinners. And, indeed, provisions are scarce and not very good. Beef is tough, bacon is indifferent, and mutton is rarely to be had; chickens and eggs are almost unheard-of delicacies, and we have to ride ten miles to get a pat of butter.

During anything like a long stay in one camp all energies very soon tend to the point of how to improve the diet, and many long rides are taken with that sole object in view, and with very various success.

If any one can boast of a leg of mutton, he considers it quite a company dish, to which friends must be invited. One of the most successful caterers is General Preston, and another is his adjutant-general, Major Owens, an old friend, who in Virginia was aide to Colonel Walton. Owens is believed to have a flock of sheep hidden away somewhere. The General gave us a splendid supper one evening, with a profusion of delicate viands, and more than one bowl of hot punch made of some capital peach-brandy.

Our own little camp was particularly well off, as Cullen came pretty well provided, and L. brought a box of good things with him from Richmond. No schoolboys can hail a hamper of prog with more gratification than a hungry lot of campaigners do, especially if they have been teetotalling rather more than they like.

After a victory in Virginia there had always been a profusion of delicacies in the Confederate camp for a long time, but from these Western people nothing had been captured but guns and empty waggons, at which there was great disappointment; and many were quite indignant, thinking themselves cheated. "Why, these Yankees are not worth killing," said General ——; "they are not a bit better off than ourselves."

L., after having one horse stolen at Richmond, had purchased another at Atlanta, and as mine had arrived with Cullen we had many a ride together. The camp was pretty extensive, and it was a three or four miles' ride to visit many of our friends.

There was a grand bombardment of Chattanooga one day, of which we had a splendid view from the top of Lookout Mountain. Not much harm was done, but it was a grand sight to see the guns blazing away far below us. On the top of the mountain is a large hotel, besides several villas and cottages. This used to be a favourite gathering-place in summer, but now every dwelling-place was deserted.

We made our way into the hotel, and purchased half-a-dozen chairs from an old woman, who said they were not hers and that she had nothing to do with them; but she took our money and made our consciences easy. And the chairs were very useful.

About this time the President came to pay a visit to the camp, and there was a general expectation that a change would take place; but none came, except in the weather, which had been dry and sunshiny, with a storm or a shower now and then, but now settled down to be wet and cold and nasty.

The President remained two days, and on the second day went with a large suite to Lookout Mountain. Homewards he rode with General Longstreet, a hundred yards in advance of the rest of the party, and they had a long confabulation, and, I believe, not a very satisfactory one. I rode with General Breckenridge, with whom, and General Custis Lee, I dined afterwards at General Gracie's. After dinner we had some capital singing by some young fellows in Gracie's brigade.

Going home, I fell in with a courier who was riding in the same direction. He was a Louisianian, and we had a long chat together. Amongst other things, he told me that if he met a negro in a fight, he should give him no quarter—that they had always treated the negroes well, and if they fought against them now, they deserved no quarter, and he, for one, should give them none. I remonstrated, saying, it was no fault of the negro that he was forced to fight by the Yankees, and that he never would fight if he could help it, &c. To all which my friend assented, with a "That's so," and I thought that I had made a convert; but when I had exhausted my arguments, although he again repeated his "That's so," he added, "For all that, I shan't give them any quarter."

Our black cook, Jeff, confided to me the other day his idea as to how the war should be carried on.

"Why, sir, why don't they do now as they used formerly to do? The generals used to dine together, and take their wine, and then one would say, 'General, I'll fight you to-morrow at such and such a place,' and then they would shake hands, and the next day they would fight their battle. That's what Napoleon used to do," Jeff concluded, "and why don't they do so now?"

A month after the battle of Chicamauga, we rode over the field of battle, which is seven or eight miles to the rear of our camp. The Yankee dead are still unburied, which is a great shame.

Perhaps General Thomas thinks it beneath his dignity to ask permission to bury them; or perhaps he thinks General Bragg will do it for him. This, however, he has no right to expect, as he is little more than a mile further from the battle-field than Bragg, who, if he sent large details of men eight miles to the rear whilst active operations are going on, would just as much have to demand a truce for the purpose as General Thomas, whose business it is. Besides, these poor fellows' friends will be very anxious that they should be identified, that they may know where to find their graves. If there be one good feeling to be found in the North, it is the respect they show to their dead; and doubtless, if these poor fellows had been identified and properly buried, very many of them would have been brought to their homes after the war, and their bones laid amongst their own kindred. Now the pigs are fattening on them—a disgusting sight to behold.

The rains had become continuous now, and the roads were nearly impassable for waggons, and no movements of importance could therefore be anticipated. The army was in a bad way. Insufficiently sheltered, and continually drenched with rain, the men were seldom able to dry their clothes; and a great deal of sickness was the natural consequence. Few constitutions can stand being wet through for a week together; and, moreover, the nights were bitterly cold, and the blankets were almost as scarce as tents. There was a great deal of discontent, which was increased by its being well known that General Bragg was on very bad terms with many of his generals.

The weather made it disagreeable to move about, and L., [Frank] V[izetelly], and I resolved to leave the army, and on the 22d of October we bade farewell to our friends, and rode over to Chicamauga station, some eight miles off.

General Joseph E. Johnston

Defending the Confederacy from the thrust aimed at cutting through her mid-section was General Joseph E. Johnston. Johnston had had a distinguished career in the United States Army and much was expected of him as a Confederate general. His reputation suffered both during and after the war because of his repeated failure to meet the enemy in a decisive battle. But he was a master of holding and withdrawing. To borrow a word made fashionable in more recent wars, he was a master of containment.

This biographical sketch of him was written by Chaplain Cross in December, 1863, just about the time that the general was settling into winter quarters at Dalton, Georgia.

GENERAL JOSEPH E. JOHNSTON

December, 1863.

"The brave man is not he who feels no fear,
For that were stupid and irrational;

But he whose noble soul its fear subdues,
And bravely dares the danger nature shrinks from.
As for your youth whom blood and blows delight,
Away! with them there is not in their crew
One valiant spirit."—*Shakespeare.*

This illustrious officer is the youngest son of the late distinguished Judge Peter Johnston, of Virginia. He was born in Prince Edward county, but received the rudiments of his education at Abingdon, where his father exercised his judicial functions. In 1825 he became a cadet at the West Point military academy, then at the very acme of its prosperity. In 1829 he graduated in the same class with General Robert E. Lee, and was immediately assigned to the Fourth artillery, with the rank of second lieutenant by brevet. Seven years after this he was appointed assistant commissary of subsistence; and, the year following, first lieutenant of topographical engineers.

In 1838 commenced the Indian war in Florida, in which his gallant conduct gave interesting presage of his future heroism. Being sent, with an escort of infantry, across a lake to make an important reconnoissance, immediately upon landing the party came upon an ambuscade of Indians. At the first fire every officer fell, and the men fled in confusion. Johnston, with great self-possession, assumed command, and rallied the affrighted fugitives. Seizing a tree, amid a perfect storm of bullets, he maintained his position till the men returned to their duty, repulsed the savages, and carried off their own dead and disabled comrades. Lieutenant Johnston was shot in the forehead, and fell; but the ball having merely grazed the skull without penetrating, he suffered no serious consequence from the wound. For this intrepid act, and other achievements during the campaign, he was rewarded

with a captaincy by brevet; and, in 1846, he became full captain by seniority.

In 1847, having been brevetted lieutenant-colonel of voltigeurs, he accompanied General Scott to Mexico, where he won additional laurels. In a reconnoissance at Cerro Gordo, venturing too near the enemy's works, he received three musket balls, which like to have terminated his military career. But

"Man is immortal till his work is done,"

and Providence had other use for the brave lieutenant-colonel. With the aid of a good constitution and a skilful surgeon, he recovered, to gather new glory at Molina del Rey, and experience another severe wound at Chapultepec.

After the Mexican war he was made colonel, and subsequently became quartermaster-general of the United States army. This office he resigned at the commencement of our present struggle, and took a position among the troops of his native state. Soon afterward, however, he offered his services to the Confederate government, was appointed major-general by President Davis, and sent to take charge of the Army of the Shenandoah. Amid great difficulties, he protected an extensive line of frontier on the Upper Potomac; and by a series of skilful movements, with ten thousand men, foiled, defeated, and held at bay for a long time, a force of twenty thousand. He prevented Patterson's junction with McClellan at Winchester, repulsed him with heavy loss at Falling Water, and afterward marched to join Beauregard at Manassas. In that terrific conflict he put the enemy to disastrous rout, reoccupied the country almost to Arlington Heights, and held his position about Centreville through the autumn and winter.

In the spring of 1862 the enemy, inflated with his suc-

cesses along the southern seaboard, on the Tennessee, the Cumberland, and the Mississippi, with an army of two hundred and twenty thousand, splendidly equipped, and confident almost to madness, made a second attempt, under the command of McClellan, to march over our little army at Manassas, and take up his quarters in the Confederate capital. He advanced early in March, "breathing out threatening and slaughter;" but Johnston had foiled him, by withdrawing his whole force to the neighborhood of Richmond, without the loss of a single life, or the abandonment of anything important to the government.

The little Napoleon now resolved to approach Richmond by another route, and so transported "The Grand Army" to the Peninsula. Johnston was ready to receive him there. He repulsed him with great slaughter at Williamsburg; met him again upon the Chickahominy; drove him back, broken and shattered, to his gunboats; and the disaster to the Federal arms would doubtless have been much greater, had not our hero received a wound which came nigh costing the Confederate cause one of its bravest champions.

Through the mercy of God, however, he is again in the field, and at the head of the Army of the West. His advent in Tennessee revived the hopes of our suffering citizens, and inspired our soldiers with new confidence and courage. It is understood that he selected the battle-ground before Murfreesboro', and suggested the disposition of the troops and the plan of the battle. The result reflected fresh credit upon his skill and fresh glory upon our arms.

Last May, under orders from Richmond, he went to take command, in person, of our forces on the Mississippi. The failure of that campaign, with the loss of Vicksburg and Port Hudson, is attributed to the insubordination of General Pemberton, who is alleged to have disobeyed every order of his superior officer, suffered himself unnecessarily to be besieged, and then shamefully surrendered the city.

On General Bragg's retirement from the Army of Tennessee, General Johnston succeeded to the command. No appointment could have been more gratifying to the troops and their officers. His appearance at their head inspired them with new confidence and zeal, and never were they in better heart for battle than to-day.

My personal acquaintance with General Johnston being but slight, I beg leave to quote another's estimate of his character and abilities as a military commander:

"The career of General Johnston has been such as the most illustrious chieftain might envy. A quick genius, a solid judgment, invincible firmness, imperturbable self-reliance, a will as resolute as that of 'the first bald Caesar,' a penetration which no device can baffle, a perseverance which no difficulty can subdue, a courage which no danger can shake, quickness of conception, promptness of action, endurance almost superhuman, and reticence as perfect as the grave—all these we take to be characteristics of a great commander; and in a high degree General Johnston possesses them all. For proof we need not go beyond the events of the last twelve months. He divined all the designs of Patterson, as if by intuition. With a force not half as strong as him, he thwarted all his plans and baffled all his enterprises. With the promptness of lightning he flew to reinforce Beauregard, as soon as he discovered that he was to be attacked. He suffered a clamor to be raised against him for not attacking McClellan, rather than permit the secret of his weakness to be known. In front of an army five times as strong as his own, he never suffered himself to be betrayed into a false movement, or lost for a single moment that perfect reliance upon his own resources which is the mark, as it is most fortunate property, of a strong understanding. He found the army a brave, but little more than half-disciplined militia; he left it a host of veterans, able to contend with any body of equal numbers that ever trod the earth. We believe that he will live to render services even more brilliant than any he has yet rendered to his country."

A small matter sometimes furnishes the key to a great character. I conclude this sketch with a scene in General Johnston's room at the Lamar House, during his visit at Knoxville, last spring. The hero was surrounded with gallant officers who had called to pay their respects, and conversation was at its floodtide, when a gentle tap was heard at the door. An officer, shining with stars and gold lace, opened it; and there stood an aged negress, with a coarse sun-bonnet upon her head and a cotton umbrella under her arm. "Is this Mr. Johnston's room?" asked the American lady of African descent. The glittering officer replied in the affirmative. "Mr. Joe Johnston's room?" "Yes." "Well, I wants to see him." And in she marched, *sans cérémonie*, and familiarly tapped the great military chieftain upon the shoulder. He turned and clasped her ebony hand in his, while she for a moment silently perused his features, and then exclaimed, with a sad voice, half-suppressed by emotion, "Massa Joe, you's gittin old." The conversation which followed is not to be recorded. Suffice it to add that, as the general held the old slave by the hand and answered her artless questions, large tears rolled down his cheeks; and the gay officers around him "albeit unaccustomed to the melting mood," found use for their pocket cambric. The sable visitant who made the stern commander of the armies of the West weep like a child was old Judy Paxton, who had "toted" Joe in her arms when he was not a general, and nobody dreamed that he ever would be.

Dinner at the Oriental

CAPTAIN FITZGERALD Ross returned to Richmond in
December, 1863. In this passage he gives some interesting insights into the public social life of the popula-
tion-swollen capital and the dietary hardships of its
citizens.

Early in December we proceeded to Richmond, accompanied by Captain Fearn. We had been introduced to the
conductor of the train, who secured us comfortable seats,
and our hospitable friends at Wilmington had provided us
with a large hamper of provisions of all sorts—a very useful
precaution before a long railroad journey in the present state
of affairs. Thus our travels were not so unpleasant as they
might otherwise have been. Thirty hours of railway brought
us to our destination, and we took up our old quarters at the
Ballard House. Richmond now presented a very different
aspect from what it had done in summer. Congress, as well
as the State Legislature of Virginia, was in session; the
shops were full of stores, and crowded with purchasers; hosts
of furloughed officers and soldiers perambulated the streets;

hotels, restaurants, and bar-rooms were crowded with guests, and the whole city presented a lively appearance.

There was some outcry, even from the pulpits, against the gaieties that were going on, but General Lee was reported to have said that the young ladies were quite right to afford the officers and soldiers on furlough as much amusement as possible; and balls, tableaux vivants, and all kinds of social gatherings, were the order of the day.

Gambling, however, as an unmitigated vice, has lately been checked by the Virginia Legislature. They debated a little whether to legalise gambling, and by making it a public amusement to check gamblers by public opinion, or whether to put it down by severe measures, and decided for the latter. All gamblers caught in the fact were to be heavily fined, and the banker to be flogged. Corporal punishment is not otherwise generally popular in this country, and has been abolished even in the army, where it is so necessary for the protection of the good soldiers, who under the lockup and imprisonment system are punished by extra duty for the faults of unworthy comrades, to whom a term of imprisonment is generally a matter of indifference, if not of positive satisfaction. Good soldiers are never flogged, and there is no more hardship or disgrace to them in bad ones being thus punished than there is to good people in murderers being hanged. And there is another consideration with regard to flogging, namely, that in time of war many men have to be shot for offences for which otherwise a sound flogging would be an adequate punishment, and, as as example, a sufficient preventive.

Colonel Brien and Major Von Borcke met us at the hotel, and carried us off to the "Oriental Saloon," when we had a capital supper, and sat talking till a late hour.

As the South is supposed just now to be in a starving condition, I will insert here the bill of fare of the Oriental Saloon, together with a little bill or two for meals partaken at that establishment:—

ORIENTAL, 8TH JANUARY 1864

BILL OF FARE.

SOUPS.

	Per Plate. Dols.
Beef,	1.50
Chicken.	
Macaroni.	
Vegetable.	
Clam.	
Oyster.	
Terrapin.	
Turtle.	
Mock turtle.	

FOWLS.

Roast turkey,	3.50
Roast goose.	
Roast ducks.	
Roast chickens,	3.50

FISH.

Rock fish,	5.00
Chub.	
Shad.	
Perch.	
Herrings.	
Crabs and lobsters.	

MEATS.

	Plate.
Roast Beef,	3.00
Roast mutton,	3.00
Roast pork,	3.00
Roast lamb,	3.00
Roast veal,	3.00

STEAKS.

	Dish.
Beef steaks,	3.50
Pork steaks,	3.50
Mutton chops,	3.50
Veal cutlets,	3.50
Venison steaks,	3.50

SUNDRIES.

Ham and eggs,	3.50
Boiled eggs,	2.00
Poached eggs,	2.00
Scrambled eggs,	3.00
Fried eggs,	3.00
Omelette,	3.00

OYSTERS.

Fried oysters,	5.00
Scalloped oysters,	5.00
Roasted oysters,	5.00
Raw oysters,	3.00

BIRDS.

Partridge, ... 3.50
Sora.
Robin.
Snipe.
Plover.
Woodcock.

VEGETABLES.

Cabbage, ... 1.00
Tomato.
Green pease.
Black-eyed pease.
Cucumbers.
Onions, ... 1.00
Lettuce.
Squashes.
Snaps.
Lima beans.
Irish potatoes, ... 1.00
Sweet potatoes, ... 1.00
Salad, ... 2.00
Asparagus.
Celery, ... 2.00

	Cup.
Pure coffee, ...	3.00
Pure tea, ...	2.00
Fresh milk, ...	2.00

WINES.

	Bottle.
Champagne, ...	50.00
Madeira, ...	50.00
Port, ...	25.00
Claret, ...	20.00
Cher[r]y, ...	35.00

LIQUORS.

	Drink.
French brandy, ...	3.00
Apple brandy, ...	2.00
Peach brandy, ...	2.00
Holland gin, ...	2.00
Rye whisky, ...	2.00

MALT LIQUORS.

	Bottle.
Porter, ...	12.00
Ale, ...	12.00
Half a bottle, ...	6.00
Fine havana, ...	1.00

Other brands of a fine quality.

CIGARS.

Bread, 50 cents—Butter, 1 dol.—Hot rolls, 1 dol. 50 cents.

GAME OF ALL KINDS IN SEASON

Terrapins served up in every style.

PETER K. MORGAN, Sen., Proprietor.

ORIENTAL SALOON, 15TH JAN. 1864.

	Dols.		Dols.
Soup for nine,	13.50	5 bottles of madeira,	250.00
Venison steak, nine,	31.50	6 bottles claret,	120.00
Fried potatoes,	9.00	1 urn cocktail,	65.00
7 birds,	24.00	Jelly,	20.00
Baked potatoes,	9.00	Cake,	20.00
Celery,	13.50	1 dozen cigars,	12.00
Bread and butter,	14.00		
Coffee,	18.00	Wines and desserts,	487.00
Apples,	12.00	Dinner,	144.50
Dinner,	144.50	Total,	631.50

These, it is true, are most remarkable for the nominal high prices of everything, but it must be remembered that the reason the paper money here is worth so little is that there is such a profusion of it. Indeed, the country has been swamped with bank-notes. For a time, such was the confidence of the people that they would eventually pay their debt, that paper was only at a small discount; but in the spring of this year (1863) Congress passed a measure enabling the Government to issue fifty millions of dollars a-month in paper money, without pledging any material guarantee for its eventual redemption, and since then the currency has naturally become more and more worthless. At present Congress is engaged in passing a measure to correct all this; the whole floating debt is to be funded, and a new currency issued on sounder principles.

But to return to the question of starvation in the Southern States, for it is true that many people here apprehended such a misfortune. I have no opportunity of seeing much of what goes on in the private houses of the poorer people, and can only judge from what I see at hotels, and eating and boarding-houses. Here, not hundreds, but thousands upon thousands of people take their meals, and one may fairly conclue that what is set before them is what they are accustomed to expect at their own homes.

I confess I never saw much universal profusion, and, I may say, waste. Hot meats and cold meats, venison pies, fish, oysters (prepared in half-a-dozen different ways), eggs, boiled, poached, "scrambled," and in omelettes, hot rolls and cakes, several kinds of bread, fruit in the season, &c., &c., are served up for breakfast, with "Confederate" (*i.e.*, artificial) coffee and tea, at hotels and boarding-houses, in quantities sufficient to satisfy an army of hungry soldiers.

At three o'clock a proportionate amount of food is served up for dinner, and the supper at eight is little less abundant. And for lodging and this board, a sum about equivalent to two shillings or half-a-crown has to be paid. At the eating-houses on the railroad, where the trains stop for meals, the supply is similar.

Accustomed to this extraordinary plenty, many families may now complain at having to content themselves with less than their former profusion, and yet the country is evidently very far from the starvation which the Yankees so charitably reckon upon as one of their chief auxiliaries in destroying the population of the South.

The Close of '63

I N REVIEWING the events of 1863, *The Southern Illustrated News* could still find "nothing in any part of them which, for a moment, should stimulate gloom or relax our energy." Here is the paper's brief summary of military prospects at the end of the year and its report of the military activities of the immediate past.

The old year has whirled into the grand mausoleum of eternity, but the ties which united the living pages of its glory to our hearts have not been sundered. We look back with pride, it may be mingled with some sadness, to the brilliant victories at Fredericksburg, the capture of Winchester, the magnificent though indecisive field of Gettysburg, the complete repulse of the enemy at Charleston, in his grand attack with plated ships and guns of unprecedented calibre and range, the bloody battles which ended after many victories, to our abandonment of Wagner and left glorious, but still victorious, old Sumter in ruins. Glancing toward the far West, though we find that we have lost Arkansas Post and been repulsed at Helena, we have to glory in the hard fought battle of Prairie Grove; at the skillful evasion of an overpowering force in lower Louisiana; the brilliant success at Brashear City, Milliken's Bend, and many successes of minor importance in Western Louisiana. Texas has been preserved almost intact, expelling the foe with shame and blood in the matchless repulses at Galveston and Sabine Pass. The gravest reverses of the year have been sustained by us in Mississippi, and resulted in the capture of Vicksburg and Port Hudson. Yet these, says the Secretary of War in his report, were, to the enemy, bloody acquisitions, and to us errors, not unredeemed by much of glory and vengeance. Our brave soldiers succumbed only to privation and exhaustion, and whatever may have been lost to the country, they at least lost not honor. But the chief hopes of the enemy have proven more elusive than the forebodings of our own people; the Mississippi remains under Confederate embargo still. In Tennessee the campaign has been conducted with more varied fortunes. By some unaccountable circumstance—treachery it is presumed—Cumberland Gap fell into the hands of the enemy, and opened up East Tennessee. At Chickamauga, soon after, the superior prowess of our arms was established in what ranks among the grandest victories of the war; but it was followed by another and more uneven battle, which gave to the enemy his lost ground. The brilliant assaults of Longstreet upon the enemy's fortified positions at Knoxville, close the catalogue of the leading events of the year. Truly we find nothing in any part of them which, for a moment, should stimulate gloom or relax our energy.

The events of the past two weeks have been of minor importance. The holidays passed off joyously and quietly. In Northern Virginia, Gen. Rosser wound up a successful raid, far within the enemy's lines, in time to enjoy a Christmas dinner with his friends in camp; but his trail was followed by the "vengeful enemy," who wreaked their ire upon the harmless shoemakers and hard working citizens of the two quiet little "alpine villages" of Sperryville and Luray. The main force of the enemy still remains north of the Rappahannock, while their pickets extend below Culpeper C. H. as far as Mitchell's station.

In Tennessee various raids have been made by Gen. Wheeler to the severe injury of the enemy's transportation, but no fighting of importance has occurred. All is quiet at Chattanooga. In East Tennessee the enemy is kept constantly alert by our army, and at present his pickets extend twelve miles east of Knoxville.

The most gentlemanly act the enemy have done during the war was performed in Charleston harbor on the evening of the 1st inst.— They fired a couple of shots over the ruins of Sumter, and when the evening gun of the brave, dismantled, but defiant old pile, boomed over the waters, they lowered their flag respectfully. But this is no offset to their inborn malignity. On Christmas day, and during the whole week, they fired at intervals into the city, doing, however, but little damage. The batteries on Johnson and Morris Islands have been playing occasionally, with unappreciable results. The last noticeable movements of the enemy are confined to the Inlet, where they were landing heavy guns, to be placed upon extensive earthworks opposite immortal little Secessionville.

General Kirby Smith has taken the field against the enemy in Arkansas. In Texas considerable excitement was created along the southwest coast by exaggerated reports of the invasion of Banks' army. The latter had seized upon several small and defenceless villages, and stolen a large quantity of cattle.

The patients in the hospitals in Richmond were treated

on New Year's day to liberal contributions of food and rai-
ment from the citizens, which will give them occasion to
remember the people—the ladies especially—of the metropo-
lis long.

The new Governor of Virginia, Major-General William
Smith, was duly inaugurated at the Capitol, on the 1st inst.
He rendered the occasion especially interesting by a patri-
otic speech, full of encouragement to the people of the Old
Dominion.

Congress continues to work with energy upon the various
matters before it. The most important measure of immediate
interest it has perfected, is the act annulling the exemptions
of persons who have furnished substitutes. The President
has fixed his signature to the act and it is now one of "the
laws of the land."

1864

President Davis' Address
to the Soldiers

ONE OF THE FIRST generally discernible signs of the doubt which was privately seeping into Confederate minds about the eventual success of the Confederacy was the whistling-Dixie sort of attitude which is represented in the next item.

It is President Davis' address to the soldiers in February, 1864, a stirring and genuinely optimistic document. Perhaps its optimism is an indication that the President was losing touch with the realities of the Confederacy's situation, for the conditions that called for such an address were, verily, a portent of hard times acoming.

Soldiers of the Army of the Confederate States:

In the long and bloody war in which your country is engaged, you have achieved many noble triumphs. You have won glorious victories over vastly more numerous hosts. You have cheerfully borne privations and toil to which you were unused. You have readily submitted to restraints upon your individual will, that the citizen might better perform his duty to the state as a soldier. To all these you have lately added another triumph—the noblest of human conquests— a victory over yourselves.

As the time drew near when you who first entered the service might well have been expected to claim relief from your arduous labors, and restoration to the endearments of home, you have heeded only the call of your suffering country. Again you come to tender your service for the public defence—a free offering, which only such patriotism as yours could make—a triumph worthy of you and of the cause to which you are devoted.

I would in vain attempt adequately to express the emotions with which I received the testimonials of confidence and regard which you have recently addressed to me. To some of those first received, separate acknowledgements were returned. But it is now apparent that a like generous enthusiasm pervades the whole army, and that the only exception to such magnanimous tender will be of those who, having originally entered for the war, cannot display anew their zeal in the public service. It is, therefore, deemed appropriate, and, it is hoped, will be equally acceptable, to make a general acknowledgement, instead of successive special responses. Would that it were possible to render my thanks to you in person, and in the name of our common country, as well as in my own, while pressing the hand of each war-worn veteran, to recognize his title to our love, gratitude and admiration.

Soldiers! By your will (for you and the people are but one) I have been placed in a position which debars me from sharing your dangers, your sufferings and your privations in the field. With pride and affection, my heart has accompanied you in every march; with solicitude, it has sought to minister to your every want; with exultation, it has marked your every heroic achievement. Yet, never in the toilsome march, nor in the weary watch, nor in the desperate assault, have you rendered a service so decisive in results, as in this last display of the highest qualities of devotion and self-sacrifice which can adorn the character of the warrior-patriot.

Already the pulse of the whole people beats in unison with yours. Already they compare your spontaneous and unanimous offer of your lives, for the defence of your country, with the halting and reluctant service of the mercenaries who are purchased by the enemy at the price of higher bounties than have hitherto been known in war. Animated by this contrast, they exhibit cheerful confidence and more resolute bearing. Even the murmurs of the weak and timid, who shrink from the trials which make stronger and firmer your noble natures, are shamed into silence by the spectacle which you present. Your brave battle-cry will ring loud and clear through the land of the enemy, as well as our own; will silence the vain-glorious boastings of their corrupt partisans and their pensioned press, and will do justice to the calumny by which they seek to persuade a deluded people that they are ready to purchase dishonorable safety by degrading submission.

Soldiers! The coming Spring campaign will open under auspices well calculated to sustain your hopes. Your resolution needed nothing to fortify it. With ranks replenished under the influence of your example, and by the aid of your representatives, who give earnest of their purpose to add, by legislation, largely to your strength, you may welcome the invader with a confidence justified by the memory of past victories. On the other hand, debt, taxation, repetition of heavy drafts, dissensions, occasioned by the strife for power, by the pursuit of the spoils of office, by the thirst for the plunder of the public treasury, and, above all, the consciousness of a bad cause, must tell with fearful force upon the overstained energies of the enemy. His campaign in 1864, must, from the exhaustion of his resources, both in men and money, be far less formidable than those of the last two years, when unimpaired means were used with boundless prodigality, and with results which are suggested by the mention of the glorious names of Shiloh and Perrysville, and Murfreesboro' and Chickamauga, and the Chickahominy and Manassas, and Fredericksburg and Chancellorsville.

Soldiers! Assured success awaits us in our holy struggle for liberty and independence, and for the preservation of all that renders life desirable to honorable men. When that success shall be reached, to you—your country's hope and pride —under Divine Providence, will it be due. The fruits of that success will not be reaped by you alone, but your children and your children's children, in long generations to come, will enjoy blessings derived from you, that will preserve your memory ever-living in their hearts.

Citizen-defenders of the homes, the liberties and the altars of the Confederacy! That the God, whom we all humbly worship, may shield you with his Fatherly care, and preserve you for safe return to the peaceful enjoyment of your friends and the association of those you most love, is the earnest prayer of your Commander-in-Chief.

JEFFERSON DAVIS.

RICHMOND, February 9th, 1864.

Gaiety as Usual in Mobile

L IFE IN THE CITIES of the deep South went on in more
normal fashion than life in besieged Richmond. Even
in blockaded Mobile there was less disruption of the
usual social life of the city, and, as in Richmond, there
was a wartime heightening of such gaieties as weddings
and balls. Here is Fitzgerald Ross's account of his visit to
the Gulf City in the winter 1863–64, an account which
mixes his reports of social activities and military preparations in an interesting historical cocktail.

Mobile had suffered very little from the war, and still carried on a brisk commerce with the outer world in spite of
the blockade. It is pleasantly situated on a broad plain, and
has a beautiful prospect of the bay, from which it receives
refreshing breezes. Large vessels cannot come directly to
the city, but pass up Spanish River six miles round a marshy
island into Mobile river, and then drop down to Mobile.

We took up our quarters at the Battle House, an enormous
caravanserai; and after a refreshing bath, and a capital break-

fast at a French restaurant, we sallied forth for a walk in the city.

Colonels Walton and Deas, who are well known here, were greeted by friends almost at every step, and we presently adjourned to the Manassas Club, where our arrival was celebrated with a "cocktail." We then paid our respects to Admiral Buchanan and to General Maury, who commands the military department of the Gulf.

In the evening we went to a grand wedding-party and ball, where all the beauty of Mobile was assembled; and the reports I had heard of the charms of the fair sex at Mobile I found to be not at all exaggerated. This was the last ball of the season, as Lent was about to commence, but they had been very gay here during the carnival. There is always a great deal of social intercourse at Mobile, and I shall ever cherish amongst my most agreeable recollections of the South the pleasant hours spent with the genial inhabitants of that city. It is usual to pay visits in the evening between seven and ten o'clock.

We were not much pleased with our accommodation at the hotel, and were removing to a boarding-house; but Colonel Scheliha, now Chief Engineer of the Department of the Gulf, whom I met in the West, insisted upon my taking up my quarters with him, which I accordingly did. He also placed his horses at my disposal, and we had many rides together. The Colonel is engaged in erecting a new line of forts round Mobile, which are perfect models of strength and judicious arrangement. They are built entirely of sand, with revetments of turf alone. The turf on the embankments is fastened down to the sand by slips of the Cherokee rose, an exceedingly prickly shrub, which when grown will become a very disagreeable obstacle to a storming party. Though I must not say much more about them, I may mention, as a proof of the solidity of these works, that the parapets are 25 feet wide, the traverses against splinters of shell are 18 feet wide, against enfilading fire, 32 feet wide. Besides these forts there are two other lines of defence at Mobile, which will soon be one of the most strongly fortified places in the world. The forts in the harbour, which are built on artificial islands, were being much strengthened; and everything was being done now with great energy, as it was reported that the Yankees designed to attack the city.

Sherman had advanced upon Jackson, but it was not supposed that an attack by land would be made from that quarter, as the country through which the Yankees would have to pass was poor and thinly populated, so that they would find it difficult to obtain supplies. To attack Mobile by land they would have to make Pascagoula their base.

One day we went down the bay to visit the outer defences in a magnificent river-steamer. The Governor of Alabama, Admiral Buchanan, General Maury, and other gentlemen and ladies, were of the party. A very good band of music from one of the regiments of the garrison played, and dancing was soon got up in the splendid saloon. They dance the "finale" of the quadrille here with all sorts of figures—one of them like the last figure in the Lancers, walking round and giving the right and left hand alternately. Admiral Buchanan, who was looking on, joined in this, and naturally by doing so created a great deal of confusion and merriment, at which he was in high glee. He is immensely popular, and the young ladies all call him a charming old gentleman, although he is at least ten years too young to be an admiral in England.

We landed at Fort Morgan and went over the place. I confess I did not like it at all. It is built in the old style, with bricks here, there, and everywhere.

Now when bricks begin to fly about violently by tons' weight at a time, which is the case when they come in contact with 15-inch shells, they make themselves very unpleasant to those who have trusted to them for protection. This was conclusively shown at Fort Sumter.

Fort Gaines, which we did not visit, was, they told me, a much better place, lately finished and strengthened on newer principles; but all agreed that these two forts were a very inadequate defence for the bay, into which the Yankees might enter whenever they chose to make the attempt.

Governor Ward made a speech to the garrison, and complimented the men who had lately re-enlisted for the war. At the commencement of the present struggle the soldiers only enlisted for three years, and in the whole army the term of enlistment was now drawing to a close. This was very awkward, as these men could not be dispensed with, and Congress would have been obliged to pass some law on the subject. But it was spared all trouble. The men knew as well as the Government that they were "bound to fight it out," and came forward voluntarily, re-enlisting with great enthusiasm for "ten years," "forty years," some even for "ninety-nine years," or "the war." The alacrity with which the army has come forward on this occasion has caused much good feeling, and the few who before were inclined to croak and despond are now again as confident as ever of ultimate success.

From Fort Morgan we went on to Fort Powell, a beautiful little sandwork in Grant's Pass. This is an inlet to the bay, through which, in former days, steamers used to take a short cut to New Orleans, paying a toll to a Mr Grant, who had deepened the channel for them, and who was rewarded by a large fortune for his enterprise. Fort Powell, which was only just being completed, had six guns, Fort Morgan about fifty. There were still strong rumours of a contemplated attack upon Mobile, but General Maury told me he did not believe in them. . . .

Whilst at Mobile we visited the men-of-war in the harbour, of which the Tennessee was the most formidable. The great difficulty is how to get this ship over the Dog River bar, which has never more than nine feet of water, whilst the Tennessee draws full thirteen. They have therefore to raise her four feet by *"camels,"* which with the dearth of mechanical appliances in the South is a very difficult operation, and Admiral Buchanan almost despaired of succeeding.

Apropos of the detention of the rams in England, Admiral Buchanan told me that during the war between the Brazils and Buenos Ayres, some sixteen years ago, he himself commanded and took out to Rio Janeiro one of two ships of war which were built at Baltimore for the Brazilians. He had given a grand entertainment—I think he said to 500 persons —on board his ship, before leaving Baltimore, and no secret was made of his destination. The Minister of Buenos Ayres at Washington was perfectly aware of what was going on, but never dreamed of making a complaint to the United States Government, and had he done so it would most certainly have been disregarded. . . .

Were it not for the friendly neutrality of the British Government towards the North, the Confederates would have had a fleet, and the war in consequence would have been over long ago.

Although the Confederates think that they have been very unhandsomely and unfairly treated by the British Government, and comment freely upon the "extraordinary conduct" of Earl Russell, I may say here that they appreciate very highly the sympathy of Englishmen, which they believe to be entirely with them; and I never in the South heard an unpleasant remark made about the people of England, whom they believe to be misrepresented by their present Foreign Secretary.

A few days after our excursion down the bay, Fort Powell was attacked by a fleet of gunboats, and underwent some shelling; but after a day or two, finding they could make no impression, the Yankees retired.

There is a capital hard "shell road," so called from being made of oyster-shells, which runs alongside the bay for some seven miles. It is the favourite drive for carriages at Mobile. At the end is a house where refreshments are taken. We drove there one day, and were in the house whilst the firing at Fort Powell was going on. When the heavy Brooks gun in the fort was fired, it shook the windows so as to make them jingle, although the distance was near thirty miles. Owing to scarcity of stone, there are very few good roads in the Southern States, except near the mountains. The sand is often so deep that horses can hardly get along. For traffic they have railways, and as Southerners, male and female, prefer riding to driving, they care little for their roads. The shell road at Mobile, however, is excellent, and at New Orleans I am told they have some equally good made of the shell of the coquille.

I met a gentleman here, the fidelity of whose negro servant (slave) deserves to be put on record. He had had to fly in haste from Natchez on the Mississippi, when that place was occupied by the Yankees, and had left very important papers and a large sum of money securely hidden at his house there. Not being able to return himself to his home, he sent his negro servant, who, with a good deal of trouble, dodged his way in and out of the Federal lines, and brought his master all his important papers and ten thousand dollars in gold (two thousand pounds). How many white servants could be trusted with a similar mission? . . .

We had decided to return by steamer up the Alabama river as far as Montgomery, as it was a much pleasanter mode of travelling than by rail. The steamers all over this continent are splendid vessels, and we were very comfortable on board our boat. The country through which we passed was fertile and cultivated, and produces much cotton.

The cultivation of cotton in America is of comparatively recent date. Colonel Deas told me, that in 1774 his grandfather, who then resided in England, wrote out to his agents in Charleston, and directed them to attempt the cultivation of a sufficient amount of cotton to supply the negroes on his plantation with homespun. At that time the great staple in the Southern States was indigo, the cultivation of which is now so entirely discontinued that they were not able to make the naval uniform in the Confederacy blue, as every one knows a naval uniform ought to be. It is now the same colour as the military uniform. I believe the reason that seamen dress in blue, is because it is the only colour which is not stained by salt water.

At Selma a large body of soldiers came on board our boat, and for the rest of our journey to Montgomery we were crowded. However, the colonels and myself took refuge in "Texas," a glass shed built high over the centre of every river-steamer, whence the vessel is piloted. The cabins below this, and above the grand saloon, where the officers of the vessel are accommodated, also belong to "Texas." Here we had chairs, plenty of room, and a fine view.

The soldiers belonged to Hardee's corps, which had been sent to reinforce General Polk, but they were now no longer required, as Sherman had retreated. He fortunately never reached the rich country about Demopolis, but the already desolate country his army passed through he devastated in the most frightful manner, both coming and going, and everybody says he deserves to be hanged.

After a short stay at Montgomery we proceeded on our journey and reached Macon the next morning. There is a magnificent railroad station here and a capital hotel, the Brown House, where we breakfasted. At the station there were a large number of Yankee prisoners, who had been picked up during Sherman's retreat.

We slept that night at Savannah and went on to Charleston next morning. Here we made a two days' rest, and I took up my quarters with Mr Ch., finding a dinner-party assembled as usual, and old friends among the guests. One of them, as a parting gift, made me a present of an enormous cigar-case full of Havannah cigars, a princely benefaction under present circumstances in Dixie, when Havannah cigars are not to be purchased at any price.

Soon after we reached Wilmington my two friends and travelling companions returned to Richmond, their leave of absence having expired, whilst I with much regret prepared to say farewell to "the sunny South." A few pleasant days flew quickly by, and then with C., whose business called him to Nassau, I embarked in the Hansa, a noble ship, which was now to run the blockade for the eighteenth time.

It was exhilarating enough when, the moon having set at midnight, we slipped out of Cape Fear river, and dashed at full speed through the blockading fleet. It was pitch dark, and not even a cigar was allowed to be alight on deck. For nearly an hour we kept peering through the night to discover whether any Yankee ship lay in our way, but we passed unobserved, and then all immediate danger was over.

The next day we saw a large number of cotton bales floating in the sea, and on arriving at Nassau we heard that they had been thrown overboard by the Alice, which had left the night before us, and had been chased for a whole day by a Yankee cruiser. A little schooner was engaged in picking them up, and as a single bale is worth 40 £ she was no doubt making a good thing of it. We performed our voyage to Nassau in about sixty hours, and were loudly cheered as we steamed into the harbour.

The Consequence of Desertion

DESERTION was a serious problem in both the Union and Confederate armies. In the Confederate Army particularly, where enlistments had been lengthened and men were long separated from their homes, extended absences without leave were commonplace. To aid in planting or harvesting a crop, to alleviate a family crisis, or simply to renew home ties, men often left the camps without the formality of permission. Most of them returned after a suitable lapse of time—sometimes to be punished, but about as often, to be accepted back into their former status without too much questioning.

The laxity exercised in disciplining such cases, however, did not apply in cases of true desertion.

On Febraury 1, 1864, the Confederates under Brigadier General R. F. Hoke forced the passage of Batchelor's Creek near Newbern, North Carolina, and attacked the Yankee-held town. In the pursuit toward the city a large number of prisoners were taken, among whom were a number who proved to be Confederate deserters. But let us hear the story in the words of Chaplain John Paris, who less than a month later preached the remarkable sermon which follows:

"Among the prisoners taken, were about fifty native North Carolinians, dressed out in Yankee uniform, with muskets upon their shoulders. Twenty-two of these men were recognized as men who had deserted from our ranks, and gone over to the enemy. Fifteen of them belonged to Nethercutt's Battalion. They were arraigned before a court martial, proved guilty of the charges, and condemned to suffer death by hanging.

"It became my duty to visit these men in prison before their execution, in a religious capacity. From them I learned that bad and mischievous influences had been used with every one to induce him to desert his flag, and such influences had led to their ruin. From citizens who had known them for many years, I learned that some of them had heretofore borne good names, as honest, harmless, unoffending citizens. After their execution I thought it proper, for the benefit of the living, that I should deliver a discourse before our brigade, upon the death of these men, that the eyes of the living might be opened, to view the horrid and ruinous crime and sin of desertion which had become so prevalent."

You are aware, my friends, that I have given public notice that upon this occasion I would preach a funeral discourse upon the death of the twenty-two unfortunate, yet wicked and deluded men, whom you have witnessed hanged upon the gallows within a few days. I do so, not to eulogize or benefit the dead. But I do so, solely, for the benefit of the living; and in doing so, I shall preach in my own way, and according to my own manner, or rule. What I shall say will either be true or false. I therefore request that you will watch me closely; weigh my arguments in the balance of truth; measure them by the light of candid reason, and compare them by the Standard of Eternal Truth, the Book of God; what is wrong, reject, and what is true, accept, for the sake of the truth, as responsible beings.

Of all deserters and traitors, Judas Iscariot . . . is undoubtedly the most infamous, whose names have found a place in history, either sacred or profane. No name has ever been more execrated by mankind: and all this has been justly done. . . .

Well may it be said that this man is the most execrable of all whose names stand on the black list of deserters and traitors that the world has furnished from the beginning until now.— Turning to the history of our own country, I find written high on the scroll of infamy the name of Benedict Arnold, who at one time stood high in the confidence of the great and good Washington. What was his crime? Desertion and treason. He too hoped to better his condition by selling his principles for money, to the enemies of his country, betraying his Washington into the hands of his foes, and committing the heaven-insulting crime of perjury before God and man. Verily, he obtained his reward; an immortality of infamy; the scorn and contempt of the good and the loyal of all ages and all countries.

Thus, gentlemen, I have brought before you two grand prototypes of desertion, whose names tower high over all on the scroll of infamy. And I now lay down the proposition, that every man who has taken up arms in defence of his country, and basely deserts or abandons that service, belongs in principle and practice to the family of Judas and Arnold. But what was the status of those twenty-two deserters whose sad end and just fate you witnessed across the river in the old field? Like you they came as volunteers to fight for the independence of their own country. Like you they received the bounty money offered by their country. Like you they took upon themselves the most solemn obligations of this oath: "I, A.B. do solemnly swear that I will bear true allegiance to the Confederate States of America, and that I will serve them honestly and faithfully against all their enemies or opposers whatsoever, and observe and obey the orders of the Confederate States, and the orders of the officers appointed over me, according to the rules and articles for the government of the Confederate States, so help me God."

With all the responsibilities of this solemn oath upon their souls, and all the ties that bind men to the land that gave them birth, ignoring every principle that pertains to the patriot, disowning that natural, as well as lawful allegiance that every man owes to the government of the State which throws around him the aegis of its protection, they went boldly, Judas and Arnold-like, made an agreement with the enemies of their country, took an oath of fidelity and allegiance to them, and agreed with them for money to take up arms and assist in the unholy and hellish work of the subjugation of the country which was their own, their native land! These men have only met the punishment meted out by all civilized nations for such crimes. To this, all good men, all true men, and all loyal men who love their country, will say, Amen!

But who were those twenty-two men whom you hanged upon the gallows? They were your fellow-beings. They were citizens of our own Carolina. They once marched under the same beautiful flag that waves over our heads; but in an evil hour, they yielded to mischievous influence, and from motives or feelings base and sordid, unmanly and vile, resolved to abandon every principle of patriotism, and sacrifice every impulse of honor; this sealed their ruin and enstamped their lasting disgrace. The question now arises, what are the influences and the circumstances that lead men into the high and damning crimes of perjury and treason? It will be hard to frame an answer that will fit every case. But as I speak for the benefit of those whom I stand before to-day, I will say I have made the answer to this question a matter of serious inquiry for more than eighteen months. The duties of my office as Chaplain have brought me much in contact with this class of men. I have visited twenty-four of them under sentence of death in their cells of confinement, and with death staring them in the face and only a few short hours between them and the bar of God, I have warned them to tell the whole truth, confess everything wrong before God and man, and yet I have not been able to obtain the full, fair and frank confession of everything relating to their guilt from even one of them, that I thought circumstances demanded, although I had baptized ten of them in the name of the Holy Trinity. In confessing their crimes, they would begin at Newbern, where they joined the enemy, saying nothing about perjury and desertion. Every man of the twenty-two, whose execution you witnessed, confessed that bad or mischievous influences had been used with him to influence him to desert. All but two, willingly gave me the names of their seducers. But none of these deluded and ruined men seemed to think he ought to suffer the penalty of death, because he had been persuaded to commit these high crimes by other men.

But, gentlemen, I now come to give you my answer to the question just asked. From all that I have learned in the prison, in the guard house, in the camp, and in the country,

I am fully satisfied, that the great amount of desertions from our army are produced by, and are the fruits of a bad, mischievous, restless, and dissatisfied, not to say disloyal influence that is at work in the country at home. If in this bloody war our country should be overrun, this same mischievous home influence will no doubt be the prime agent in producing such a calamity. Discontentment has, and does, exist in various parts of the State. We hear of these malcontents holding public meetings, not for the purpose of supporting the Government in the prosecution of the war, and maintenance of our independence, but for the purpose of finding fault with the Government. Some of these meetings have been dignified with the name of "peace meetings;" some have been ostensibly called for other purposes, but they have invariably been composed of men who talk more about their "rights," than about their duty and loyalty to their country. These malcontents profess to be greatly afflicted in mind about the state of public affairs. In their doleful croakings they are apt to give vent to their melancholy lamentations in such words as these: "The country is ruined!" "We are whipt!" "We might as well give up!" "It is useless to attempt to fight any longer!" "This is the rich man's war and the poor man's fight;" &c. Some newspapers have caught the mania and lent their influence to this work of mischief; whilst the pulpit, to the scandal of its character for faith and holiness, has belched forth in some places doctrines and counsels through the ministrations of unworthy occupants, sufficient to cause Christianity to blush under all the circumstances. I would here remark, standing in the relation which I do before you, that the pulpit and the press, when true and loyal to the Government which affords them protection, are mighty engines for good; but when they see that Government engaged in a bloody struggle for existence, and show themselves opposed to its efforts to maintain its authority by all constitutional and legal means, such a press, and such pulpits should receive no support for an hour from a people that would be free. The seal of condemnation should consign them to oblivion.

Office Board of Examiners—Examination of a Conscript.

Such sentiments as we have just alluded to, are sent in letters to our young men in the army, by writers professing to be friends; often with an urgent and pressing invitation to come home; and some have even added that execrable and detestable falsehood, the quintessence of treason, "the State is going to secede." Letters coming into our camps on the

Rappahannock and Rapidan sustain this position. What are the effects produced upon our young men in the ranks? With the illiterate, they are baleful indeed. The incautious youth takes it for granted that the country is ruined and that the Government is his enemy. The poisonous contagion of treason from home gets hold in his mind and steals into his feelings. This appeal from home has overcome him. The young man of promise and of hope once, now becomes a deserter. Is guilty by one false step of the awful crimes of perjury and desertion. The solemn obligations of his oath are disregarded; he takes to the woods, traverses weary roads by night for days, until he reaches the community in which he claims his home; but for what? To engage in any of the honorable vocations of life? No, gentlemen. But to lie hidden from the face of all good, true and loyal men. But for what purpose? To keep from serving his country as a man and a citizen. To consume the provisions kept in the country for the support of the women and children, families of soldiers who are serving their country, indeed; and lastly, to get his living in part, at least, by stealing and robbing. And here allow me to say, I am not sufficiently skilled in language to command words to express the deep and unutterable detestation I have of the character of a deserter. If my brother were to be guilty of such a high crime, I should certainly make an effort to have his name changed to something else, that I, and my children after me, might not feel the deep and lasting disgrace which his conduct had enstamped upon it.

I hold, gentlemen, that there are few crimes in the sight of either God or man, that are more wicked and detestable than desertion. The first step in it is perjury. Who would ever believe such an one in a court of justice again? The second, is treason. He has abandoned the flag of his country; thus much he has aided the common enemy. These are startling crimes, indeed, but the third is equally so. He enstamps disgrace upon the name of his family and children.

From amidst the smoke and flames of Sinai God has declared that He "is a jealous God, visiting the iniquities of the fathers upon the children unto the third and fourth generations of them that hate me." The infamy that the act of disloyalty on the part of a father places his children in after him, is a disability they cannot escape: it was his act, not theirs; and to them it has become God's visitation according to the text quoted above. The character of infamy acquired by the tories of the revolution of 1776, is to this day imputed to their descendants, in a genealogical sense. Disloyalty is a crime that mankind never forget and but seldom forgive; the grave cannot cover it.

Many cry out in this the day of our discontent, and say, "we want peace." This is true, we all want peace, the land mourns on account of the absence of peace, and we all pray for peace. You have often heard me pray for peace, but I think you will bear me witness to-day that you have never heard me pray for peace without independence. God forbid that we should have a peace that brought no independence. . . .

I think you will bear me witness that I have never been hopeful of an early peace in my intercourse among you. But to-day I fancy that I can discover a little cloud, in the political heavens as large as a man's hand at least, that seems to portend peace. Take courage, then, companions in arms. All things around us to-day bid us be of good courage. History fails to tell us of ten millions of freemen being enslaved, who had determined to be free. A braver or more patriotic army than we have, never followed their chief to victory. Their endurance challenges the admiration of the world. When I have seen our brave men in winter's cold and summer's heat, marching from battle-field to battle-field, barefooted as they were born, and without a murmur, I could not doubt our final success. *Such men as these, were never born to be slaves.* Again, when I have turned my eye homeward from the camp, and witnessed the labors of our fair country women, in preparing clothing to meet the wants of the suffering in the field and witnessed their untiring devotion to the relief of the sick and wounded in the hospitals, I knew that the history of no country, and of no age afforded anything like a parallel, and my faith assured me we never were born to be the slaves of Yankees. Then let your trust to-day be strong in the God of nations.

Surely, then, no man can be found in all our land who owes allegiance to his country, that is so lost to himself, and to all that is noble and patriotic, as to say, "I am for the Union as it was." Such an one could only merit the good man's scorn, and desire the tory's infamy for himself, and disgrace for his children. . . .

Then, to-day, in the light of this beautiful Sabbath sun, let us take courage, and with renewed trust in God, resolve to do our whole duty as patriots and soldiers, and leave the event to the Arbiter of nations. *Amen!*

Theatricals in the Army

BUT CAMP MORALE could be good as well as bad, and it is surprising to find that in most cases Confederate morale was exceptionally good. Soldier amusements were not provided by any government or nationally organized agency. There were various state and local relief societies in the Confederacy, but for their own welfare and amusements the men in the armies were left pretty much to their own devices.

Camp amusements consisted of card playing, gambling of every conceivable description, snowballing and swimming in season, occasional ball games, and entertainment by amateur talent among the soldiers themselves. Bands were not widespread in the Confederate Army, but there were a few. Portable musical instruments, however, provided entertainment in almost every camp. There were occasional performances of amateur theatricals. Such a performance is described in the following communication to *The Southern Illustrated News.*

THEATRICALS IN THE ARMY.

A correspondent in the army writes to us as follows:

CAMP GREGG'S BRIGADE, FIELD'S DIVISION, ⎫
ZOLLICOFFER, EAST TENNESSEE, April 15, 1864.⎭

Mr. Editor:—As a portion of your valuable journal is devoted to the drama, I take the liberty to ask a small space therein, in order to bring before the public an enterprise in this far-famed corner of the Confederacy—vulgarly called "East Tenn."

I dare say a majority of your readers will be surpised to learn that the drama (not Ogden's legitimate) is prospering among Longstreet's war-worn veterans. Such is the case, however, as I shall soon show. Mrs. Bailey, a member of the *quondam* "Bailey Troupe," being on a visit to her husband, leader of the 3d Arkansas band, kindly tendered her efforts toward relieving the dull monotony of camp life. Thereupon, Mr. J. A. Bailey, calling to his assistance his brother, Geo. A. Bailey, together with several members of "Hood's Minstrels," determined to give a theatrical performance. "Where there's a will there's a way;" and despite the weather—April weather—lack of conveniences, &c., they at once set to work to extemporize a *stage* under the broad canopy of Heaven.

The spot selected for this model "Temple of the Muses" is, as the accompanying drawing [not published] shows, a natural amphitheatre, close to the track of the East Tenn. & Va. railroad, and about one mile from Zollicoffer. The *stage* consisted of planks used for shipping horses on the cars, and was kindly furnished by an obliging quartermaster. The *infernal regions* from which "Banquo's Ghost" issues forth to astonish "Macbeth," were, of course, omitted. The back scen-

ery was formed by a tent-fly from General Anderson's headquarters; the ladies' dressing-room, to the left, by a wall-tent,
captured at Lenoir Station, from Burnside & Co., and the
gentlemen's *ditto*, by a so-called *A* tent. As to boxes, par-
quette, reserved seats, and other modern improvements, our
opera-house was almost destitute; a dozen or so of benches,
borrowed from a neighboring church, supplying the whole.
In fact, "standing seats" were found more convenient, and
the hill in front served as an admirable substitute for these
sometimes indispensable articles.— Tallow candles, screened
by a board as reflector, supplied the place of footlights; but
"pale-faced Luna," who was expected to shed her benign
rays over the assembled multitude, deemed it proper to hide
her features behind a veil of sable clouds, and the audience
was thus thrown into darkness. I am thus explicit in detailing
the minutiae of this novel theatre as I consider it important
for future reference as a guide to all who intend to seek
"pleasure under difficulties."

The first performance was given on the 5th April, and commenced at the hour usually designated as "early candle
light," the band of the 3d Arkansas playing the overture—
"La Sonnambula."

The programme opened with, "The Soldier Boy's Court-
ship," Mr. George A. Bailey (soldier boy) being *the* character par excellence; his side-splitting humor convulsing the
"house," and instituting him, at once, the favorite.— "The
Soldier Lad I Adore," was sung by Mrs. Bailey, with exquisite taste and feelings and failed not to carry every heart
with it. "Highland Fling," danced by Mr. D. Stetter, of
"Hood's Minstrels," in Ethiopian costume, (female) was
executed to perfection—so much so, that no one would have
imagined the little drummer of the 4th Texas to be sailing
under false colors. Mrs. Bailey followed in that charming

ballad, "Annie of the Vale," in which, if possible, she surpassed her first effort. Mr. George A. Bailey, who has already proved himself complete master of the humorous, appeared next, with unbounded success in the execution of a comic hornpipe; in fact, we have seen but few to equal him, and still fewer to surpass him. The farce of "Lucy Long," in which "Hood's Minstrels" appeared as a body was well rendered. Messrs. Chandler and Jett brought out the negro's character in a manner which might make the "Buckley's" look to their laurels. Albert Pike's "Fine Arkansas Gentleman" was sung next by Mr. G. A. Bailey, and here again his well-modulated voice, comic gestures, and inimitable performance, carried the audience by *storm*, as we soldiers say. The performance concluded with "P. T. Barnum's ball," the principal character (negro Pete) being sustained by Mr. Jett, in his usual excellent style. His dance with the soldier, (Mr. G. B.) especially, was most humorous, and brought down the "house" as well as himself, for he was skillfully tripped by his nimble antagonist. Such, Mr. Editor, was one of our most pleasant nights in camp, and we do not think that this performance has ever been equalled in the army.

The performers, each and all, deserve the thanks of their fellow-soldiers, and especially Mrs. Bailey, who, by her fine acting and vocal powers, elevated the whole affair to the rank of a first class entertainment.

All hail to the Messrs. Baileys and Hood's Minstrels.— Long may they meet the plaudits with which they were greeted is the wish of one who, with many others, varied camp life by a pleasant evening among the Muses.

NEMO

The Bishop-General, Leonidas Polk

S HERMAN left his camp near Chattanooga May 8, 1864, to begin his campaign against Atlanta. Among the Confederate generals opposing him was the celebrated churchman-warrior, General Leonidas Polk. By June 14 the Confederates had fallen back to a range of small mountains just north and west of Marietta. It was here that General Polk was killed by a shot from a Yankee battery.

General Johnston expressed the feelings of the country in the General Field Order he published on the day of Polk's death:

"COMRADES! You are called to mourn your first captain, your oldest companion-in-arms. Lieutenant-General Polk fell to-day at the outpost of this army—the army he raised and commanded—in all of whose trials he has shared—to all of whose victories he contributed.

"In this distinguished leader we have lost the most courteous of gentlemen, the most gallant of soldiers.

"The christian, patriot soldier, has neither lived nor died in vain. His example is before you—his mantle rests with you."

Here is a portion of the sketch of General Polk which Chaplain Cross had written in December, 1863, for his book *Camp and Field.*

Lieutenant-General Polk is a man of brilliant mind; well informed on all subjects; lively and imaginative; prompt, ardent, and energetic; remarkably neat in personal appearance; dignified, yet courteous, in manner; as brave in battle as eloquent in discourse; and looks as much the general as the bishop.

A good story was told of him soon after he entered the army, which went the rounds of the Southern newspaper press. On a journey he entered a hotel where he was a stranger. The proprietor met him at the door, and saluted him as "Judge." "You mistake me, sir," said the bishop; "I am no judge." "General, then, perhaps," rejoined the publican. "And no general," was the reply. "Bishop, then, I am sure," exclaimed his host. "Very well," said the traveller; "but why do you take me for judge, general, or bishop?" "Why, sir," answered the other, "having kept a hotel for a long series of years, and seeing constantly so many strangers, I have accustomed myself to the study of character, and am seldom wrong in my judgment. As soon as you entered my house, I perceived that you were a professional gentleman; and it needed no second look to assure me that, whatever your profession, you must be at the head of it."

Perhaps the story is not true, but it *might* be. No officer in the Confederate army has more the port of a leader than Lieutenant-General Polk. Manifestly, he was made to command.

The following is furnished me in a letter by the Rev. Dr. Quintard, the general's chaplain and intimate friend. I give it in his own words:

"The other day, as we were riding out and talking very familiarly on various subjects, General Polk mentioned a singular incident that occurred to him some years ago. His oldest son—now Captain Hamilton Polk—when in college, purchased a walking-stick for his father. Wishing his father's name and Episcopal seal engraved upon the head of the cane, he carried it to an engraver in New York and gave him a picture of the bishop's seal, as printed in the 'Church Almanac.' The seal was a simple shield, having for its device a cross in the centre, with key and crosier laid across it. On calling for the cane, young Polk found that the engraver, by some strange hocus-pocus, had engraved, plainly and distinctly, a sword in place of a key. Now you may speculate on that to your heart's content; for it has the advantage over most stories, of being true."

I have the best authority for saying that the remarkable yarn, first spun in the Chattanooga Rebel, of the presentation to the bishop, by his brother, of a bowie-knife and a brace of pistols as an outfit for him after his consecration to the Episcopate, was a sheer fabrication.

To the same category, doubtless, belongs a certain story of him in connection with the Battle of Perryville. It is said that General Cheatham, in a furious charge, exhorted his troops to drive the Yankees to a certain place supposed to be not far from every battle-field; and that General Polk, dashing by, waved his sword and shouted, "Drive them, my brave fellows! drive them—where General Cheatham told you to drive them!"

The following, however, did actually occur on that bloody field. Near the close of the day a large force appeared on our right, enfilading General Polk's corps with terrible effect. Thinking them to be some of our own troops who had mistaken him for the enemy, he ordered his men to suspend their action and rode forward alone. Approaching the force in question, he was surprised to find them in Federal uniform. With great presence of mind he rode near the general in command and cried, with an authoritative voice, "Cease firing, general! Don't you see that you are slaughtering our own men?" The officer, with a somewhat doubtful and puzzled look, responded, "Excuse me, sir; but who are you? I have not the honor of knowing you." To which General Polk replied, "You cease firing, and in five minutes you shall hear from me." Then, putting spurs to his horse, he galloped back to his command and shouted, "Boys, they are your enemies! Fire!" The instant crash which followed was as if all the thunders of heaven had united their voices; and when the blue battle-cloud rose, the enfilading foe had disappeared, but the ground where he had stood was heaped with the wounded and the dead.

Bishop Polk, though he has laid aside his lawn, has not put off his religion. As far as practicable in the army, he hallows the Sabbath, and avails himself of every opportunity of attending public worship. At Harrodsburg, two days before the battle, he invited Dr. Quintard to accompany him to the Episcopal church, which is one of the most beautiful in the West. As they walked up the aisle alone, the general exclaimed, with emotion, "O for the days when we went up to the house of the Lord and compassed His altar with the voice of praise and thanksgiving!" Reaching the chancel, he said to the doctor, "Can we not have prayers?" and they kneeled down and poured out their hearts to God; and the general left the sanctuary with a face all bathed in tears. Such soldiers do not fight for fame.

A Plea for the Reliable Gentleman

EVEN WITH THE WAR reaching deeper and deeper into the South, the Confederates could still laugh at themselves, though the humor was sometimes sardonic.

Here is a typical sketch by a Confederate humorist, a sketch that has application not only to the war of the Confederates but to all wars. The article appeared in *The Southern Illustrated News* with an illustration by the distinguished Confederate artist, W. L. Sheppard. Although unsigned, "A Plea for the Reliable Gentleman" was probably written by Dr. George W. Bagby.

A PLEA FOR THE RELIABLE GENTLEMAN.

"Adde parum parvo, magnus acervus erit."

If the barbarities of this "cruel" war are to be summed up at its close, none will strike a then calm and refrigerated public as more unprovoked and inhuman in their character than those which have been perpetrated upon that innocent and unoffending man now known as "The Reliable Gentleman," whose name has become a reproach in the house of his friends—if he has any—and a jest in the mouth of his enemies. An unfriendly press, which took him by the hand at the commencement of the war, has turned upon him with a merciless ferocity, and an unthinking people, taking the cue, have pursued him with unrelenting inhumanity. He is represented as wandering about on the railroads, with his carpet-bag full of the most marvellous stories with which to gull his fellow-citizens and take in unsuspecting newspaper reporters. Even his private character has been made the subject of animadversion, and we not unfrequently see allusions in the press to incorrect rumors which it says must have originated with The Reliable Gentleman, after taking "one snifter too many."

Now I know the charges against him are grave enough. After a heavy outlay of the old currency, I have succeeded in obtaining a copy of them. Among the more serious, I find that last spring he, in company with one Louis Napoleon, did recognize and declare free and independent, the Confederate States of America, and that shortly after The Reliable Gentleman, at the head of fifty thousand French troops, was on the Rio Grande, carpet-bag in hand, awaiting an opportunity to cross. A few weeks after he ran out of England with seven iron-clads, and was to break the blockade at Charleston all to flinders—if he ever reached it—which he didn't. On the 3d of July last, I find him charged with taking forty thousand prisoners at Gettysburg, but, owing to some difficulty in getting transportation for his carpet-bag or some other serious cause, failing to bring them into the Confederate lines. A few days before that, through his instrumentality, Grant lost sixty thousand men before Vicksburg by a "slow fever," and virtually gave up the siege. In another specification, he is accused of having arrived nine times at Spottswood Hotel, in company with a delegation from Illinois, empowered to form a treaty of peace with the Confederacy. He is charged, also, with having re-captured New Orleans (with the aid of the Mobile papers) almost every week since its fall, and with spending what time he had to spare from this operation in leading brigades of deserters from the Yankee army who were "tired of the war," and had thrown down their arms. In an exodus of this kind, other brigades have been represented as falling upon him fiercely, but only to result in those other brigades being "totally destroyed" by those centurions who had thrown down their arms. In the flanking business, his conduct (if the indictment were true, which I utterly deny) would appear to have been peculiarly flagrant. In company with some distinguished general, he is always on the enemy's flank, having just gotten through Snickers' Gap, or some other gap, in time to get a favorable opportunity to open on the unsuspecting foe, of whose artillery he has already pocketed two or three dozen pieces by way of an eye-opener. In those flank movements it is alleged that he is always with "the cavalry in hot pursuit," from which hot pursuit nothing is ever heard "at the War Department." The captured artillery is generally found to be entirely used up in those caloric chases, and is not sent down to the armory. These I believe may be set down as the more serious of the charges. His captures of immense wagon trains and some minor matters are omitted. Now against all these on behalf of The Reliable Gentleman, I put in an *alibi*. I shall contend that that much abused gentleman had no agency in the circulation of these reports, that he has been sitting down quietly at home, and that it is the Public which has deceived itself. Taking this Public for my jury, I shall submit the following statement of facts as evidence:

A few weeks since I traveled the entire length of one of the railroads in Virginia. I carried no baggage, with the exception of two baskets of postage stamps, given me by the conductor in taking my fare out of a Confederate I. O. U., and having nothing about me that any of the passengers could steal, I looked around with an unclouded mind. As we approached a station where a good deal of artillery had been encamped, I descried a tall countryman, (exempt from conscription, probably an account of his having no shoes and very few pantaloons that I could see,) sitting on a worm-fence. Just as we reached the station, this exempt, in reply to a question from a neighbor, used these remarkable words: "Yes! old Dillory moved it 'bout 9 o'clock this morning."

"Eh! what's that?" ejaculated a nervous gentleman in front of me; "all the artillery moved? 'Here, my friend, (to the man on the fence) do you know whether Captain Three-bars' battery went?' "

(Man on the fence)—"Cappen w-h-a-t?"

(Old gent, cars now moving off)—"Captain Three-bars' bat—"

Here the man was out of sight. "Bless my soul, this is too bad; I've got a son in that battery."

Here the old gentleman explained to his neighbor on the next seat that the man had said that all the artillery had moved up to the front at 9 o'clock, "and" he added, "they must be fighting by this time!"

At the next station, a countryman who was on the cars got off, and rushing up to a party of his chums at the grocery door, breathlessly jerked out the following information: "Fighting like thunder in front—commenced at 9 o'clock—been going it all day—Captain Three-bars killed—battery cut all to pieces—his father's on the train now—old man takes it mighty hard—we got the best of it—drove 'em ten miles—lots of prisoners."

Two stations below this the report had grown into such dimensions as to include Lieut. Gen Blanks' corps in the fight, and the capture of several thousand prisoners, the several being soon changed into the definitive numeral seven as a more satisfactory statement. A wounded cavalryman on the cars, (who *had* been in the skirmish the day before) was set upon and besieged with questions. He could not tell much of the "scrummage," as he had been wounded early in the day, and brought off, but though all might have happened which was stated, as "they was 'gaging in right peert, when he left."

I need not occupy your space with a detailed statement of how the rumor grew. When we reached the end of the road, the newspaper reporters rushed upon the scene, and in a remarkably short time had every thing every body knew, and a great deal they didn't know, winding up by carrying off the cavalryman bodily. The daily journals next morning contained the following:

"Highly Important from the Army—Heavy Engagement Yesterday—Large Captures of Prisoners—Threebars' Battery Cut to Pieces:

"The city was much excited last evening by rumors of a heavy engagement which took place yesterday morning on the Cross-it-or-die river, in which our troops were victorious, routing the enemy with great slaughter, and taking seven thousand prisoners. From a conversation with a gentleman who was wounded in the action, and other passengers who came down on the train, we are enabled to give a brief but Gen. Blank. The infantry fighting commenced at daybreak, reliable account. The corps engaged on our side was that of and our artillery, which was ordered up at 9 o'clock, arrived on the ground in admirable condition, and opened fire about 11 o'clock. The fighting on both sides was of a most determined character, but an irresistible charge of our men broke the lines of the enemy, and the cowardly foe retreated in great confusion, leaving 7,000 prisoners, including many field officers, in our hands.

"Capt. Threebars' battery bore a most gallant part in the action, and was literally cut to pieces. It repulsed seven distinct charges of three whole divisions of the enemy, the men fighting with their rammers after their ammunition gave out. One private killed twenty-seven of the enemy, including three lieutenant colonels, with a priming wire. A gallant fellow, acting as No. 3 at the gun, used a thumb-stall so effectually that the ground for miles around him was strewed with the slain. Capt. Threebars set a noble example to his men, standing by his guns until pierced by nineteen 100-pounder Parrot shells. His body was brought down on the train last evening in charge of his afflicted father.

"The prisoners may be expected here some time this morning. No official details of this engagement had been received at the war department last night, though something from Gen. Blank may be expected during the day."

Now did The Reliable Gentleman do this? I respectfully submit not; and gentlemen of the jury you will agree with me. Well, now, let me read you an extract from the same journals published the day after:

"It appears that the statements brought to this city night before last by 'the reliable gentleman,' about the fight that morning, were grossly exaggerated, so much so, indeed, that that most veracious (?) gentleman is supposed to have been under the effects of a drop too much when he communicated the intelligence."

I am sure that if I were to rest the case of my client here, my jury immediately upon retiring would find itself guilty of murder in the first degree, and insist on being hung. This, however, is not the object of The Reliable Gentleman, and to calm the remorse of the jury I will cite a case to show that it is not only in war matters that rumors grow without much aid, but that they thrive finely even in the social circle. I have a friend named Smith, a sober, amiable, peaceable man, who, I don't think, would intentionally hurt a chicken. Not long ago Smith threw a rock, and accidentally hitting Mrs. Jones' cat in his garden, killed it. He afterwards put the cat over the fence. Now, here is what I heard of Smith's character in company a few weeks afterwards: I heard that he drank; that he had a violent temper; that when this temper was up he was worse than an Indian, and didn't make anything of executing a war dance on top of the dinner-table, which he immediately followed up by falling upon his family and tomahawking a couple of them by way of keeping his hand in; that only a few weeks before he had seized a brickbat, knocked his neighbor, Mrs. Jones, off her fence, and then thrown her body over into the next yard!

With this conclusion, which I flatter myself is a settler, I rest the case of The Reliable Gentleman with a High-minded, Honorable, Intelligent and Just Public.

The Jews in Richmond

As a minority in the South (though they contributed the most distinguished member of President Davis' Cabinet) the Jews were attacked as speculators and shirkers. Here is Maximilian Michelbacher's defense of his people, published as a preface to the eminent rabbi's sermon delivered on one of the days of national prayer recommended by the President.

ᴊᴜᴜᴜᴜᴢ₯ ₢ᴇᴠᴠᴠᴠᴋ

Brethren of the House of Israel: It is due to you, to whom I always speak of your faults, without fear, favour or affection, to say: I have carefully investigated your conduct from the commencement of this war to the present time, and I am happy in coming to the unbiassed conclusion, that you have fulfilled your duties as good citizens and as men, who love their country. It has been charged by both the ignorant and the evil-disposed against the people of our faith, that the Israelite does not fight in the battles of his country! All history attests the untruthfulness of this ungracious charge, generated in the cowardly hearts and born between the hypocritical lips of ungenerous and prejudiced foes. The Israelite

287

has never failed to defend the soil of his birth, or the land of his adoption—the Emperors of France and Russia will bear evidence to the verity of this assertion. In respect to those Israelites, who are now in the army of the Confederate States, I will merely say, that their patriotism and valor have never been doubted by such men as have the magnanimous souls of Lee, Johnston, Jackson and others of like manhood. The recorded votes and acts of the Israelites of this Confederacy, amply prove their devotion to the support of its Government. They well understand their duties as citizens and soldiers, and the young men do not require the persuasion of conscription to convert them into soldiers, to defend, as they verily believe, the only free government in North America. Many of our young men have been crippled for life, or slain upon the field of battle, in the service of the Confederate States, and there are several thousands yet coursing the campaigns of the war against those enemies of our Confederacy, who are as detestable to them, as were the Philistines to David and his countrymen.

The humanity and providence of the Israelite for the distressed families of the soldiers of our army, have allayed the pangs of poverty and brought comfort to households, wherein before were only seen hopelessness and misery. In this you have performed your duties as Israelites and as citizens—and, for this, may the God of our fathers shower upon you all the blessings which He confers upon His favourite children!

There is another cry heard, and it was even repeated in the Halls of Congress, that the Israelite is oppressing the people—that he is engaged in the great sin of speculating and extorting in the bread and meat of the land. To discover the character of this accusation, I have made due inquiry—the information I have acquired upon this head, from sources that extend from the Potomac to the Rio Grande, plainly present the fact, that the Israelites are not speculators nor extortioners. As traders and as merchants, they buy merchandise and sell the same *immediately*; the merchandise is never put aside, or hoarded to enhance its value, by withdrawing it from the market. Flour, meal, wheat, corn, bacon, beef, coal and wood are hardly ever found in the mercantile magazines or storehouses of the Israelite—he buys some of these articles for his own consumption, but he buys none of them to sell again—he does not extort—it is obvious to the most obtuse mind that the high prices of the Israelite would drive all his customers into the stores of his Christian neighbours; but is such the effect of the price of the Israelite's goods?

The peculiar characteristic of the Jewish merchant is seen in his undelayed, rapid and instant sales; his temperament does not allow him, by hoarding his goods, to risk time with his money, which, with him, is as restless as the waves of the sea that bears the ships that convey the manufactured goods of his customers. I thank God, that my investigation has proved to me that the cry against the Jew is a false one—this cry, though cunningly devised after the most approved model of villainy, will not subserve the base and unjust purpose of hindering the virtuous indignation of a suffering people, from tracing the true path of the extortioner, and awarding to him, who deals in the miseries, life and blood of our fellow-citizens, that punishment, which the traitor to the happiness and liberties of his country deserves to have measured unto him.

Spending the Seed Corn

As Sherman's army drove deep into Georgia, all the resources of the Confederacy and of the state were called upon to check the advance on Atlanta. President Davis relieved General Johnston as commander of the Confederate troops defending the city and replaced him with General John B. Hood. Time proved the inadequacy of the President's supposed remedy for a grave situation, but public opinion was demanding a general who would cease the withdrawals toward the city he was protecting and give issue to the campaign.

Georgia's governor, Joseph Emerson Brown, who had been among the severest critics of the administration, was now forced to use the men he had withheld from the Confederate Army by special state exemptions. Wholehearted cooperation with General Hood might have done much to lighten the fix in which the Confederates found themselves, but, even on the brink of disaster, Governor Brown could make the transfer of men and ordnance to the use of the Confederacy full of difficulties.

Among local troops which participated in the futile defense of Atlanta was the body of cadets from the Georgia

Military Institute, a small school near Marietta which died with the war. The service of the cadets was inconsiderable, but it was typical of the spirit with which teenagers and old men alike came to the defense of their homes.

The Georgia cadets were typical of the spirit with which the whole people of the Confederacy waged war. The feats of individual youngsters are legion and uncounted. In Virginia another group of cadets, young soldiers from "Stonewall" Jackson's V.M.I., won a hard fight at New Market on May 15, 1864. The reports on the two groups of schoolboy soldiers follow.

Headquarters Battalion of Cadets,
And Georgia Military Institute,
Milledgeville, Oct. 27th, 1864.

Maj. Gen. H. C. Wayne,
Adj. and Inspector General of Georgia.

Sir—Your order of the 12th, May 1864, to report myself to General Jos. E. Johnston commanding the Army of Tennessee and "to hold the corps of Cadets in readiness, to obey his orders during the present emergency," was joyfully received and promptly executed. The Cadets of the Georgia Military Institute, have sought active field service from the beginning of the war. This desire had become almost a passion. Under its influence we had lost our higher classes and might have lost the existence of the Institute, but for the hopes inspired by your reply to the petition of last year and their positive realization in your order of May 12th.

The service of the Battalion has been as follows. On the 27th of May, under a special field-order from General Johnston we reported to you in Atlanta, where you were organizing the Militia. By your order the Battalion was sent to West Point, where we remained until the third (3d) of July, when by order of Maj. General G. W. Smith, we reported for duty at Turner's Ferry on the Chattahoochee. There for the first time, the Cadets exchanged shots with the enemy. I remember with pride that the style of their march across the river on the afternoon of the 6th, under fire, elicited applause from veterans.

On the 12th July the following special order from General Johnston, detached the Battalion from General Smith's command, viz:

Headquarters Army of Tennessee,
July 12th, 1864, 11 A.M.

General:

General Johnston directs you to send the Battalion of Georgia State Cadets, Maj. Capers commanding, to West Point, Georgia, without delay.

Most respectfully, your obedient servant,

(Signed)   A. P. Mason,
Major & A. A. G.

On the 25th July the Battalion was ordered back to the division; and marched to position in the trenches of Atlanta, in the night of the 27th.

On the 14th August the Battalion was ordered here by his Excellency the Governor.

In no single instance, whatever may have been the duties

assigned them or the position occupied by them, have our expectations been disappointed in either the bearing or efficiency of the command. There was fatigue and blood and death in their ranks but no white feather.

Considering the nature of our services in the trenches and on the picket lines of Atlanta, we have reason to be grateful to God that our list of casualties is so small. . . .

Very respectfully,

Your obedient servant,

F. W. Capers,
Major Commanding.

❋ ❋ ❋ ❋ ❋

Head Quarters, Corps Cadets,
July 4, 1864.

General:

In obedience to General Orders, No. —, head quarters, Virginia Military Institute, June 27th, 1864, I have the honor to submit the following report of the operations of the corps of cadets, under my command in the field, from May 11th to June 25th, inclusive.

In obedience to orders from Maj. Gen. Breckinridge, communicated through you, at 7 A.M. on the morning of May 11th, the corps of cadets, consisting of a battalion of four companies of infantry, and a section of three inch rifle guns, took up the line of march for Staunton. The march to Staunton was accomplished in two days. I preceded the column, on the second day, some hours, for the purpose of reporting to Gen. Breckinridge, and was ordered by him to put the cadets in camp one mile south of Staunton. On the morning of the 13th I received orders to march at daylight on the road to

A gallant boy my love was born:
The Yankee name he holds in scorn;
He's always faithful, loving, brave,
And risks his life this land to save.
He knows right well how oft my thoughts
Hover around him day and night;
How oft to Heaven I upward look,
And pray for him, my life! my light!

George Dunn & Comp'y, Publishers, Richmond, Va.

294

I shall be a son of Mars
When Iv'e been at many wars,
When I show my cuts and scars
    To the sound of the drum.
But this nasty, weary drill,
Of it I have had my fill,
And if I had my will,
    To it would never come.
                [ARDENT RECRUIT

George Dunn & Comp'y, Publishers. Richmond, Va.

Harrisonburg, taking position in the column in rear of Echols' brigade. We marched eighteen miles, and encamped—moved at daylight on the 14th, marched sixteen miles, and encamped. At 12 o'clock on the night of the 14th, received orders to prepare to march immediately, without *beat* of drum, and as noiselessly as possible. We moved from camp at half past one o'clock, taking position in the general column, in rear of Echols' brigade, being followed by the column of artillery under the command of Major McLaughlin. Having accomplished a distance of six miles, and approached the position of the enemy, as indicated by occasional skirmishing with his pickets in front, a halt was called, and we remained on the side of the road two or three hours, in the midst of a heavy fall of rain. The general having determined to receive the attack of the enemy, made his dispositions for battle, posting the corps in reserve. He informed me that he did not wish to *put the cadets in*, if he could avoid it, but that should occasion require it, he would use them very freely. He was also pleased to express his confidence in them, and I am happy to believe that his expectations were not disappointed, for when the tug of battle came, they bore themselves gallantly and well.

The enemy not making the attack as was anticipated, or not advancing as rapidly as was desired, the line was deployed into column, and the advance resumed. Here I was informed by one of Gen. Breckinridge's aids, that my battalion, together with the battalion of Col. G. M. Edgar, would constitute the reserve, and was instructed to keep the section of artillery with the column, and to take position, after the deployments should have been made, 250 or 300 yards in rear of the front line of battle, and to maintain that distance. Having begun a flank movement to the left, about two miles south of New Market, the nature of the ground was such as to render it impossible that the artillery should continue with the infantry column. I ordered Lieut. Minge to join the general artillery column in the main road, and to report to Major McLaughlin; after that, I did not see the section of artillery until near the close of the engagement. Major McLaughlin, under whose command they served, was pleased to speak of the section in such complimentary terms, that I was satisfied they had done their duty. Continuing the advance on the ground to the left of the main road, and south of New Market, at 12½ P.M. we came under the fire of the enemy's batteries. Having advanced a quarter of a mile under the fire, we were halted, and the column was deployed, the march up to this time having been by flank in column. The ground in front was open, with skirts of woods on the left. The General's plans seem to have undergone some modification. Instead of one line, with a reserve, he formed his infantry in two, artillery in rear and to the right; the cavalry deployed and guarding the right flank, left flank resting on a stream. Wharton's brigade of infantry constituted the first line; Echols' brigade the second; the battalion of cadets, brigaded with Echols, was the last battalion but one from the left of the second line, Edgar's battalion being on the left. The lines having been adjusted, the order to advance was passed. As Wharton's line ascended a knoll, it came in full view of the enemy's batteries, which opened a heavy fire, but not having gotten the range, did but little damage. By the time the second line reached the same ground, the Yankee gunners had gotten the exact range, and their fire began to tell on our line with fearful accuracy. It was here that Captain Hill and others fell. Great gaps were made through the ranks; but the cadet, true to his discipline, would close in to the centre to fill the interval, and push steadily forward. The alignment of the battalion, under this terrible fire, which strewed the ground with killed and wounded for more than a mile, on open ground, would have been creditable even on a field day.

The advance was thus continued until, having passed Bushong's house, a mile or more beyond New Market, and still to the left of the main road, the enemy's batteries, at 250 or 300 yards, opened upon us with canister and case shot, and their long lines of infantry were put into action at the same time. The fire was withering. It seemed impossible that any living creature could escape; and here we sustained our heaviest loss, a great many being wounded, and numbers knocked down, stunned, and temporarily disabled. I was here disabled for a time, and the command devolved upon Capt. H. A. Wise, company A. He gallantly pressed onward. We had before this gotten into the front line. Our line took a position behind a fence. A brisk fusillade ensued; a shout; a rush—and the day was won. The enemy fled in confusion, leaving killed, wounded, artillery and prisoners in our hands. Our men pursued in hot haste, until it became necessary to halt, draw ammunition, and re-establish the lines for the purpose of driving them from their last position on Rude's hill, which they held with cavalry and artillery to cover the passage of the river, about a mile in their rear. Our troops charged and took the position without loss. The enemy withdrew, crossed the river, and burnt the bridge. The engagement closed at 6½ P.M. The cadets did their duty, as the long list of casualties will attest. Numerous instances of gallantry might be mentioned—but I have thought it better to refrain from specifying individual cases, for fear of making invidious distinctions, or from want of information, withholding praise where it may have been justly merited. It had rained almost incessantly during the battle, and at its termination the cadets were well nigh exhausted. Wet, hungry, and many of them shoeless—for they had lost their shoes and socks in the deep mud through which it was necessary to march—they bore their hardships with that uncomplaining resignation, which characterizes the true soldier. . . .

I am, General, very respectfully,
Your obedient servant,

S. Ship,
Lieut. Col. and Commandant
Maj. Gen. F. H. Smith, Superintendent

Peace Negotiations

A n *Address* of the Confederate Congress in 1864
summed up the situation and reiterated the South's
desire for peace. It was interpreted by amateur peace-
makers as an invitation to negotiations to end the war.
The most important of several abortive attempts at peace
was the mission of Colonel James F. Jacquess and J. R.
Gilmore to Richmond.

Jacquess and Gilmore came with the knowledge of
Lincoln, but they were not sent by him. Their representations gained them an audience with President Davis,
but the conversations reached a stalemate on Davis' in-
sistence on the already published Confederate conditions
for peace—terms which had not altered from the outbreak
of the war.

The conferees in Richmond agreed upon secrecy, but
accounts of the conference were printed in the North,
and Secretary of State Judah P. Benjamin felt free to
release to the public the letter he had written Commissioner James M. Mason in Paris as a report of the
conference.

DEPARTMENT OF STATE. ⎫
Richmond, Va., August 25, 1864. ⎭

Sir,—Numerous publications which have recently appeared in the journals of the United States on the subject of informal overtures for peace between two Federations of States now at war on this continent, render it desirable that you should be fully advised of the views and policy of this Government on a matter of such paramount importance. It is likewise proper that you should be accurately informed of what has occurred on the several occasions mentioned in the published statements.

You have heretofore been furnished with copies of the manifesto issued by the Congress of the Confederate States, with the approval of the President, on the 14th June last, and have doubtless, acted in conformity with the resolution which requested that copies of this manifesto should be laid before foreign governments. "The principles, sentiments, and purposes, by which these States have been, and are still actuated," are set forth in that paper with all the authority due to the solemn declaration of the Legislative and Executive Departments of this Government, and with a clearness which leaves no room for comment or explanation.—In a few sentences it is pointed out that all we ask is immunity from interference with our internal peace and prosperity "and to be left in the undisturbed enjoyment of those inalienable rights of life, liberty, and the pursuit of happiness, which our common ancestors declared to be the equal heritage of all parties to the social compact. Let them forbear aggressions upon us, and the war is at an end. If there be questions which require adjustment by negotiation, we have ever been willing, and are still willing, to enter into communication with our adversaries in a spirit of peace, of equity, and manly frankness."

The manifesto closed with the declaration that "we commit our cause to the enlightened judgment of the world, to the sober reflections of our adversaries themselves, and to the solemn and righteous arbitrament of Heaven."

Within a very few weeks after the publication of this manifesto, it seemed to have met with a response from President Lincoln. In the early part of last month a letter was received by General LEE from Lieutenant-General GRANT, in the following words:

"Headquarters Armies of the United States,
"City Point, Va., July 8, 1864.

"General R. E. LEE, commanding Confederate forces near Petersburg, Virginia:

"GENERAL,—I would request that Colonel JAMES F. JACQUESS, Seventy-third Illinois volunteer infantry, and J. R. GILMORE, Esq., be allowed to meet Colonel ROBERT OULD, Commissioner for the Exchange of Prisoners, at such a place between the lines of the two armies as you may designate. The object of the meeting is legitimate with the duties of Colonel OULD as Commissioner.

"If not consistent for you to grant the request here asked, I would beg that this be referred to President DAVIS for his action.

"Requesting as early an answer to this communication as you may find it convenient to make, I subscribe myself,

"Very respectfully, Your ob't serv'nt,

"U. S. GRANT.
"Lieutenant-General, U. S. A."

On the reference of this letter to the President, he authorized Colonel Ould to meet the persons named in General Grant's letter; and Colonel Ould, after seeing them, returned to Richmond, and reported to the President, in the presence of the Secretary of War and myself that Messrs. Jacquess and Gilmore had not said anything to him about his duties as Commissioner for Exchange of Prisoners, but that they asked permission to come to Richmond for the purpose of seeing the President; that they came with the knowledge and approval of President Lincoln, and under his pass; that they were informal messengers, sent with a view of paving the way for a meeting of formal commissioners authorized to negotiate for peace, and desired to communicate to President Davis the views of Mr. Lincoln, and to obtain the President's views in return, so as to arrange for a meeting of commissioners. Colonel Ould stated that he had told them repeatedly that it was useless to come to Richmond to talk of peace on any other terms than the recognized independence of the Confederacy, to which they said that they were aware of that, and that they were, nevertheless, confident that their interview would result in peace. The President, on this report of Colonel Ould, determined to permit them to come to Richmond under his charge.

On the evening of the 16th of July, Colonel Ould conducted these gentlemen to a hotel in Richmond, where a room was provided for them, in which they were to remain under surveillance during their stay here, and the next morning I received the following letter:

"SPOTSWOOD HOUSE ⎫
"RICHMOND, VA., JULY 17, 1864.⎰

"*Hon.* J. P. BENJAMIN, *Secretary of State of Confederate States of America:*

"DEAR SIR,—The undersigned, JAMES F. JACQUESS, of Illinois, and JAMES R. GILMORE, of Massachusetts, most respectfully solicit an interview with President DAVIS. They visit Richmond as private citizens, and have no official character or authority; but they are fully possessed of the views of the United States Government relative to an adjustment of the differences now existing between the North and the South and have little doubt that a free interchange of views between President DAVIS and themselves would open the way to such *official* negotiations as would ultimate in restoring PEACE to the two sections of our distracted country.

"They therefore ask an interview with the President, and, awaiting your reply, are

"Most truly and respectfully,
"Your obedient servants,

"JAMES F. JACQUESS,
"JAMES R. GILMORE."

The word "official" is underscored, and the word "peace" doubly understored, in the original.

After perusing the letter, I invited Colonel Ould to conduct the writers to my office; and on their arrival, stated to them that they must be conscious they could not be admitted to an interview with the president without informing me more fully of the object of their mission, and satisfying me that they came by request of Mr. Lincoln. Mr. Gilmore replied that they came unofficially, but with the knowledge, and at the desire, of Mr. Lincoln; that they thought the war had gone far enough; that it could never end except by some sort of agreement; that the agreement might as well be made now as after further bloodshed; that they knew by the recent address of the Confederate Congress that we were willing to make peace; that they admitted that proposals ought to come from the North, and that they were prepared to make these proposals by Mr. Lincoln's authority; that it was necessary to have a sort of informal understanding in advance of regular negotiations, for if commissioners were appointed without some such understanding, they would meet, quarrel, and separate, leaving the parties more bitter against each other than before; that they knew Mr. Lincoln's views, and would state them if pressed by the President to do so, and desired to learn his in return.

I again insisted on some evidence that they came from Mr. Lincoln; and in order to satisfy me, Mr. Gilmore referred to the fact that permission for their coming through our lines had been asked officially by General Grant in a letter to General Lee, and that General Grant in that letter had asked that this request should be referred to President Davis. Mr. Gilmore then showed me a card, written and signed by Mr. Lincoln requesting General Grant to aid Mr. Gilmore and friend in passing through his lines into the Confederacy. Colonel Jacquess then said that his name was not put on the card for the reason that it was earnestly desired that their visit should be kept secret; and he had come into the Confederacy a year ago, and had visited Petersburg on a similar errand, and that it was feared if his name should become known, that some of those who had formerly met him in Petersburg would conjecture the purpose for which he now came. He said that the terms of peace which they would offer to the President would be honorable to the Confederacy; that they did not desire that the Confederacy should accept any other terms, but would be glad to have my promise, as they gave theirs, that their visit should be kept a profound secret if it failed to result in peace; that it would not be just that either party should seek any advantage by divulging the fact of their overture for peace, if unsuccessful. I assented to this request, and then, rising, said: "Do I understand you to state distinctly that you come as messengers from Mr. Lincoln for the purpose of agreeing with the President as to the proper mode of inaugurating a formal negotiation for peace, charged by Mr. Lincoln with authority for stating his own views and receiving those of President Davis?" Both answered in the affirmative, and I then said that the President would see them at my office the same evening at 9 P.M.; that, at least, I presumed he would, but if he objected, after hearing my report, they should be informed. They were then recommitted to the charge of Colonel Ould, with the understanding that they were to be reconducted to my office at the appointed hour unless otherwise directed.

This interview, connected with the report previously made by Colonel Ould, left on my mind the decided impression that Mr. Lincoln was averse to sending formal commissioners to open negotiations, lest he might thereby be deemed to have recognized the independence of the Confederacy, and that he was anxious to learn whether the conditions on which alone he would be willing to take such a step would be yielded by the Confederacy; that with this view he had placed his messengers in a condition to satisfy us that they really came from him, without committing himself to anything in the event of a disagreement as to such conditions as he considered to be indispensable. On informing the President, therefore, of my conclusions, he determined that no question of form or etiquette should be an obstacle to his receiving any overtures that promised, however remotely, to result in putting an end to the carnage which marked the continuance of hostilities.

The President came to my office at 9 o'clock in the evening, and Colonel Ould came a few moments later, with Messrs. Jacquess and Gilmore. The President said to them that he had heard, from me, that they came as messengers of peace from

Mr. Lincoln; that as such they were welcome; that the Confederacy had never concealed its desire for peace, and that he was ready to hear whatever they had to offer on that subject.

Mr. Gilmore then addressed the President, and in a few minutes had conveyed the information that these two gentlemen had come to Richmond impressed with the idea that this Government would accept a peace on the basis of a reconstruction of the Union, the abolition of slavery, and the grant of an amnesty to the people of the States as repentant criminals. In order to accomplish the abolition of slavery, it was proposed that there should be a general vote of all the people of both federations, in mass, and the majority of the vote thus taken was to determine that as well as all other disputed questions. These were stated to be Mr. Lincoln's views. The President answered, that as these proposals had been prefaced by the remark that the people of the North were a majority, and that a majority ought to govern, the offer was, in effect, a proposal that the Confederate States should surrender at discretion, admit that they had been wrong from the beginning of the contest, submit to the mercy of their enemies, and avow themselves to be in need of pardon for crimes; that extermination was preferable to such dishonor.

He stated that if they were themselves so unacquainted with the form of their own government as to make such propositions, Mr. Lincoln ought to have known, when giving them his views, that it was out of the power of the Confederate Government to act on the subject of the domestic institutions of the several States, each State having exclusive jurisdiction on that point, still less to commit the decision of such a question to the vote of a foreign people; that the separation of the States was an accomplished fact: that he had no authority to receive proposals for negotiation except by virtue of his office as President of an independent confederacy; and on this basis alone must proposals be made to him.

At one period of the conversation, Mr. Gilmore made use of some language referring to these States as "rebels" while rendering an account of Mr. Lincoln's views, and apologized for the word. The President desired him to proceed, that no offence was taken, and that he wished Mr. Lincoln's language to be repeated to him as exactly as possible. Some further conversation took place, substantially to the same effect as the foregoing, when the President rose to indicate that the interview was at an end. The two gentlemen were then recommitted to the charge of Colonel Ould, and left Richmond the next day.

This account of the visit of Messrs. Gilmore and Jacquess to Richmond has been rendered necessary by publications made by one or both of them since their return to the United States, notwithstanding the agreement that their visit was to be kept secret. They have, perhaps, concluded that as the promise of secrecy was made at their request, it was permissible to disregard it. We had no reason for desiring to conceal what occurred, and have therefore, no complaint to make of the publicity given to the fact of the visit. The extreme inaccuracy of Mr. Gilmore's narrative will be apparent to you from the foregoing statement.

You have no doubt seen, in the Northern papers, an account of another conference on the subject of peace, which took place in Canada, at about the same date, between Messrs. C. C. Clay and J. P. Holcombe, Confederate citizens of the highest character and position, and Mr. Horace Greeley, of New York, acting with authority of President Lincoln. It is deemed not improper to inform you that Messrs. Clay and Holcombe, although enjoying, in an eminent degree, the confidence and esteem of the President, were strictly accurate in their statement that they were without any authority from this Government to treat with that of the United States on any subject whatever. We had no knowledge of their conference with Mr. Greeley, nor of their proposed visit to Washington, till we saw the newspaper publications. A significant confirmation of the truth of the statement of Messrs. Gilmore and Jacquess, that they came as messengers from Mr. Lincoln, is to be found in the fact that the views of Mr. Lincoln, as stated by them to the President, are in exact conformity with the offensive paper addressed to "whom it may concern," which was sent by Mr. Lincoln to Messrs. Clay and Holcombe by the hands of his private secretary, Mr. Hay, and which was properly regarded by those gentlemen as an intimation that Mr. Lincoln was unwilling that this war should cease while in his power to continue hostilities.

I am, very respectfully,
Your obedient servant,

J. P. BENJAMIN,
Secretary of State.

HON. JAMES M. MASON, Commissioner to the Continent, &c., &c., &c., PARIS

Victories in the Indian Territory

THE WAR in the West was sometimes forgotten in the rush of political and military activity in Virginia and Georgia and has almost as often been overlooked by historians of the war. It raged with its particular kind of guerrilla fury and produced its particular kind of heroes and heroism. The Confederates made good use of the Indian troops and worked with them effectively in the Indian Territory.

Events in the fall of 1864 called forth three General Orders which were printed in pamphlet form so that the soldiers of the West could send them to their families as mementos of a memorable campaign.

CIRCULAR.

HEAD QUARTERS, DIST. IND. TER'Y.⎱
Fort Towson, C. N., Oct. 17th, 1864. ⎰

There having been many applications within the last few days for copies of Gen'l Orders No. 61, current series from these Head Quarters, the Major General Commanding this military District has ordered that another supply embracing General Orders No. 81 current series from Head Quarters Trans-Mississippi Department, and General Orders No. 26, current series from Gen'l Cooper's Head Quarters, be printed for the use of the troops of this District, to enable them to furnish copies to their friends at home.

By Order of   MAJOR GEN'L. MAXEY

T. M. Scott, A. A. Gen'l.

HEAD QUARTERS INDIAN DIVISION.⎫
Camp Bragg. Sept. 30th, 1864. ⎬

GENERAL ORDERS⎫
    No. 26.   ⎬

I. The thanks of this command are hereby tendered to the gallant officers and men, of Gano's & Watie's Brigades and Howell's Battery, for the signal successes they have gained over the enemy within his lines, and in rear of his fortifications, north of the Arkansas River by destroying his Forage Camps and capturing a magnificent train of 255 loaded wagons, and other property (valued at one and one half millions of dollars in U. S. currency) a large proportion of which they secured and brought out, marching over 300 miles in fourteen days, engaging the enemy victoriously four times, with small loss on our side in numbers. We mourn the death of the honored few, among them the promising young soldier, Adjt. D. R. Patterson of the Seminole Regiment whose career of usefulness was suddenly terminated at Cabin Creek, while at the side of the gallant Chieftain John Jumper charging the enemy's right. The enemy lost 97 killed, many wounded and 111 prisoners. The brilliancy and completeness of this expedition has not been excelled in the history of the war. Firm, brave and confident, the officers had but to order and the men cheerfully executed. The whole having been conducted, with perfect harmony between the war-worn veterans, Stand Watie, the chivalrous Gano and their respective commands, ending with the universal expression that they may again participate in like enterprises. The commanding Genl. hopes that they, and the rest of the command may soon have an opportunity to gather fresh laurels on other fields.

II. In the departure of Genl. Gano he takes the best wishes of the Comdg. Gen'l. and it is a matter of pride to record, in General Orders, the gallant bearing, energy and promptness which has characterized that officer in the execution of every order and instruction—from his brilliant dash at Diamond Grove, to the splendid achievement at Cabin Creek. While the circumstances attending require his immediate transfer, the Comdg. Gen'l hopes that it may be of short duration.

By Command of   BRIG. GEN'L. D. H. COOPER.

T. B. HEISTON, Capt. A. A. Gen'l.

HEAD QUARTERS, DIST. IND. TER'Y.⎱
Fort Towson C. N., *Oct. 7th,* 1864.   ⎰

GENERAL ORDERS⎱
    No. 61   ⎰

The Major General Commanding announces with pride and pleasure the series of brilliant victories on the 16th, 17th, 19th and 20th ultimo, north of the Arkansas River, by the Troops under the leadership of the gallant and chivalrous Gano, and the noble old hero Stand Watie, accompanied by Howell's Battery.

Of this expedition Gen. Gano in his official Report says:

"For three days and nights our boys were without sleep, except such as they could snatch in the saddle or at watering places.

"They dug down banks, cut out trees, rolled wagons and Artillery up hill and down by hand, kept cheerful and never wearied in the good cause, and came into Camps, all rejoicing on the 28th.

"We were out fourteen days, marched over four hundred miles, killed ninety-seven, wounded many, and captured one hundred and eleven prisoners, burned six thousand tons of hay, and all the reapers and mowers, destroyed altogether (from the Federals) one and a half millions of dollars worth of property, bringing safely into our lines nearly one third of that amount estimated in Green Back."

Officers and men behaved gallantly. Of Gen. Watie, he says, "Gen. Watie was by my side, cool and brave as ever."

Of the whole command he says: "The men all did their duty and laid up for themselves imperishable honors."

Throughout the expedition I am rejoiced to say perfect harmony and good will prevailed between the white and Indian troops, all striving for the common good of our beloved country.

For gallantry, energy, enterprise, dash and judgment, and completeness of success, this raid has not been surpassed during the war.

The Major General Commanding deems this a fit occasion to say that not the least of the glorious results of this splendid achievement is the increased cheerfulness and confidence of all in their prowess, and ability to whip anything like equal numbers. Throughout the year the MORALE of the command has been steadily on the increase. For the Troops of the Indian Territory, this has been a year of brilliant success.

Your Arkansas campaign is part of the recorded history of the country.

Since your return, almost every part of the command has been engaged.

A steam boat laden with valuable stores has been captured, a regiment has been almost demolished in sight of the guns of Fort Smith, the survivors captured and the camp destroyed.

Many guns and pistols have been taken,—mail after mail has been captured,—hay camps almost without number have been destroyed and the hay burned; horses, mules and cattle have been wrested from the enemy and driven into our lines. Vast amounts of Sutlers Stores have been captured. Wagons have been burned in gun shot of Fort Smith; the enemy has been virtually locked up in his Forts, and your successes have culminated in this most glorious victory, over which the Telegraph informs us the enemy is *now* wailing.

In our rejoicings let us not forget our gallant comrades in arms who have offered up their lives upon their country's altar of Freedom, priceless sacrifices to their country's redemption. If there be widows and orphans of these gallant men seek them out and deliver this poor tribute to their worth.

And let us remember the sufferings of our wounded, and offer them the tears of sympathy.

Soldiers! There is a cruel enemy still cursing your country. There is still work to do. You have proven what you can do —Remember that strict and cheerful obedience to orders, strict discipline, and thorough drill, will render you still more efficient as soldiers of the holy cause. Your Commanding General has every confidence in your ability and willingness to take and perform any part you may yet have in the ensuing campaign.

II. It is ordered that this order be read at the head of every regiment and battalion, and company of artillery, and at every post in this District.

III. A copy will be forwarded of this order and the commendatory order of Brig. Gen. D. H. Cooper, to the Head Quarters Trans-Mississippi Department.

	S. B. MAXEY.
Official,	Maj. Gen'l. Comdg.
M. L. BELL A. A. Gen'l.	

HEAD QUARTERS, TRANS-MISS. DEPARTMENT,
Shreveport, La., Oct. 12th, 1864.

GENERAL ORDERS,⎫
    No. 81   ⎭

The General Commanding announces to the army the complete success of one of the most brilliant raids of the war.

The expedition under Brigadier Generals Gano and Stand Watie, penetrating far within the enemy's lines, has captured his forage camp and train, destroyed five thousand tons of hay, and brought out one hundred and thirty captured wagons, loaded with stores, after destroying as many more, which were disabled in the action.

These, with one hundred and thirty-five prisoners, and more than two hundred of the enemy killed and wounded, attest the success of the expedition.

The celerity of the movement, the dash of the attack, and their entire success, entitle the commands engaged to the thanks of the country.

By command of   GEN'L. E. KIRBY SMITH.

S. S. ANDERSON, A. Ad't. Gen'l.

Sherman in Atlanta

S HERMAN had whipped Hood at Peachtree Creek in late July. Hard battles around the city sealed the fate of Atlanta. After the battle at Jonesboro on September 2, Atlanta's ordnance stores were fired and Hood's soldiers marched out of the city to the plaintive strains of "Lorena."

Inspired by a visit from President Davis, Hood set to harassing Sherman's lines of communication and promised a drive to the north through Tennessee. Unperturbed, Sherman prepared to continue his March Through Georgia as a March to the Sea. The following informal report of Yankee doings in Atlanta was published on Turnwold Plantation (near Eatonton, Georgia)—in the line of march toward Savannah—just the day before Sherman turned his men south from Atlanta.

Eatonton, Ga., Nov. 4, 1864.

J. A. Turner, Esq.,

Dear Sir:— At your request, I have written down all the points of interest, furnished me by my friend, connected with her leaving Atlanta, &c. I have written it hastily, and leave it for you to condense, as you may deem proper. Hoping its publication may prove of some interest to your readers, I proceed, as follows:

I had pleasure of meeting with a very intelligent lady, a few days since, one of the exiles from Atlanta, under the late order of Gen. Sherman, banishing the citizens from that place, who furnished me with some facts, which may prove of interest to your readers. As soon as the yankees obtained possession of the city, the officers began to hunt up comfortable quarters, and the lady of whom I speak, found herself under the necessity of taking three of them as boarders, or of submitting to the confiscation of her house to the purpose of sheltering our foe. Those who boarded with Mrs. —— proved to be very gentlemanly fellows, and rendered her service in protecting her from the intrusion of the private soldiers, besides aiding her in disposing of her cows, and hogs, when she was compelled to leave. A neighbor of hers, whose husband had rendered himself obnoxious to the yankees, by his service to the south, was ordered by a yankee general, to vacate her premises, in two hours, and a guard was stationed to prevent her from moving her effects. This lady appealed to Gen. Sherman, who immediately ordered the removal of the guard, and permitted her to remove, or sell, any, or all, of her furniture, and other valuables, at her discretion. The lady with whom I conversed, was under the necessity of calling upon Gen. Sherman, after the publication of the edict of banishment, and she represents him as being very kind, and conciliatory in his deportment towards her, and others who visited him. He expressed much regret at the necessity which compelled him to order the citizens of Atlanta from their homes, but stated, in justification of his course, that he intended to make Atlanta a second Gibraltar; that when he completed his defensive works, it would be impregnable; and as no communication could be held with their friends, in the south, they (the citizens) would suffer for food; that it was impossible for him to subsist his army, and feed the citizens, too, by a single line of railroad; and that as he intended to hold Atlanta, at all hazards, he thought it was humanity to send them out of the city, where they could obtain necessary supplies. He took the little child of my friend in his arms, and patted her rosy cheeks, calling her "a poor little exile," and saying he was sorry to have to drive her away from her comfortable home, but that war was a cruel, and inexorable thing, and its necessities compelled him to do many things, which he heartily regretted. In conversation with the lady, he paid a just and well merited tribute to the valor of our arms. He remarked, that it would be no disgrace to us, if we were finally subjugated—as we certainly would be—as we had fought against four or five times our number, with a degree of valor which had excited the admiration of the world; and that the United States government would gain no honor, nor credit, if they succeeded in their purposes, as they had thus far failed, with five men in the field, to our one. He regarded the southern soldiers as the bravest in the world, and admitted, that in a fair field fight, we could whip them two to our one, but he claimed for himself, and his compeers, the credit of possessing more strategic ability than our generals. "You can beat us in fighting, madam," said he, "but we can out-manœuvre you; your generals do not work half enough; we work day and night, and spare no labor, nor pains, to carry out our plans."

Referring to his evacuation of the trenches, around the city, he asked the lady, if they did not all think he was retreating; and when she replied that some did think so, he laughed heartily at the idea and remarked, "I played Hood a real *yankee trick*, that time, didn't I? He thought I was running away, but he soon had to pull up stakes, and run himself." (I wonder whose turn it is to laugh now?)

The lady, from whom these facts were obtained, says that Sherman had a vast number of applications from ladies, and others, in reference to their moving, and that, as far as she could learn, he was very patient, gentlemanly, and obliging, as much so as he could be to them consistently with his prescribed policy. He permitted her to bring out her horse, and rockaway, although his army was greatly needing horses at the time; and, also, to send her provisions to some suffering relatives within his lines. She speaks in high terms of the discipline of the yankee army; says that the privates are more afraid of their officers than our slaves are of their masters, and that, during her stay, there was no disorderly conduct to be seen anywhere, but that quiet, and good order, prevailed throughout the city.

An instance of yankee kindness deserves to be mentioned here: A widow lady, whose husband had been a member of the masonic fraternity, died, shortly after the occupation of the city by the enemy. The yankee officers gave her remains a decent and respectable burial, and took her three orphan children, and sent them to their own homes, to be educated at some masonic institute, at the north.

From the facts which I report, on the authority of a lady

of unquestioned veracity, and respectability, it will be seen that our barbarous foes are not entirely lost to all the dictates, and impulses of humanity. Would to God that the exhibitions of it were more frequent in their occurrence.

Respectfully, yours,

Geo. G. N. MacDonell.

In a Yankee Prison

O F THE THOUSANDS of Confederates who spent months or years in Federal prisons at Point Lookout, Fort Warren, Johnson's Island, Elmira, and other prison pens during the war, only three told their stories in books for the homefolks. One of these was Anthony M. Keiley, a prominent citizen of Petersburg, who was taken prisoner early in 1864 and spent five months at Point Lookout and Elmira before he was exchanged through the lines.

Keiley's account of his experiences paints little prettier a picture of the Yankee camps that the Union soldiers' stories did of Andersonville, Millen, Salisbury, and other Southern prisons. In the chapter that follows he describes the routine at Point Lookout, Maryland.

The routine of prison-life at Point Lookout was as follows: Between dawn and sunrise a "reveille" horn summoned us into line by companies, ten of which constituted each division—of which I have before spoken—and here the roll was called. This performance is hurried over with as much haste as is ascribed to certain marital ceremonies in a poem that it would be obviously improper to make more particular allusion to—and those whose love of a nap predominates over fear of the Yankees usually tumble in for another snooze. About 8 o'clock the breakfasting begins. This operation consists in the forming of the companies again into line, and introducing them under lead of their Sergeants, into the mess-rooms, where a slice of bread and a piece of pork or beef—lean in the former and fat in the latter being contraband of war— are placed at intervals of about twenty inches apart. The meat is usually about four or five ounces in weight. These we seized upon, no one being allowed to touch a piece, however, until the whole company entered, and each man was in position opposite his ration (universally *and properly* pronounced *raytion,* among our enemies, as it is almost as generally called, with the "a" short among ourselves). . . . The men then busy themselves with the numberless occupations, which the fertility of American genius suggests, of which I will have something to say hereafter, until dinner time, when they are again carried to the mess-houses, where another slice of bread, and rather over a half pint of a watery slop, by courtesy called "soup," greets the eyes of such ostrich-stomached animals, as can find comfort in that substitute for nourishment. About sundown the roll is again called, on a signal by the horn, and an hour after, "taps" sounds, when all are required to be in their quarters—and this, in endless repetition and without a variation, is the routine life of prison.

The Sanitary Commission, a benevolent association of exempts in aid of the Hospital Department of the Yankee army, published in July last, a "Narrative of Sufferings of United States Officers and Soldiers, Prisoners of War," in which a parallel is drawn, between the treatment of prisoners on both sides, greatly to the disadvantage of course, of "Dixie."

Among other statements, in glorification of the humanity of the Great Republic, is one on page 89, from Miss Dix, the grand female dry nurse of Yankee Doodle, who by the by, gives unpardonable offence to the pulchritude of Yankeedom by persistently *refusing to employ any but ugly women as nurses*—the vampire—which affirms that the prisoners at Point Lookout, "were supplied with vegetables, with the best of wheat bread, and fresh and salt meat three times daily in abundant measures."

Common gallantry forbids the characterization of this remarkable extract in harsher terms than to say it is untrue *in every particular*.

It is quite likely that some Yankee official at Point Lookout, made this statement to the benevolent itinerant, and her only fault may be in suppressing the fact that she "*was informed*," &c., &c. But it is altogether inexcusable in the Sanitary Commission, to attempt to palm such a falsehood upon the world, knowing its falsity, as they must. For my part, I never saw any one get enough of any thing to eat at Point Lookout, except the soup, and a tea spoonful of that was *too much* for ordinary digestion.

These digestive discomforts are greatly enhanced by the villainous character of the water, which is so impregnated with some mineral as to offend every nose, and induce diarrhoea in almost every alimentary canal. It colors every thing black in which it is allowed to rest, and a scum rises on the top of a vessel if it is left standing during the night, which reflects the prismatic colors as distinctly as the surface of a stagnant pool. Several examinations of this water have been made by chemical analysis, and they have uniformly resulted in its condemnation by scientific men, but the advantages of the position to the Yankees, so greatly counterbalance any claim of humanity, that Point Lookout is likely to remain a prison camp until the end of the war, especially as there are wells outside of "the Pen," which are not liable to these charges, the water of which is indeed perfectly pure and wholesome, so that the Yanks suffer no damage therefrom. I was not surprised therefore on my return to the Point, after three months absence, to find many preparations looking to the permanent occupancy of the place. It has already served the purposes of a prison, since the 25th of July, 1863, when the Gettysburg prisoners, or a large portion of them, were sent thither from the "Old Capitol," Fort McHenry and Fort Delaware, and the chances are that it will play the part of a jail until the period of the promised redemption of our National Currency.

Another local inconvenience is, the exposed location of the post. Situated on a low tongue of land jutting out into the bay, and, as I have before remarked, but a few inches above ordinary high tide, it is visited in winter by blasts whose severity has caused the death of several of the well-clad sentinels, even, altho' during the severest portion of the winter of 1863–4, they were relieved every thirty minutes—two hours being the usual time of guard duty. And when a strong easterly gale prevails for many hours in winter, a large portion of the camp is flooded by the sea, which finds convenient access by means of ditches constructed for the drainage of camp. When this calamity befalls the men, their case is pitiable indeed. The supply of wood issued to the prisoners during the winter was not enough to keep up the most moderate fires for two hours out of the twenty-four, and the only possible way of avoiding freezing, was by unremitting devotion to the blankets. This, however, became impossible when everything was afloat, and I was not surprised, therefore, to hear some pitiable tales of suffering during the past winter from this cause.

This latter evil might be somewhat mitigated but for a barbarous regulation peculiar, I believe, to this "pen," under which the Yanks stole from us any bed clothing we might possess, *beyond one blanket!* This petty larceny was effected through an instrumentality they call *inspections.* Once in every ten days an inspection is ordered, when all the prisoners turn out in their respective divisions and companies in *marching order.* They range themselves in long lines between the rows of tents, with their blankets and haversacks—those being the only articles considered orthodox possessions of a rebel. A Yankee inspects each man, taking away his extra blanket, if he has one, and appropriating any other superfluity he may chance to possess, and this accomplished, he visits the tents and seizes everything therein that under the convenient nomenclature of the Federals, is catalogued as "contraband,"—blankets, boots, hats, anything. The only way to avoid this, is by a judicious use of greenbacks,—and a trifle will suffice—it being true, with a few honorable exceptions, of course, that Yankee soldiers are very much like ships: to move them, you must "slush the ways."

In the matter of clothing, the management at Point Lookout is simply infamous. You can receive nothing in the way of clothing without giving up the corresponding article which you may chance to possess; and so rigid is this regulation, that men who come there bare-footed have been compelled to beg or buy a pair of worn out shoes to carry to the office in lieu of a pair sent them by their friends, before they could receive the latter. To what end this plundering is committed I could never ascertain, nor was I ever able to hear any better, or indeed any other reason advanced for it than that the possession of extra clothing would enable the prisoners to bribe their guards! Heaven help the virtue that a pair of second-hand Confederate breeches could seduce!

As I have mentioned the guards, and as this is a mosaic chapter, I may as well speak here as elsewhere of the method by which order is kept in camp. During the day the platform around the pen is constantly paced by sentinels chiefly of the Invalid (or, as it is now called, the Veteran Reserve) Corps, whose duty it is to see that the prisoners are orderly, and particularly, that no one crosses "the dead line." This is a shallow ditch traced around within the enclosure, about fifteen feet from the fence. The penalty for stepping over this is death, and although the sentinels are probably instructed to warn any one who may be violating the rule, the order does not seem to be imperative, and the negroes, when on duty, rarely troubled themselves with this superfluous formality. These were on duty during my stay at the Point, every third day, and their insolence and brutality were intolerable.

Besides this detail of day guard, which of course is preserved during the night, a patrol makes the rounds constantly from "taps," the last *horn* at night, to "reveille." These were usually armed with pistols for greater convenience, and as they are shielded from scrutiny by the darkness, the indignities and cruelties they oftentimes inflict on prisoners, who for any cause may be out of their tents between those hours, especially when the patrol are black, are outrageous. Many of these are of a character which could not by any periphrase be decently expressed,—they are, however, precisely the acts which a set of vulgar brutes, suddenly invested with irresponsible authority, might be expected to take delight in, and, as it is of course impossible to recognize them, redress is unattainable, even if one could brook the sneer and insult which would inevitably follow complaint. Indeed, most of the Yankees do not disguise their delight at the insolence of these Congoes.

To the Friends of the Southern Cause

THE EFFORTS of the Southern women in support of the war were seldom formally organized, but they were priceless. Their services in feeding and aiding traveling soldiers in the Wayside Homes and Hospitals supplied an essential need not taken care of by the government. Their work with the sick and wounded released men for service in the field. And their help in keeping up individual morale was inestimable.

In late 1864 the good ladies of South Carolina planned a bazaar to raise money and collect supplies for the use of the soldiers. This is the circular in which they set forth the objects of their Soldiers' Relief Association.

To the Friends of the Southern Cause at Home.

In May last we addressed our friends abroad. This appeal is to those at home. We will be satisfied if our second appeal shall be as successful at the first—if our home people respond as well as strangers have done. Our first Circular was sent to Nassau and Europe. It set forth the greatness and duration of our struggle—the vast expenditures of money and the sacrifice of life by our ruthless foe for our subjugation. But while it was showed how vain were his efforts, it set forth also our great sacrifices, and explained to those whose want of local knowledge rendered information necessary how much exertion was required to provide for the comfort and well-being of our soldiers and seamen in health and in sickness. We devoted attention especially to Wayside Homes and Hospitals, and explained to our distant friends how essential they had proved in a country having such a large area as ours—with so many soldiers in the field and so many battles being fought, and with so many sick and wounded passing to and fro. And, finally, we mentioned that one of the most honorable missions of the war—the care for the sick and wounded—had been confided, to a considerable extent, to our females, and that we had accepted the trust in humble dependence upon the Divine guidance, and with it would labor to the end. That in the discharge of these duties we felt the need of many articles, such as bed clothing, groceries, shoes, for the seamen, etc., and that in aid of this object we intended during the fall to hold a bazaar in the city of Columbia, where we would collect articles of domestic use, such as sugar, tea, coffee, candles, soap, crockeryware, cooking utensils, shoes, blankets, gloves, and articles of clothing for both sexes and for children; and after devoting such of them as were necessary to the use of the Homes and Hospitals, we would sell the remainder at reasonable prices.

We appealed to our foreign friends to send us any of the articles enumerated or any others that occurred to them—or if they preferred it to remit funds in aid of our plans. The response to this appeal, as we remarked in the outset, has been most encouraging. In Nassau and in Liverpool our friends have been particularly zealous, and the undersigned are already in possession of such contributions as inspire them with every hope of success. This, however, cannot be complete without the co-operation of our friends at home, and it is the object of this paper to solicit your warmest efforts in an enterprise which commends itself to the heart of every patriot. We cannot expect to succeed in so large a work without the active assistance of all classes; but that of the planters and farmers is indispensable. It will be remembered that in these times every product of the farmer is in great demand. These we solicit of every kind. There is nothing that the farmer produces and manufactures, from a bale of cotton or barrel of flour or fresh and salt meat to a straw broom or a wooden bowl, that will not be acceptable. Pickles, catsups, vinegar, syrup, are all useful and valuable for hospital purposes.

We would especially invite attention to the numberless articles of a useful and fancy kind which the taste and ingenuity of the ladies have developed during the war, as for instance straw and palmetto bonnets and hats, cloth hats, knitting of every description, crochet and tatting, camp bags, tobacco pouches, pin and needle cases. And, in a word, to all the handiwork of the busy fingers which have plied so industriously in obedience to the promptings of earnest hearts in the cause of our country.

Such of these as are perishable will be sold, the remainder will be devoted to the use of the Hospitals and Homes. So large an undertaking has required time and preparation, which has resulted in postponement heretofore. As the bazaar will have for sale articles comprised in the separate departments of business, for example, dry goods, groceries, fresh and salt meats, fancy articles, etc., all to be sold in separate departments, there was no building in Columbia but the

State House that would answer our purpose. It had been our expectation to have had our sales opened in November, but the delays of the blockade and the sitting of the Legislature have compelled a postponement until January. Before that time the public will be duly informed through the newspapers of all the necessary arrangements. For the present we desire to let it be known that such a scheme as we have described is, we hope, in successful progress, and to invite our friends to give it their earnest consideration and that generous support to which it is so well entitled from every motive of humanity and patriotism.

Mrs. Dr. John Fisher, Columbia.
Mrs. M. A. Snowden, Charleston.
Miss Eliza P. Hayne, Charleston.
Mrs. F. H. Elmore, Columbia.
Mrs. A. W. Leland, Columbia.
Mrs. D. E. Huger, Charleston.
Mrs. A. M. Manigault, Charleston.
Miss L. S. Porter, Charleston.

Columbia, S. C., November 5, 1864.

Discipline in Lee's Army

EVEN THE SOLDIERS under so noble a commander as
General Lee were not immune to the faults that have
been the faults of soldiers since wars began. As supplies
became scarcer in the Confederate Army, scrounging became more and more an acceptable, and necessary, way
of procuring necessities. It was inevitable that some
soldiers should overstep the bounds of discipline in appropriating stores for their own use. Here is General
Lee's order against such practices.

HEAD QUARTERS ARMY OF NORTHERN VA.
12th December, 1864.

GENERAL ORDERS,}
    No. 71   }

The General Commanding has heard with pain and mortifi-
cation that outrages and depredations amounting in some
cases to flagrant robbery, have been perpetrated upon citizens
living within the lines, and near the camps of the army. Poor
and helpless persons have been stripped of the means of sub-

sistence and suffered violence by the hands of those upon whom they had a right to rely for protection. In one instance an atrocious murder was perpetrated upon a child by a band of ruffians whose supposed object was plunder.

The General Commanding is well aware that the great body of the army which so unselfishly devotes itself to the defence of the country, regards these crimes with abhorrence; and that they are committed by a few miscreants unworthy of the name of soldiers. But he feels that we cannot escape the disgrace that attends these evildoers, except by the most strenuous exertions on our part to restrain their wickedness and bring upon them the just punishment of their offences. This can only be accomplished by the united efforts of those good and true men who are no less desirous of being esteemed for virtue by their countrymen, than of being respected for courage by their enemies. Laws and orders will prove ineffectual unless sustained by the hearty cooperation of those who feel that the existence of the evil is a reproach to themselves. The aid of all such is earnestly and confidently invoked to remove this stain from the fair name of the army. Let each man guard its honor as zealously as his own, regarding those who bring reproach upon it, as enemies of his own reputation, and remembering that to withhold information that might lead to the detection of these criminals is to become morally a participant of their guilt.

The attention of officers is particularly directed to this subject. Their responsibility is greatest, for upon their care and vigilance necessarily depend, in a great degree, the prevention and detection of unlawful acts by these men.

Those commanding regiments, companies, or in charge of camps, hospitals, or detachments, will be required to account for all who fail to attend the roll calls under existing orders, or for such of their officers and men as may be arrested absent from their commands without proper authority, by the guards and pickets of the army.

Corps commanders will habitually keep out patrols to arrest all who are improperly absent and to protect the persons and property of those residing in the vicinity of their commands. When arrested the parties, themselves, and the officers responsible for their conduct will be brought to trial without delay.

By command of General LEE.

W. H. TAYLOR,
A. A. General.

In Sherman's Wake

As 1864 drew to a close General Hood was in Tennessee on a daring and disastrous campaign. Sherman had left Atlanta undefended to march to the coast. With the bulk of the Confederate Army in Tennessee with Hood, Wheeler's Cavalry was all that stood before Sherman to block his advance. Wheeler's troops were not strong enough to provide anything more than harassing actions, but for individual courage and determination they were unmatched.

The first of the next pair of selections is General Joe Wheeler's address to his troops at the close of 1864, thanking them for past braveries and exhorting them to renewed endeavor.

As Wheeler's men, as well as Sherman's, had of necessity to live off the country in which they were fighting, their presence in Georgia was almost as much feared as that of the Yankees themselves. "The whole land mourns, on account of Wheeler's cavalry," wrote Joseph Addison Turner in *The Countryman*. "Here in middle Georgia, they are dreaded fully as much, if not more, than the yankees." The second of these selections concerning

Wheeler's Cavalry is a letter published in *The Country-man* in January, 1865, which describes the passage of both the Yankees and the Confederates through Scriven County, Georgia.

HEAD QUARTERS, CAVALRY CORPS,
December 31st, 1864.

My brave Soldiers:

The close of the year terminates a campaign of eight months, during which you have engaged in continuous and successful fighting.

From Dalton to Atlanta you held the right of our army. Opposed almost continuously by a force of infantry ten times your number, you repulsed every assault, inflicting upon the enemy a loss in killed and wounded numerically greater than your entire strength. Every attempt on the part of the enemy to turn or strike our right flank was met and repulsed by your valor and determined courage. It should be a proud reflection to you all, that during the entire campaign, the Army of Tennessee never lost a position by having the flank turned which it was your duty to protect.

During every movement of our lines, you have been between our infantry and the enemy hurling back his exulting advance, and holding his entire army at bay until our troops had quietly prepared to receive and repulse his gigantic assaults. Having failed by other means to drive our army from the position in front of Atlanta, he now sends three heavy columns of cavalry to destroy our communications, to release prisoners of war, and march in triumph with them through our country. You promptly strike one column and drive it back discomfited; then quickly assailing the two others, you defeat them and complete their destruction and capture. This, alone, cost the enemy more than five thousand men, horses, arms and equipment, besides material, colors and cannon. This was due to your valor, and is without parallel in the history of this war.

Having been detached and sent to the rear of the enemy you captured his garrison, destroyed his stores and broke his communications more effectually and for a larger period than any other cavalry force, however large, has done.

During Sherman's march through Georgia you retarded his advance and defeated his cavalry daily, preventing his spreading over and devastating the country.

During the last five months you have traveled nearly three thousand miles, fighting nearly every day, and always with success. You must have been victorious in more than fifty pitched battles, and a hundred minor affairs placing a number of the enemy *hors du combat* fully four times the greatest number you ever carried into action.

I desire, my brave soldiers, to thank you for your gallantry, devotion and good conduct. Every charge I have asked you to make, has been brilliantly executed. Every position I have asked you to hold, has been held until absolutely untenable. Your devotion to your country fills my heart with gratitude. You have done your full duty to your country and to me; and I have tried to do my full duty to you. Circumstances have forced upon you many and great deprivations. You have been deprived of the issues of clothing and many of the comforts and conveniences which other troops have enjoyed and have borne all without a murmur.

Soldiers of Kentucky, Tennessee, Texas and Arkansas! you deserve special commendation for your sacrifices and fortitude. Separated from your homes and families you have nobly done all that gallant devoted men could do. Soldiers from Alabama and Georgia! your homes have nearly all been overrun and destroyed, yet without complaint you have stood to your colors like brave and patriotic men. Your country and your God will one day reward you.

The gallant Kelly whom we all loved so well is dead. Many other brave spirits whose loss we deeply feel sleep with him. They fell—the price of victory.

Allen, Humes, Anderson, Dibbrell, Hagan, Crews, Ashby, Harrison and Breckenridge, and many other brave men whose gallantry you have so often witnessed are here still to guide and lead you in battles yet to be fought and victories yet to be won.

Another campaign will soon open in which I only ask you to fight with the same valor I have always seen you exhibit upon the many fields where your determined courage has won victory for our cause.

J. WHEELER,
Major General.

❖   ❖   ❖   ❖   ❖

Mobley's Pond, Scriven Co., Ga.

Mr. Countryman:—I accidentally met with a number of your delightful paper, The Countryman, and felt, while reading it, that I had met an old friend, so much rejoiced was I to again hear from a section of country where I have left some dear friends. Being deprived entirely of a mail, I have, for some time past, felt much anxiety about the welfare of the people of Milledgeville, and vicinity—having heard the yankees destroyed much property—but trust the rumors are somewhat exaggerated. Allow me to congratulate you, on such a lucky deliverance of your Countryman from the hands of the northern vandals.

I have been residing in Scriven county, for several weeks past, and thought, if there was any place secure from the enemy, it was here. It seems no place is so safe, but they can compass it out. They passed through this part of the country, committing great depredations, such as burning gin-houses, corn-cribs, and even dwellings of those who had not courage to meet the dreaded foe. Some have no corn left; others were more fortunate, as the yankees were in a considerable hurry, and could not visit every place. Watches and money were carried off in large quantities. One wealthy farmer suffered much by them. He buried his valuables in the graveyard, but was betrayed by one of his servants; so they carried off his gold, and silver, his watches, and a large amount of confederate money, and bonds. Many have suffered in like manner. All the stock was killed, and carried off, in some places.

I must tell you how shamefully Gen. Wheeler's men acted. Though they have a wide-spread reputation of being the greatest horse thieves in the country, they never acted worse than they have recently. While the enemy were burning and destroying property, on one side of Briar creek, they were stealing horses, and mules on the other. Only a few yankees crossed over on our side, and there was a large force of Wheeler's men dodging about, who could have captured, and killed all the enemy, and saved much property.

Some of the neighbors ran themselves, and stock to Carolina, for safe keeping; some took to the swamps, while only a few were captured. Some were exceedingly lucky, having returned home safely, after being politely stripped of everything, and paroled by their blue-coated friends; while others, not so fortunate, are sojourning with them still, and, report says, are penned up at night like hogs, feeding on roasted potatoes. One of the citizens was severely whipped. They found him armed, and gave him two hundred lashes. He has not since been heard from.—It is now getting more quiet. The past two weeks have been very exciting. The roads were strewn with dead horses, and several dead yankees have been found. At last accounts, the enemy had surrounded Savannah. Fort McAllister has fallen. It is only thirty miles from here to Savannah, and when an engagement is going on, we hear the cannon very distinctly. . . .

Respectfully yours,

BERTHA.

1865

"Forbid It Heaven!"

A CTIVITY in Virginia was slowed to a mire truce by winter, but operations in the deep South continued. Sherman took Savannah in time to offer it to President Lincoln as a Christmas gift. Though the people of Charleston feared that their city, the birthplace of secession, was next and would receive a particularly thorough "Shermanizing," the astute old redhead turned northeast and headed for Columbia.

Despite the threats to the cities of their heartland, the soldiers of the South were not yet officially downhearted. Here are the resolutions passed by McGowan's Brigade, one of the most distinguished units of South Carolina soldiers.

RESOLUTIONS

Adopted by McGowan's Brigade, South Carolina Volunteers.

The soldiers and officers of McGowan's Brigade do
Resolve, 1st. That the war in which we are engaged is a war of self-defence; that in the beginning, nearly four years ago, we took up arms in defence of the right to govern ourselves, and to protect our country from invasion, our homes from desolation, and our wives and children from insult and outrage.

2d. That the reasons which induced us to take up arms at the beginning have not been impaired, but, on the contrary, infinitely strengthened by the progress of the war. Outrage and cruelty have not made us love the perpetrators. If we then judged that the enemy intended to impoverish and oppress us, we *now know* that they propose to subjugate, enslave, disgrace and destroy us.

3d. As we were actuated by principle when we entered the service of the Confederate States, we are of the same opinion still. We have had our share of victories, and we must expect some defeats. Our cause is righteous and must prevail. In the language of General Greene, during the darkest hours of the Revolution, when he was struggling to recover South Carolina, then entirely overrun and suffering under the scourge of Tarl[e]ton, "Independence is certain, if the people have the fortitude to bear and the courage to persevere."

4th. To submit to our enemies now, would be more infamous than it would have been in the beginning. It would be cowardly yielding to power what was denied upon principle. It would be to yield the cherished right of self-government, and to acknowledge ourselves wrong in the assertion of it; to brand the names of our slaughtered companions as traitors; to forfeit the glory already won; to lose the fruits of all the sacrifices made and the privations endured; to give up independence now nearly gained, and bring certain ruin, disgrace and eternal slavery upon our country. Therefore, unsubdued by past reverses, and unawed by future dangers, we declare our determination to battle to the end, and not to lay down our arms until independence is secured. Is life so dear, or peace so sweet, as to be purchased at the price of chains and slavery? Forbid it Heaven!

"Humiliation Spreads Her Ashes"

B UT THERE WAS NOTHING in the South to stem the tide
sweeping over her. William Gilmore Simms, the dean
of Southern literary men, was then a resident of Columbia. As the city rose from the ashes left in Sherman's wake
he published, first in the *Daily Phoenix* and then in a
pamphlet printed on paper originally intended for Confederate bank notes, a remarkable account of the "sack
and destruction" of the city.

"It has pleased God," begins Simms' introduction, "in
that Providence which is so inscrutable to man, to visit
our beautiful city with the most cruel fate which can ever
befall States or cities. He has permitted an invading army
to penetrate our country almost without impediment; to
rob and ravage our dwellings, and to commit three-fifths
of our city to the flames. . . . The schools of learning,
the shops of art and trade, of invention and manufacture;
shrines equally of religion, benevolence and industry;
are all buried together, in one congregated ruin. Humiliation spreads her ashes over our homes and garments, and
the universal wreck exhibits only one common aspect of
despair. It is for us, as succinctly but as fully as possible,

and in the simplest language, to endeavor to make the melancholy record of our wretchedness as complete as possible."

Here is a portion of Simms' account.

The end was rapidly approaching. The guns were resounding at the gates. Defence was impossible. At a late hour on Thursday night, the Governor, with his suite and a large train of officials, departed. The Confederate army began its evacuation, and by daylight few remained who were not resigned to the necessity of seeing the tragedy played out. After all the depletion, the city contained, according to our estimate, at least twenty thousand inhabitants, the larger proportion being females and children and negroes. Hampton's cavalry . . . lingered till near 10 o'clock the next day, and scattered groups of Wheeler's command hovered about the Federal army at their entrance into the town.

The inhabitants were startled at daylight, on Friday morning, by a heavy explosion. This was the South Carolina Railroad Depot. It was accidentally blown up. Broken open by a band of plunderers, among whom were many females and negroes, their reckless greed precipitated their fate. This building had been made the receptacle of supplies from sundry quarters, and was crowded with stores of merchants and planters, trunks of treasure, innumerable wares and goods of fugitives—all of great value. It appears that, among its contents, were some kegs of powder. The plunderers paid, and suddenly, the penalties of their crime. Using their lights freely and hurriedly, the better to *pick*, they fired a train of powder leading to the kegs. The explosion followed, and the number of persons destroyed is variously estimated, from seventeen to fifty. It is probable that not more than thirty-five suffered, but the actual number perishing is unascertained.

At a nearly hour on Friday, the commissary and quartermaster stores were thrown wide, the contents cast out into the streets and given to the people. The negroes especially loaded themselves with plunder. All this might have been saved, had the officers been duly warned by the military authorities of the probable issue of the struggle. Wheeler's cavalry also shared largely of this plunder, and several of them might be seen, bearing off huge bales upon their saddles.

It was proposed that the white flag should be displayed from the tower of the City Hall. But General Hampton, whose command had not yet left the city, and who was still eager to do battle in its defence, indignantly declared that if displayed, he should have it torn down.

The following letter from the Mayor to General Sherman was the initiation of the surrender:

MAYOR'S OFFICE
COLUMBIA, S. C., February 17, 1865.

TO MAJOR-GENERAL SHERMAN: The Confederate forces having evacuated Columbia, I deem it my duty, as Mayor and representative of the city, to ask for its citizens the treatment accorded by the usages of civilized warfare. I therefore respectfully request that you will send a sufficient guard in advance of the army, to maintain order in the city and protect the persons and property of the citizens.

Very respectfully, your obedient servant,
T. J. GOODWYN, Mayor.

At 9 o'clock, on the painfully memorable morning of the 17th February, (Friday,) a deputation from the City Council, consisting of the Mayor, Aldermen McKenzie, Bates and Stork, in a carriage bearing a white flag, proceeded towards the Broad River Bridge Road. Arriving at the forks of the Winnsboro Road, they discovered that the Confederate skirmishers were still busy with their guns, playing upon the advance of the Federals. These were troops of General Wheeler. This conflict was continued simply to afford the main army all possible advantages of a start in their retreat. General Wheeler apprised the deputation that his men would now be withdrawn, and instructed them in what manner to proceed. The deputation met the column of the Federals, under Captain Platt, who send them forward to Colonel Stone, who finally took his seat with them in the carriage. The advance belonged to the 15th corps.

The Mayor reports that on surrendering the city to Colonel Stone, the latter assured him of the safety of the citizens and of the protection of their property, *while under his command.* He could not answer for General Sherman, who was in the rear, but he expressed the conviction that he would fully confirm the assurances which he (Colonel Stone) had given. Subsequently, General Sherman did confirm them, and that night, seeing that the Mayor was exhausted by his labors of the day, he counselled him to retire to rest, saying, "Not a finger's breadth, Mr. Mayor, of your city shall be harmed. You may lie down to sleep, satisfied that your town shall be as safe in my hands as if wholly in your own." Such was very nearly the language in which he spoke; such was the substance of it. He added: "It will become my duty to destroy some of the public or Government buildings: but I will reserve this performance to another day. It shall be done to-

morrow, provided the day be calm." And the Mayor retired
with this solemnly asserted and repeated assurance.

About 11 o'clock, the head of the column, following the
deputation—the flag of the United States surmounting the
carriage—reached Market Hall, on Main street, while that of
the corps was carried in the rear. On their way to the city,
the carriage was stopped, and the officer was informed that a
large body of Confederate cavalry was flanking them. Colonel Stone said to the Mayor, "We shall hold you responsible
for this." The Mayor explained, that the road leading to
Winnsboro, by which the Confederates were retreating, ran
nearly parallel for a short distance with the river road, which
accounted for the apparent flanking. Two officers, who arrived in Columbia ahead of the deputation, (having crossed
the river at a point directly opposite the city,) were fired
upon by one of Wheeler's cavalry. We are particular in men-
tioning this fact, as we learn that, subsequently, the incident
was urged as a justification of the sack and burning of the
city.

Hardly had the troops reached the head of Main street,
when the work of pillage was begun. Stores were broken open
within the first hour after their arrival, and gold, silver, jewels
and liquors, eagerly sought. The authorities, officers, soldiers,
all seemed to consider it a matter of course. And woe to him
who carried a watch with a gold chain pendant; or who wore
a choice hat, or overcoat, or boots or shoes. He was stripped
in the twinkling of an eye. It is computed that, from first to
last, twelve hundred watches were transferred from the
pockets of their owners to those of the soldiers. Purses shared
the same fate; nor was the Confederate currency repudi-
ated. . . .

At about 12 o'clock, the jail was discovered to be on fire
from within. This building was immediately in rear of the

Market, or City Hall, and in a densely built portion of the city. The supposition is that it was fired by some of the prisoners—all of whom were released and subsequently followed the army. The fire of the jail had been preceded by that of some cotton piled in the streets. Both fires were soon subdued by the firemen. At about half-past 1 P. M., that of the jail was rekindled, and was again extinguished. Some of the prisoners, who had been confined at the Asylum, had made their escape, in some instances, a few days before, and were secreted and protected by citizens.

No one felt safe in his own dwelling; and, in the faith that General Sherman would respect the Convent, and have it properly guarded, numbers of young ladies were confided to the care of the Mother Superior, and even trunks of clothes and treasure were sent thither, in full confidence that they would find safety. Vain illusions! The Irish Catholic troops, it appears, were not brought into the city at all; were kept on the other side of the river. But a few Catholics were collected among the corps which occupied the city, and of the conduct of these, a favorable account is given. One of them rescued a silver goblet of the church, used as a drinking cup by a soldier, and restored it to the Rev. Dr. O'Connell. This priest, by the way, was severely handled by the soldiers. Such, also, was the fortune of the Rev. Mr. Shand, of Trinity (the Episcopal) Church, who sought in vain to save a trunk containing the sacred vessels of his church. It was violently wrested from his keeping, and his struggle to save it only provoked the rougher usage. We are since told, on reaching Camden, General Sherman restored what he believed were these vessels to Bishop Davis. It has since been discovered that the plate belonged to St. Peter's Church in Charleston.

And here it may be well to mention, as suggestive of many clues, an incident which presented a sad commentary on that

confidence in the security of the Convent, which was entertained by the great portion of the people. This establishment,
under the charge of the sister of the Right Rev. Bishop Lynch,
was at once a convent and an academy of the highest class.
Hither were sent for education the daughters of Protestants,
of the most wealthy classes throughout the State; and these,
with the nuns and those young ladies sent thither on the
emergency, probably exceeded one hundred. The Lady Superior herself entertained the fullest confidence in the immu-
nites of the establishment. But her confidence was clouded,
after she had enjoyed a conference with a certain major of
the Yankee army, who described himself as an editor, from
Detroit. He visited her at an early hour in the day, and announced his friendly sympathies with the Lady Superior and
the sisterhood; professed his anxiety for their safety—his purpose to do all that he could to insure it—declared that he
would instantly go to Sherman and secure a chosen guard;
and, altogether, made such professions of love and service, as
to disarm those suspicions, which his bad looks and bad manners, inflated speech and pompous carriage, might otherwise
have provoked. The Lady Superior with such a charge in her
hands, was naturally glad to welcome all shows and prospects
of support, and expressed her gratitude. He disappeared, and
soon after re-appeared, bringing with him no less than eight
or ten men—none of them, as he admitted, being Catholics.
He had some specious argument to show that, perhaps, her
guard had better be one of Protestants. This suggestion stag-
gered the lady a little, but he seemed to convey a more potent
reason, when he added, in a whisper: *"For I must tell you,
my sister, that Columbia is a doomed city!"* Terrible doom!
This officer, leaving his men behind him, disappeared, to
show himself no more. The guards so left behind were finally
among the most busy as plunderers. The moment that the

inmates, driven out by the fire, were forced to abandon their house, they began to revel in its contents,

Quis custodiet ipsos custodes?—who shall guard the guards? —asks the proverb. In a number of cases, the guards provided for the citizens were among the most active plunderers; were quick to betray their trusts, abandon their posts, and bring their comrades in to join in the general pillage. The most dextrous and adroit of these, it is the opinion of most persons, were chiefly Eastern men, or men of immediate Eastern origin. The Western men, including the Indiana, a portion of the Illinois and Iowa, were neither so dextrous nor unscrupulous—were frequently faithful and respectful; and, perhaps, it would be safe to assert that many of the houses which escaped the sack and fire, owed their safely to the presence or the contiguity of some of these men. But we must retrace our steps.

It may be well to remark that the discipline of the soldiers upon their first entry into the city, was perfect and most admirable. There was no disorder or irregularity on the line of march, showing that their officers had them completely in hand. They were a fine looking body of men, mostly young and of vigorous formation, well clad and well shod, seemingly wanting in nothing. Their arms and accoutrements were in bright order. The negroes accompanying them were not numerous, and seemed mostly to act as drudges and body servants. They groomed horses, waited, carried burdens, and, in almost every instance under our eyes, appeared in a purely servile, and not a military capacity. The men of the West treated them generally with scorn or indifference, sometimes harshly, and not unfrequently with blows.

But if the entrance into town and while on duty, was indicative of admirable drill and discipline, such ceased to be the case the moment the troops were dismissed. Then, whether by tacit permission or direct command, their whole deportment underwent a sudden and rapid change. The saturnalia soon began. We have shown that the robbery of the persons of the citizens and the plunder of their homes commenced within one hour after they had reached the Market Hall. It continued without interruption throughout the day. Sherman, at the head of his cavalry, traversed the streets everywhere—so did his officers. Subsequently, these officers were everywhere on foot, yet beheld nothing which required the interposition of authority. And yet robbery was going on at every corner—in nearly every house. Citizens generally applied for a guard at their several houses, and, for a time, these guards were alloted them. These might be faithful or not. In some cases, as already stated, they were, and civil and respectful; considerate of the claims of women, and never trespassing upon the privacy of the family; but, in numbers of cases, they were intrusive, insulting and treacherous—leaving no privacy undisturbed, passing without a word into the chambers and prying into every crevice and corner.

But the reign of terror did not fairly begin till night. In some instances, where parties complained of the misrule and robbery, their guards said to them, with a chuckle: "This is nothing. Wait till tonight, and you'll see h-ll."

Among the first fires at evening was one about dark, which broke out in a fithy purlieu of low houses, of wood, on Gervais street, occupied mostly as brothels. Almost at the same time, a body of the soldiers scattered over the Eastern outskirts of the city, fired severally the dwellings of Mr. Secretary Trenholm, General Wade Hampton, Dr. John Wallace, J. U. Adams, Mrs. Starke, Mr. Latta, Mrs. English, and many others. There were then some twenty fires in full blast, in as many different quarters, and while the alarm sounded from these quarters a similar alarm was sent up almost simultaneously from Cotton Town, the Northernmost limit of the city, and from Main street in its very centre, at the several stores or houses of O. Z. Bates, C. D. Eberhardt, and some others, in the heart of the most densely settled portion of the town; thus enveloping in flames almost every section of the devoted city. At this period, thus early in the evening, there were few shows of that drunkenness which prevailed at a late hour in the night, and only after all the grocery shops on Main street had been rifled. The men engaged in this were well prepared with all the appliances essential to their work. They did not need the torch. They carried with them, from house to house, pots and vessels containing combustible liquids, composed probably of phosphorous and other similar agents, turpentine, &c.; and, with balls of cotton saturated in this liquid, with which they also overspread floors and walls, they conveyed the flames with wonderful rapidity from dwelling to dwelling. Each had his ready box of Lucifer matches, and, with a scrape upon the walls, the flames began to rage. Where houses were closely contiguous, a brand from one was the means of conveying destruction to the other.

The winds favored. They had been high throughout the day, and steadily prevailed from South-west by West, and bore the flames Eastward. To this fact we owe the preservation of the portions of the city lying West of Assembly street.

The work, begun thus vigorously, went on without impediment and with hourly increase throughout the night. Engines and hose were brought out by the firemen, but these were soon driven from their labors—which were indeed idle against such a storm of fire—by the pertinacious hostility of the soldiers; the hose was hewn to pieces, and the firemen, dreading worse usage to themselves, left the field in despair. Meanwhile, the flames spread from side to side, from front to rear, from street to street, and where their natural and inevitable progress was too slow for those who had kindled them, they helped them on by the application of fresh combustibles and more rapid agencies of conflagration. By midnight, Main street, from its Northern to its Southern extremity, was a solid wall of fire. By 12 o'clock, the great blocks, which included the banking houses and the Treasury buildings, were consumed; Janney's (Congaree) and Nickerson's Hotels; the magnificent manufactories of Evans & Cogswell —indeed every large block in the business portion of the city; the old Capitol and all the adjacent buildings were in ruins. The range called the "Granite" was beginning to flame at 12, and might have been saved by ten vigorous men, resolutely working.

At 1 o'clock, the hour was struck by the clock of the Market Hall, which was even then illuminated from within. It was its own last hour which it sounded, and its tongue was silenced forevermore. In less than five minutes after, its spire went down with a crash, and, by this time, almost all the buildings within the precinct were a mass of ruins.

Very grand, and terrible, beyond description, was the awful spectacle. It was a scene for the painter of the terrible. It was the blending of a range of burning mountains stretched in a continuous series of more than a mile. Here was Ætna, sending up its spouts of flaming lava; Vesuvius, emulous of like display, shooting up with loftier torrents, and Stromboli, struggling, with awful throes, to shame both by its superior volumes of fluid flame. The winds were tributary to these convulsive efforts, and tossed the volcanic torrents hundreds of feet in air. Great spouts of flame spread aloft in canopies of sulphurous cloud—wreaths of sable, edged with sheeted lightnings, wrapped the skies, and, at short intervals, the falling tower and the tottering wall, avalanche-like, went down with thunderous sound, sending up at every crash great billowy showers of glowing fiery embers.

Throughout the whole of this terrible scene the soldiers continued their search after spoil. The houses were severally and soon gutted of their contents. Hundreds of iron safes, warranted "impenetrable to fire and the burglar," it was soon satisfactorily demonstrated, were not "Yankee proof." They were split open and robbed, yielding, in some cases, very largely of Confederate money and bonds, if not of gold and silver. Jewelry and plate in abundance was found. Men could be seen staggering off with huge waiters, vases, candelabra, to say nothing of cups, goblets and smaller vessels, all of solid silver. Clothes and shoes, when new, were appropriated—the rest left to burn. Liquors were drank with such avidity as to astonish the veteran Bacchanals of Columbia; nor did the parties thus distinguishing themselves hesitate about the vintage. There was no idle discrimination in the matter of taste, from that vulgar liquor, which Judge Burke used to say always provoked within him "an inordinate propensity to sthale," to the choicest red wines of the ancient cellars. In one vault on Main street, seventeen casks of wine were stored away, which, an eye-witness tells us, barely sufficed, once broken into, for the draughts of a single hour —such were the appetites at work and the numbers in possession of them. Rye, corn, claret and Madeira all found their way into the same channels, and we are not to wonder, when told that no less than one hundred and fifty of the drunken creatures perished miserably among the flames kindled by their own comrades, and from which they were unable to escape. The estimate will not be thought extravagant by those who saw the condition of hundreds after 1 o'clock A. M. By others, however, the estimate is reduced to thirty; but the number will never be known. Sherman's officers themselves are reported to have said that they lost more men in the sack and burning of the city (including certain explosions) than in all their fights while approaching it. It is also suggested that the orders which Sherman issued at daylight, on Saturday morning, for the arrest of the fire, were issued in consequence of the loss of men which he had thus sustained.

One or more of his men were shot, by parties unknown, in some dark passages or alleys—it is supposed in consequence of some attempted outrages which humanity could not endure; the assassin taking advantage of the obscurity of the situation and adroitly mingling with the crowd without. And while these scenes were at their worst—while the flames were at their highest and most extensively raging—groups might be seen at the several corners of the streets, drinking, roaring, revelling—while the fiddle and accordion were playing their popular airs among them. There was no cessation of the work till 5 A. M. on Saturday.

A single thought will suffice to show that the owners or lodgers in the houses thus sacrificed were not silent or quiet spectators of a conflagration which threw them naked and homeless under the skies of night. The male population, consisting mostly of aged men, invalids, decrepits, women and children, were not capable of very active or powerful exertions; but they did not succumb to the fate without earnest pleas and strenuous efforts. Old men and women and children were to be seen, even while the flames were rolling and raging around them, while walls were crackling and rafters tottering and tumbling, in the endeavor to save their clothing and some of their most valuable effects. It was not often that they were suffered to succeed. They were driven out headlong.

Ladies were hustled from their chambers—their ornaments plucked from their persons, their bundles from their hands. It was in vain that the mother appealed for the garments of her children. They were torn from her grasp and hurled into the flames. The young girl striving to save a single frock, had it rent to fibres in her grasp. Men and women bearing off their trunks were seized, despoiled, in a moment the trunk burst asunder with the stroke of axe or gun-butt, the contents laid bare, rifled of all the objects of desire, and the residue sacrificed to the fire. You might see the ruined owner, standing woebegone, aghast, gazing at his tumbling dwelling, his scattered property, with a dumb agony in his face that was inexpressibly touching. Others you might hear, as we did, with wild blasphemies assailing the justice of Heaven, or invoking, with lifted and clenched hands, the fiery wrath of the avenger. But the soldiers plundered and drank, the fiery work raged, and the moon sailed over all with as serene an aspect as when she first smiled upon the ark resting against the slopes of Ararat.

"The Glory of History Is Honour"

Edward A. Pollard was a remarkable and forceful Confederate editor. Although he violently opposed nearly everything that President Davis ever did, his loyalty to the South cannot be questioned. Pollard was the chief contemporary historian of the Confederacy and is well remembered for his year-by-year history of the war and for his pamphlets on individual battles.

In May, 1864, Pollard undertook to go to England to work with his publishers in London on his forthcoming volume about the war. (Publishing conditions in Richmond had deteriorated so that his book was a project beyond the capacities there.) Passage on blockade runners to Bermuda cost at that time $8,000 in Confederate money ($400 in gold), but Pollard had the good fortune to sail as the guest of the captain of the British owned *Greyhound.* His good fortune, however, was short-lived. The *Greyhound* was captured by Union blockaders, and Pollard was sent to Fort Warren, the Union prison in Boston harbor. He stayed there until August, when he was released on parole. After four months as a prisoner at large he was returned to the Confederacy.

Pollard prepared a short book of his experiences as a prisoner, *Observations in the North,* which vies with Keiley's prison narrative for the honor of the last Confederate book published in Richmond. But the publication of the book took some time, and, inveterate reporter that he was, he put out as an interim message to his countrymen a small pamphlet reviewing the political situation and urging continued resistance. Although he urged resistance and put up a front of optimism, here in Pollard's open letter is the first real statement of the Confederacy as "The Lost Cause." "The glory of history," he says, "is indifferent to events; it is simply Honour."

The grand conclusion to which the observations I made in the North last summer lead is this: that if we can ever regain substantially nothing more than the *status quo* of seven months ago; if we can ever present to the North the same prospect of a long war we did then, and put before them the weary task of overcoming the fortitude of a brave people, we shall have peace and independence in our grasp. It is a vulgar mistake that to accomplish our success in this war we have to retrieve all of the past and recover by arms all the separate pieces of our territory. It is to be remembered that we are fighting on the defensive, and have only to convince the enemy that we are able to protect the vital points of our country to compel him to a peace in which all is surrendered that he has overrun, and all the country that he holds by the ephemeral and worthless title of invasion, falls from him as by the law of gravitation. The price of our peace has come to be now but a moderate measure of endeavour—a measure

I am persuaded only large enough to convince the Yankee of another link drawn out in the prolongation of the war. Let but his present animated hope of dispatching the Confederacy in a few months be exploded, and I predict that peace will be the result; for he will have then an occasion of discouragement far greater than that of last summer, as each later prolongation of the war will bring with it a larger tax on patience and a new train of necessities—among them the dreaded one of *conscription*, no longer to be put off by the present comfortable expedients which have reached their *maximum* in the substitution of the foreigner and the negro.

My friends, it is not extravagant to say that the time has come when only such endeavour as will put us in anything like the situation we were in a few months ago—or only such proof of endurance as will convince the North of another lease of the war—will assure us peace and independence. I wish that I could insert this conviction in every fibre of the Southern mind. The task before us is not very great. If we can only regain the situation of last summer, or even if we can only give a proof to the enemy that we are not at the extremity of our resources or at the last limits of resolution —that we are able and determined to fight this war indefinitely, we have accomplished the important and vital conditions of peace. And I believe we can easily do the first— recover substantially, in all important respects, the losses of the past few months, and even add to the *status quo* of last summer new elements of advantage for us. Defeat Sherman at any stage short of Richmond and it re-opens and recovers all the country he has overrun. Leave him if you please the possession of the seaports; but these have have no value to us as ports of entry and are but picket posts in our system of defences. His campaign comes to nought if he cannot reach Grant; nothing left of it but the brilliant zig-zag of a raid,

vanishing as heat lightning in the skies. Follow the consequences of Sherman's misadventure. Grant's army of mon-
grels alone, without the looked for aid from the Carolinas,
can no more take Richmond than it can surmount the sky.
If that army is the only assailant of Richmond, then the ctiy
never was more feebly threatened. It is true that Grant is
within a few miles of our capital, when, this time last year,
he was on the Rapidan. But that is a fool's measure of danger;
for in each case we have the same army shielding Richmond,
and whether that shield is broken ten or a hundred miles
away is of no importance to the interest it covers. Again,
Grant had on the Rapidan the finest army the enemy had
ever put in the field. He has now on the lines around Richmond the poorest army that has ever been assembled under
the Yankee flag; and the last dregs of the recruiting offices
have been sifted out to make it.

Is there anything really desperate in our situation, unless
to fools and cowards who draw lines on paper to show how
the Yankees are at this place and at that place, and think
that this cob-web occupation of the country, where the
enemy has no garrisons and no footholds, indicates the extent
of Yankee conquest and gives the true measure of the remnant of the Confederacy! And yet this is too much the popular fashion of the time in estimating the military situation.
Men are drawing for themselves pictures of despair out of
what are to those who think profoundly and bravely no more
important than the passages of the hour—

> Light and shade
> Upon a waving field, chasing each other.

I am determined to express the truth, no matter how painful to myself or unwelcome to others. In the first periods of
this war who was not proud of the Confederacy and its

heroic figure in history! Yet now it is to be confessed that a large portion of our people have fallen below the standards of history, and hold no honourable comparison with other nations that have fought and struggled for independence. It is easy for the tongue of the demagogue to trip with flattery on the theme of war; but when we come to the counsels of the intelligent the truth must be told. We are no longer responding to the lessons and aspirations of history. You speak of the scarcity of subsistence. But Prussia in her wars, drained her supplies until black bread was the only thing to eat in the king's palace; and yet, under Frederick, she won not only her independence, but a position among the Five Great Powers of Europe. You speak of the scarcity of men. Yet with a force not greater than that with which we have only to hold an invaded country and maintain the defensive, Napoleon fought his splendid career, and completed a circle of victories that touched the boundaries of Europe.

It is enough then to sicken the heart with shame and vexation that now, when of all times, it is most important to convince the enemy of our resolution—now, when such a course, for peculiar reasons, will insure our success—there are men who not only whine on the streets about making terms with the enemy, but intrude their cowardice into the official places of the Government, and sheltered by secret sessions and confidential conversations, roll the word "reconstruction" under the tongue. Shame upon the Congress that closed its doors that it might better consult of dishonourable things! Shame upon those leaders who should encourage the people and yet have broken down their confidence by private conversations, and who, while putting in newspapers some cheap words of patriotism, yet in the same breath suggest their despair by a suspicious cant about trusting in Providence, and go off to talk submission with their intimates in a corner! Shame upon those of the people who have now no other feeling in the war than an exasperated selfishness; who are ready to sink, if they can carry down in their hands some little trash of *property*; who will give their sons to the army, but not their precious negro slaves; who are for hurrying off embassies to the enemy to know at what price of dishonour they may purchase some paltry remnant of their possessions! Do these men ever think of the retributions of history?

When Cato the Younger was pursued to Utica by the victorious arms of Caesar, Plutarch relates of him on this occasion certain conversation and sentiments which singularly apply to our own condition in a besieged city, and may almost be taken as repeated in the streets of Richmond:

"One of the Council," writes Plutarch, "observed the expediency of a decree for enfranchising the slaves, and many commended the motion. Cato, however, said: 'He would not do that, because it was neither just nor lawful; but such as their masters would voluntarily discharge, he would receive, provided they were of proper age to bear arms.' This many promised to do; and Cato withdrew, after having ordered lists to be made out of all that should offer. . . . All of the patrician order with great readiness enfranchised and armed their slaves; but as for the three hundred, who dealt in traffic and loans of money at high interest, and whose slaves were a considerable part of their fortune, the impression which Cato's speech had made upon them did not last long. As some bodies readily receive heat, and as easily grow cold again when the fire is removed, so the sight of Cato warmed and liberalized these traders; but when they came to consider the matter among themselves, the dread of Caesar soon put to flight their reverence for Cato and for virtue. For thus they talked: 'What are we, and what is the man whose orders we refuse to receive? Is it not Caesar, into whose hands the whole power of the Roman empire is fallen? And surely none of us is a Scipio, a Pompey, or a Cato. Shall we, at a time when their fears make all men entertain sentiments beneath their dignity—shall we, in Utica, fight for the liberty of Rome with a man against whom Cato and Pompey the Great durst not make a stand in Italy? Shall we enfranchise our slaves to oppose Caesar, who have no more liberty ourselves than that conqueror is pleased to leave us? Ah! what wretches that we are! Let us at last know ourselves, and send deputies to intercede with him for money.' . . . They told Cato that they had resolved to send deputies to Caesar to intercede first and principally for him. If that request should not be granted, they would have no obligation to him for any favour to themselves, but as long as they had breath would fight for Cato. Cato made his acknowledgments for their regard, and advised them to send immediately to intercede for themselves. 'For me,' said he, 'intercede not. It is for the conquered to turn suppliants, and for those who have done an injury to beg pardon. For my part, I have been unconquered through life, and superiour in the things I wished to be; for in justice and honour I am Caesar's superiour.' "

The arguments of the traders and time-servers in Utica are not unknown in Richmond. But shall we not also find in this city something of the aspirations of Cato—a determination, even if we are overcome by force, to be unconquered in spirit, and, in any and all events, to remain superiour to the enemy—in honour.

I do not speak to you, my countrymen, idle sentimentalism. I firmly believe that the great Commonwealth of Virginia, and this city, which has a peculiar title to whatever there is of good and illustrious report in this war, have been recently, and are yet in some measure on the verge of questions which involve an interest immeasurably greater than has yet been disclosed in this contest—that of their historical and immortal honour.

My friends, this is not rubbish. The glory of History is indifferent to events: it is simply Honour. The name of Virginia in this war is historically and absolutely more important to us than any other element of the contest; and the coarse time-server who would sell an immortal title of honour as a trifling sentimentalism, and who has constantly in his mouth the phrase of "substantial interests," is the inglorious wretch who laughs at history and grovels in the calculations of the brute.

Those who have lived entirely in the South since the commencement of this war have little idea of the measure of honour which Virginia has obtained in it, and the consideration she has secured in the eyes of the world. One away from home finds even in intercourse with our enemies, that the name of Virginia is an ornament to him, and that the story of this her heroic capital—the record of Richmond—is universally accepted in two hemispheres as the most illustrious episode of the war. Honour such as this is not a piece of rhetoric or a figure of speech; it is something to be cherished under all circumstances, and to be preserved in all events.

It is scarcely necessary to say that I regard subjugation but as the vapour of our fears. But if remote possibilities are to be regarded, I have simply to say, that in all events and extremities, all chances and catastrophes, I am for Virginia going down to history, proudly and starkly, with the title of a subjugated people—a title not inseparable from true glory, and which has often claimed the admiration of the world—rather than as a people who ever submitted, and bartered their honour for the mercy of an enemy—in our case a mercy whose *pittance* would be as a mess of pottage weighed against an immortal patrimony!

The issue I would put before you is: No Submission; No State Negotiations with the Enemy; No Conventions for such objects, however proper for others. Let Virginia stand or fall by the fortunes of the Confederate arms, with her spotless honour in her hands.

If Virginia accepts the virtuous and noble alternative, she saves in all events, her honour, and by the resolution which it implies, may hope to secure a positive and glorious victory; and I, among the humblest of her citizens, will be proud to associate myself with a fate which, if not happy, at least can never be ignoble. But, if she chooses to submit, and make terms for Yankee clemency, the satisfaction will at least remain to me of not sharing in the dishonour of my native State, and of going to other parts of the world, where I may say: "I, too, was a Virginian, but not of those who sold the jewels of her history for the baubles and cheats of her conquerours."

EDWARD A. POLLARD

"Great Disasters Have Overtaken Us"

TIME WAS RUNNING OUT for the Confederacy. For accounts of the last days of the war we must turn to later publications. The Confederates were no longer able, physically or spiritually, to publish them. And there was little point in doing so. The propaganda value of accounts of a nation in its death throes would have been nil. And transportation had become so disrupted that publications could no longer be distributed to a wide audience.

Grant opened his spring campaign against the Richmond-Petersburg line, and the Virginia defense finally gave way. Richmond was evacuated on April 2 and Lee surrendered to Grant at Appomattox Court House on April 9. Only Johnston blocked Sherman's path toward joining his army with that of Grant. Resistance in the East was no longer effective. President Davis and the remnants of his Cabinet were fleeing south and west.

For there was still a forlorn hope in the West. If the President could make his way across the Mississippi and join the troops of General Edmund Kirby Smith, all might not yet be lost. In one of the very last of Confederate

$100,000
DEWARD!
IN GOLD.

Hea quarters Cav. Corp.,
Military Divi ion Mississippi,
Macón Ga., May 6, 1865.

One Hundred Thousand Dollars Reward

in Gold, will be paid to any person or persons who wil apprehend and deliver JEFFERSON DAVIS to any of the Military authorities of the United States.

Several millions of specie, reported to be with him, will become the
property of the captors.

J, H. WILSO

publications General Kirby Smith urged his troops to maintain the hopes of the dying nation.

Head Quarters Trans-Miss. Department,

SHREVEPORT, LA., APRIL 21 1865.

SOLDIERS OF THE TRANS-MISSISSIPPI ARMY:

The crisis of our revolution is at hand. Great disasters have overtaken us. The Army of Northern Virginia and our Commander-in-Chief are prisoners of war. With you rest the hopes of our nation, and upon your action depends the fate of our people. I appeal to you in the name of the cause you have so heroically maintained,—and in the name of your fire-sides and families so dear to you,—in the name of your bleeding country whose future is in your hands. Show that you are worthy of your position in history. Prove to the world that your hearts have not failed in the hour of disaster, and that at the last moment you will sustain the holy cause which has been so gloriously battled for, by your brethren east of the Mississippi.

You possess the means of long resisting invasion. You have hopes of succor from abroad—protract the struggle, and you will surely receive the aid of nations who already deeply sympathize with you.

Stand by your colors—maintain your discipline. The great resources of this Department, its vast extent, the numbers, the discipline, and the efficiency of the Army, will secure to our country terms that a proud people can with honor accept, and may, under the Providence of God, be the means of checking the triumph of our enemy and of securing the final success of our cause.

E. KIRBY SMITH,
General.

Secession Runs Its Course

JOHNSTON surrendered to Sherman near Hillsboro, North Carolina. President Davis met with the remaining members of his Cabinet for the last time at Washington, Georgia, May 4. Here he talked optimistically of re-establishing the government in Kirby-Smithdom west of the Mississippi. But the midshipmen who had accompanied him from Richmond as his guard were released from their assignment, and the Cabinet was allowed to disperse to take their chances individually.

Two days later, from his headquarters at Macon, Federal General J. H. Wilson issued an order that was soon posted on the buildings and fences in the heart of the Confederacy:

"One hundred thousand dollars reward in gold, will be paid to any person or persons who will apprehend and deliver Jefferson Davis to any of the military authorities of the United States. Several million of specie, reported to be with him, will become the property of the captors."

Four days later President Davis was captured at Irwinville, Georgia.

Secession had run its course.

Index

Abrams, Alexander St. Clair, 195–96, 209; his *A Full and Detailed History of the Siege of Vicksburg*, quoted, 196–208

Acquia (i.e., Aquia) Creek, Va., 145

Adams, J. U., 354

Address of the Confederate Congress, 300

Advertiser & Register (Mobile), 30

Agrippa (slave), 112

Alabama, 9

Alabama (ship), 149–54

Alabama River, 259

Albuquerque, New Mexico Territory, 72, 73

Aldie, Va., 170

Alexander, J. W., 66

Alexandria, Va., 37

Alice (ship), 261

Alleyton, Tex., 178

amateur theatricals, 272–75

amusements, 58, 272

Anderson (Confederate officer), 274

Anderson, Robert, 7, 10, 12, 13, 14, 15, 22, 23

Anderson, Samuel S., 315

Andersonville, 321

"Annie of the Vale" (song), 275

Appomattox, xxiv

Appomattox Court House, Va., 369

Aquia Creek, Va., 145

Arizona campaign, 186. *See also* New Mexico and Arizona Campaign.

Arkansas, 24, 38, 244

Arkansas campaign, 314

Arkansas Post, 242

Arkansas River, 311, 312

Arlington Heights, Va., 232

Army Argus, The, 124

Arnold, Herman C., 12

As You Like It, 164

Ashby, Mr., 337

Atlanta, 196, 290, 292, 293, 316–20, 334, 335

Bagby, George William, 280

Bailey, George A., 273, 274, 275

Bailey, J. A., 273, 275

Bailey, Mrs. J. A., 273, 274

Baldwin, William E., 205

Ball, Dabney, 54

A CATALOG OF SELECTED
DOVER BOOKS
IN ALL FIELDS OF INTEREST

A CATALOG OF SELECTED DOVER
BOOKS IN ALL FIELDS OF INTEREST

DRAWINGS OF REMBRANDT, edited by Seymour Slive. Updated Lippmann, Hofstede de Groot edition, with definitive scholarly apparatus. All portraits, biblical sketches, landscapes, nudes. Oriental figures, classical studies, together with selection of work by followers. 550 illustrations. Total of 630pp. 9⅛ × 12¼.
21485-0, 21486-9 Pa., Two-vol. set $29.90

GHOST AND HORROR STORIES OF AMBROSE BIERCE, Ambrose Bierce. 24 tales vividly imagined, strangely prophetic, and decades ahead of their time in technical skill: "The Damned Thing," "An Inhabitant of Carcosa," "The Eyes of the Panther," "Moxon's Master," and 20 more. 199pp. 5⅜ × 8½. 20767-6 Pa. $3.95

ETHICAL WRITINGS OF MAIMONIDES, Maimonides. Most significant ethical works of great medieval sage, newly translated for utmost precision, readability. Laws Concerning Character Traits, Eight Chapters, more. 192pp. 5⅜ × 8½.
24522-5 Pa. $4.50

THE EXPLORATION OF THE COLORADO RIVER AND ITS CANYONS, J. W. Powell. Full text of Powell's 1,000-mile expedition down the fabled Colorado in 1869. Superb account of terrain, geology, vegetation, Indians, famine, mutiny, treacherous rapids, mighty canyons, during exploration of last unknown part of continental U.S. 400pp. 5⅜ × 8½. 20094-9 Pa. $7.95

HISTORY OF PHILOSOPHY, Julián Marías. Clearest one-volume history on the market. Every major philosopher and dozens of others, to Existentialism and later. 505pp. 5⅜ × 8½. 21739-6 Pa. $9.95

ALL ABOUT LIGHTNING, Martin A. Uman. Highly readable non-technical survey of nature and causes of lightning, thunderstorms, ball lightning, St. Elmo's Fire, much more. Illustrated. 192pp. 5⅜ × 8½. 25237-X Pa. $5.95

SAILING ALONE AROUND THE WORLD, Captain Joshua Slocum. First man to sail around the world, alone, in small boat. One of great feats of seamanship told in delightful manner. 67 illustrations. 294pp. 5⅜ × 8½. 20326-3 Pa. $4.95

LETTERS AND NOTES ON THE MANNERS, CUSTOMS AND CONDITIONS OF THE NORTH AMERICAN INDIANS, George Catlin. Classic account of life among Plains Indians: ceremonies, hunt, warfare, etc. 312 plates. 572pp. of text. 6⅛ × 9¼. 22118-0, 22119-9, Pa. Two-vol. set $17.90

ALASKA: The Harriman Expedition, 1899, John Burroughs, John Muir, et al. Informative, engrossing accounts of two-month, 9,000-mile expedition. Native peoples, wildlife, forests, geography, salmon industry, glaciers, more. Profusely illustrated. 240 black-and-white line drawings. 124 black-and-white photographs. 3 maps. Index. 576pp. 5⅜ × 8½. 25109-8 Pa. $11.95

CATALOG OF DOVER BOOKS

THE BOOK OF BEASTS: Being a Translation from a Latin Bestiary of the Twelfth Century, T. H. White. Wonderful catalog real and fanciful beasts: manticore, griffin, phoenix, amphivius, jaculus, many more. White's witty erudite commentary on scientific, historical aspects. Fascinating glimpse of medieval mind. Illustrated. 296pp. 5⅜ × 8¼. (Available in U.S. only) 24609-4 Pa. $6.95

FRANK LLOYD WRIGHT: ARCHITECTURE AND NATURE With 160 Illustrations, Donald Hoffmann. Profusely illustrated study of influence of nature—especially prairie—on Wright's designs for Fallingwater, Robie House, Guggenheim Museum, other masterpieces. 96pp. 9¼ × 10¾. 25098-9 Pa. $7.95

FRANK LLOYD WRIGHT'S FALLINGWATER, Donald Hoffmann. Wright's famous waterfall house: planning and construction of organic idea. History of site, owners, Wright's personal involvement. Photographs of various stages of building. Preface by Edgar Kaufmann, Jr. 100 illustrations. 112pp. 9¼ × 10.
23671-4 Pa. $8.95

YEARS WITH FRANK LLOYD WRIGHT: Apprentice to Genius, Edgar Tafel. Insightful memoir by a former apprentice presents a revealing portrait of Wright the man, the inspired teacher, the greatest American architect. 372 black-and-white illustrations. Preface. Index. vi + 228pp. 8¼ × 11. 24801-1 Pa. $10.95

THE STORY OF KING ARTHUR AND HIS KNIGHTS, Howard Pyle. Enchanting version of King Arthur fable has delighted generations with imaginative narratives of exciting adventures and unforgettable illustrations by the author. 41 illustrations. xviii + 313pp. 6⅛ × 9¼. 21445-1 Pa. $6.95

THE GODS OF THE EGYPTIANS, E. A. Wallis Budge. Thorough coverage of numerous gods of ancient Egypt by foremost Egyptologist. Information on evolution of cults, rites and gods; the cult of Osiris; the Book of the Dead and its rites; the sacred animals and birds; Heaven and Hell; and more. 956pp. 6⅛ × 9¼.
22055-9, 22056-7 Pa., Two-vol. set $21.90

A THEOLOGICO-POLITICAL TREATISE, Benedict Spinoza. Also contains unfinished *Political Treatise*. Great classic on religious liberty, theory of government on common consent. R. Elwes translation. Total of 421pp. 5⅜ × 8½.
20249-6 Pa. $6.95

INCIDENTS OF TRAVEL IN CENTRAL AMERICA, CHIAPAS, AND YUCATAN, John L. Stephens. Almost single-handed discovery of Maya culture; exploration of ruined cities, monuments, temples; customs of Indians. 115 drawings. 892pp. 5⅜ × 8½. 22404-X, 22405-8 Pa., Two-vol. set $15.90

LOS CAPRICHOS, Francisco Goya. 80 plates of wild, grotesque monsters and caricatures. Prado manuscript included. 183pp. 6⅞ × 9⅜. 22384-1 Pa. $5.95

AUTOBIOGRAPHY: The Story of My Experiments with Truth, Mohandas K. Gandhi. Not hagiography, but Gandhi in his own words. Boyhood, legal studies, purification, the growth of the Satyagraha (nonviolent protest) movement. Critical, inspiring work of the man who freed India. 480pp. 5⅜ × 8½. (Available in U.S. only)
24593-4 Pa. $6.95

ILLUSTRATED DICTIONARY OF HISTORIC ARCHITECTURE, edited by Cyril M. Harris. Extraordinary compendium of clear, concise definitions for over 5,000 important architectural terms complemented by over 2,000 line drawings. Covers full spectrum of architecture from ancient ruins to 20th-century Modernism. Preface. 592pp. 7½ × 9⅜. 24444-X Pa. $15.95

THE NIGHT BEFORE CHRISTMAS, Clement Moore. Full text, and woodcuts from original 1848 book. Also critical, historical material. 19 illustrations. 40pp. 4⅝ × 6. 22797-9 Pa. $2.50

THE LESSON OF JAPANESE ARCHITECTURE: 165 Photographs, Jiro Harada. Memorable gallery of 165 photographs taken in the 1930's of exquisite Japanese homes of the well-to-do and historic buildings. 13 line diagrams. 192pp. 8⅜ × 11¼. 24778-3 Pa. $10.95

THE AUTOBIOGRAPHY OF CHARLES DARWIN AND SELECTED LETTERS, edited by Francis Darwin. The fascinating life of eccentric genius composed of an intimate memoir by Darwin (intended for his children); commentary by his son, Francis; hundreds of fragments from notebooks, journals, papers; and letters to and from Lyell, Hooker, Huxley, Wallace and Henslow. xi + 365pp. 5⅜ × 8. 20479-0 Pa. $6.95

WONDERS OF THE SKY: Observing Rainbows, Comets, Eclipses, the Stars and Other Phenomena, Fred Schaaf. Charming, easy-to-read poetic guide to all manner of celestial events visible to the naked eye. Mock suns, glories, Belt of Venus, more. Illustrated. 299pp. 5¼ × 8¼. 24402-4 Pa. $7.95

BURNHAM'S CELESTIAL HANDBOOK, Robert Burnham, Jr. Thorough guide to the stars beyond our solar system. Exhaustive treatment. Alphabetical by constellation: Andromeda to Cetus in Vol. 1; Chamaeleon to Orion in Vol. 2; and Pavo to Vulpecula in Vol. 3. Hundreds of illustrations. Index in Vol. 3. 2,000pp. 6⅛ × 9¼. 23567-X, 23568-8, 23673-0 Pa., Three-vol. set $38.85

STAR NAMES: Their Lore and Meaning, Richard Hinckley Allen. Fascinating history of names various cultures have given to constellations and literary and folkloristic uses that have been made of stars. Indexes to subjects. Arabic and Greek names. Biblical references. Bibliography. 563pp. 5⅜ × 8½. 21079-0 Pa. $8.95

THIRTY YEARS THAT SHOOK PHYSICS: The Story of Quantum Theory, George Gamow. Lucid, accessible introduction to influential theory of energy and matter. Careful explanations of Dirac's anti-particles, Bohr's model of the atom, much more. 12 plates. Numerous drawings. 240pp. 5⅜ × 8½. 24895-X Pa. $5.95

CHINESE DOMESTIC FURNITURE IN PHOTOGRAPHS AND MEASURED DRAWINGS, Gustav Ecke. A rare volume, now affordably priced for antique collectors, furniture buffs and art historians. Detailed review of styles ranging from early Shang to late Ming. Unabridged republication. 161 black-and-white drawings, photos. Total of 224pp. 8⅜ × 11¼. (Available in U.S. only) 25171-3 Pa. $13.95

VINCENT VAN GOGH: A Biography, Julius Meier-Graefe. Dynamic, penetrating study of artist's life, relationship with brother, Theo, painting techniques, travels, more. Readable, engrossing. 160pp. 5⅜ × 8½. (Available in U.S. only) 25253-1 Pa. $4.95

HOW TO WRITE, Gertrude Stein. Gertrude Stein claimed anyone could understand her unconventional writing—here are clues to help. Fascinating improvisations, language experiments, explanations illuminate Stein's craft and the art of writing. Total of 414pp. 4⅜ × 6⅜. 23144-5 Pa. $6.95

ADVENTURES AT SEA IN THE GREAT AGE OF SAIL: Five Firsthand Narratives, edited by Elliot Snow. Rare true accounts of exploration, whaling, shipwreck, fierce natives, trade, shipboard life, more. 33 illustrations. Introduction. 353pp. 5⅜ × 8½. 25177-2 Pa. $8.95

THE HERBAL OR GENERAL HISTORY OF PLANTS, John Gerard. Classic descriptions of about 2,850 plants—with over 2,700 illustrations—includes Latin and English names, physical descriptions, varieties, time and place of growth, more. 2,706 illustrations. xlv + 1,678pp. 8½ × 12¼. 23147-X Cloth. $75.00

DOROTHY AND THE WIZARD IN OZ, L. Frank Baum. Dorothy and the Wizard visit the center of the Earth, where people are vegetables, glass houses grow and Oz characters reappear. Classic sequel to *Wizard of Oz*. 256pp. 5⅜ × 8. 24714-7 Pa. $4.95

SONGS OF EXPERIENCE: Facsimile Reproduction with 26 Plates in Full Color, William Blake. This facsimile of Blake's original "Illuminated Book" reproduces 26 full-color plates from a rare 1826 edition. Includes "The Tyger," "London," "Holy Thursday," and other immortal poems. 26 color plates. Printed text of poems. 48pp. 5¼ × 7. 24636-1 Pa. $3.50

SONGS OF INNOCENCE, William Blake. The first and most popular of Blake's famous "Illuminated Books," in a facsimile edition reproducing all 31 brightly colored plates. Additional printed text of each poem. 64pp. 5¼ × 7. 22764-2 Pa. $3.50

PRECIOUS STONES, Max Bauer. Classic, thorough study of diamonds, rubies, emeralds, garnets, etc.: physical character, occurrence, properties, use, similar topics. 20 plates, 8 in color. 94 figures. 659pp. 6⅛ × 9¼. 21910-0, 21911-9 Pa., Two-vol. set $15.90

ENCYCLOPEDIA OF VICTORIAN NEEDLEWORK, S. F. A. Caulfeild and Blanche Saward. Full, precise descriptions of stitches, techniques for dozens of needlecrafts—most exhaustive reference of its kind. Over 800 figures. Total of 679pp. 8⅛ × 11. Two volumes. Vol. 1 22800-2 Pa. $11.95
Vol. 2 22801-0 Pa. $11.95

THE MARVELOUS LAND OF OZ, L. Frank Baum. Second Oz book, the Scarecrow and Tin Woodman are back with hero named Tip, Oz magic. 136 illustrations. 287pp. 5⅜ × 8½. 20692-0 Pa. $5.95

WILD FOWL DECOYS, Joel Barber. Basic book on the subject, by foremost authority and collector. Reveals history of decoy making and rigging, place in American culture, different kinds of decoys, how to make them, and how to use them. 140 plates. 156pp. 7⅞ × 10¾. 20011-6 Pa. $8.95

HISTORY OF LACE, Mrs. Bury Palliser. Definitive, profusely illustrated chronicle of lace from earliest times to late 19th century. Laces of Italy, Greece, England, France, Belgium, etc. Landmark of needlework scholarship. 266 illustrations. 672pp. 6⅛ × 9¼. 24742-2 Pa. $14.95

ILLUSTRATED GUIDE TO SHAKER FURNITURE, Robert Meader. All furniture and appurtenances, with much on unknown local styles. 235 photos. 146pp. 9 × 12. 22819-3 Pa. $8.95

WHALE SHIPS AND WHALING: A Pictorial Survey, George Francis Dow. Over 200 vintage engravings, drawings, photographs of barks, brigs, cutters, other vessels. Also harpoons, lances, whaling guns, many other artifacts. Comprehensive text by foremost authority. 207 black-and-white illustrations. 288pp. 6 × 9. 24808-9 Pa. $8.95

THE BERTRAMS, Anthony Trollope. Powerful portrayal of blind self-will and thwarted ambition includes one of Trollope's most heartrending love stories. 497pp. 5⅜ × 8½. 25119-5 Pa. $9.95

ADVENTURES WITH A HAND LENS, Richard Headstrom. Clearly written guide to observing and studying flowers and grasses, fish scales, moth and insect wings, egg cases, buds, feathers, seeds, leaf scars, moss, molds, ferns, common crystals, etc.—all with an ordinary, inexpensive magnifying glass. 209 exact line drawings aid in your discoveries. 220pp. 5⅜ × 8½. 23330-8 Pa. $4.95

RODIN ON ART AND ARTISTS, Auguste Rodin. Great sculptor's candid, wide-ranging comments on meaning of art; great artists; relation of sculpture to poetry, painting, music; philosophy of life, more. 76 superb black-and-white illustrations of Rodin's sculpture, drawings and prints. 119pp. 8⅜ × 11¼. 24487-3 Pa. $7.95

FIFTY CLASSIC FRENCH FILMS, 1912-1982: A Pictorial Record, Anthony Slide. Memorable stills from Grand Illusion, Beauty and the Beast, Hiroshima, Mon Amour, many more. Credits, plot synopses, reviews, etc. 160pp. 8¼ × 11. 25256-6 Pa. $11.95

THE PRINCIPLES OF PSYCHOLOGY, William James. Famous long course complete, unabridged. Stream of thought, time perception, memory, experimental methods; great work decades ahead of its time. 94 figures. 1,391pp. 5⅜ × 8½. 20381-6, 20382-4 Pa., Two-vol. set $23.90

BODIES IN A BOOKSHOP, R. T. Campbell. Challenging mystery of blackmail and murder with ingenious plot and superbly drawn characters. In the best tradition of British suspense fiction. 192pp. 5⅜ × 8½. 24720-1 Pa. $3.95

CALLAS: PORTRAIT OF A PRIMA DONNA, George Jellinek. Renowned commentator on the musical scene chronicles incredible career and life of the most controversial, fascinating, influential operatic personality of our time. 64 black-and-white photographs. 416pp. 5⅜ × 8¼. 25047-4 Pa. $8.95

GEOMETRY, RELATIVITY AND THE FOURTH DIMENSION, Rudolph Rucker. Exposition of fourth dimension, concepts of relativity as Flatland characters continue adventures. Popular, easily followed yet accurate, profound. 141 illustrations. 133pp. 5⅜ × 8½. 23400-2 Pa. $3.95

HOUSEHOLD STORIES BY THE BROTHERS GRIMM, with pictures by Walter Crane. 53 classic stories—Rumpelstiltskin, Rapunzel, Hansel and Gretel, the Fisherman and his Wife, Snow White, Tom Thumb, Sleeping Beauty, Cinderella, and so much more—lavishly illustrated with original 19th century drawings. 114 illustrations. x + 269pp. 5⅜ × 8½. 21080-4 Pa. $4.95

SUNDIALS, Albert Waugh. Far and away the best, most thorough coverage of ideas, mathematics concerned, types, construction, adjusting anywhere. Over 100 illustrations. 230pp. 5⅜ × 8½. 22947-5 Pa. $4.95

PICTURE HISTORY OF THE NORMANDIE: With 190 Illustrations, Frank O. Braynard. Full story of legendary French ocean liner: Art Deco interiors, design innovations, furnishings, celebrities, maiden voyage, tragic fire, much more. Extensive text. 144pp. 8⅞ × 11¾. 25257-4 Pa. $10.95

THE FIRST AMERICAN COOKBOOK: A Facsimile of "American Cookery," 1796, Amelia Simmons. Facsimile of the first American-written cookbook published in the United States contains authentic recipes for colonial favorites—pumpkin pudding, winter squash pudding, spruce beer, Indian slapjacks, and more. Introductory Essay and Glossary of colonial cooking terms. 80pp. 5⅜ × 8½. 24710-4 Pa. $3.50

101 PUZZLES IN THOUGHT AND LOGIC, C. R. Wylie, Jr. Solve murders and robberies, find out which fishermen are liars, how a blind man could possibly identify a color—purely by your own reasoning! 107pp. 5⅜ × 8½. 20367-0 Pa. $2.50

THE BOOK OF WORLD-FAMOUS MUSIC—CLASSICAL, POPULAR AND FOLK, James J. Fuld. Revised and enlarged republication of landmark work in musico-bibliography. Full information about nearly 1,000 songs and compositions including first lines of music and lyrics. New supplement. Index. 800pp. 5⅜ × 8¼. 24857-7 Pa. $15.95

ANTHROPOLOGY AND MODERN LIFE, Franz Boas. Great anthropologist's classic treatise on race and culture. Introduction by Ruth Bunzel. Only inexpensive paperback edition. 255pp. 5⅜ × 8½. 25245-0 Pa. $6.95

THE TALE OF PETER RABBIT, Beatrix Potter. The inimitable Peter's terrifying adventure in Mr. McGregor's garden, with all 27 wonderful, full-color Potter illustrations. 55pp. 4¼ × 5½. (Available in U.S. only) 22827-4 Pa. $1.75

THREE PROPHETIC SCIENCE FICTION NOVELS, H. G. Wells. *When the Sleeper Wakes, A Story of the Days to Come* and *The Time Machine* (full version). 335pp. 5⅜ × 8½. (Available in U.S. only) 20605-X Pa. $6.95

APICIUS COOKERY AND DINING IN IMPERIAL ROME, edited and translated by Joseph Dommers Vehling. Oldest known cookbook in existence offers readers a clear picture of what foods Romans ate, how they prepared them, etc. 49 illustrations. 301pp. 6⅛ × 9¼. 23563-7 Pa. $7.95

SHAKESPEARE LEXICON AND QUOTATION DICTIONARY, Alexander Schmidt. Full definitions, locations, shades of meaning of every word in plays and poems. More than 50,000 exact quotations. 1,485pp. 6½ × 9¼. 22726-X, 22727-8 Pa., Two-vol. set $29.90

THE WORLD'S GREAT SPEECHES, edited by Lewis Copeland and Lawrence W. Lamm. Vast collection of 278 speeches from Greeks to 1970. Powerful and effective models; unique look at history. 842pp. 5⅜ × 8½. 20468-5 Pa. $11.95

THE BLUE FAIRY BOOK, Andrew Lang. The first, most famous collection, with many familiar tales: Little Red Riding Hood, Aladdin and the Wonderful Lamp, Puss in Boots, Sleeping Beauty, Hansel and Gretel, Rumpelstiltskin; 37 in all. 138 illustrations. 390pp. 5⅜ × 8½. 21437-0 Pa. $6.95

THE STORY OF THE CHAMPIONS OF THE ROUND TABLE, Howard Pyle. Sir Launcelot, Sir Tristram and Sir Percival in spirited adventures of love and triumph retold in Pyle's inimitable style. 50 drawings, 31 full-page. xviii + 329pp. 6½ × 9¼. 21883-X Pa. $7.95

AUDUBON AND HIS JOURNALS, Maria Audubon. Unmatched two-volume portrait of the great artist, naturalist and author contains his journals, an excellent biography by his granddaughter, expert annotations by the noted ornithologist, Dr. Elliott Coues, and 37 superb illustrations. Total of 1,200pp. 5⅜ × 8.
Vol. I 25143-8 Pa. $8.95
Vol. II 25144-6 Pa. $8.95

GREAT DINOSAUR HUNTERS AND THEIR DISCOVERIES, Edwin H. Colbert. Fascinating, lavishly illustrated chronicle of dinosaur research, 1820's to 1960. Achievements of Cope, Marsh, Brown, Buckland, Mantell, Huxley, many others. 384pp. 5¼ × 8¼. 24701-5 Pa. $7.95

THE TASTEMAKERS, Russell Lynes. Informal, illustrated social history of American taste 1850's–1950's. First popularized categories Highbrow, Lowbrow, Middlebrow. 129 illustrations. New (1979) afterword. 384pp. 6 × 9.
23993-4 Pa. $8.95

DOUBLE CROSS PURPOSES, Ronald A. Knox. A treasure hunt in the Scottish Highlands, an old map, unidentified corpse, surprise discoveries keep reader guessing in this cleverly intricate tale of financial skullduggery. 2 black-and-white maps. 320pp. 5⅜ × 8½. (Available in U.S. only) 25032-6 Pa. $6.95

AUTHENTIC VICTORIAN DECORATION AND ORNAMENTATION IN FULL COLOR: 46 Plates from "Studies in Design," Christopher Dresser. Superb full-color lithographs reproduced from rare original portfolio of a major Victorian designer. 48pp. 9¼ × 12¼. 25083-0 Pa. $7.95

PRIMITIVE ART, Franz Boas. Remains the best text ever prepared on subject, thoroughly discussing Indian, African, Asian, Australian, and, especially, Northern American primitive art. Over 950 illustrations show ceramics, masks, totem poles, weapons, textiles, paintings, much more. 376pp. 5⅜ × 8. 20025-6 Pa. $6.95

SIDELIGHTS ON RELATIVITY, Albert Einstein. Unabridged republication of two lectures delivered by the great physicist in 1920–21. *Ether and Relativity* and *Geometry and Experience*. Elegant ideas in non-mathematical form, accessible to intelligent layman. vi + 56pp. 5⅜ × 8½. 24511-X Pa. $2.95

THE WIT AND HUMOR OF OSCAR WILDE, edited by Alvin Redman. More than 1,000 ripostes, paradoxes, wisecracks: Work is the curse of the drinking classes, I can resist everything except temptation, etc. 258pp. 5⅜ × 8½. 20602-5 Pa. $4.95

ADVENTURES WITH A MICROSCOPE, Richard Headstrom. 59 adventures with clothing fibers, protozoa, ferns and lichens, roots and leaves, much more. 142 illustrations. 232pp. 5⅜ × 8½. 23471-1 Pa. $3.95

PLANTS OF THE BIBLE, Harold N. Moldenke and Alma L. Moldenke. Standard reference to all 230 plants mentioned in Scriptures. Latin name, biblical reference, uses, modern identity, much more. Unsurpassed encyclopedic resource for scholars, botanists, nature lovers, students of Bible. Bibliography. Indexes. 123 black-and-white illustrations. 384pp. 6 × 9. 25069-5 Pa. $8.95

FAMOUS AMERICAN WOMEN: A Biographical Dictionary from Colonial Times to the Present, Robert McHenry, ed. From Pocahontas to Rosa Parks, 1,035 distinguished American women documented in separate biographical entries. Accurate, up-to-date data, numerous categories, spans 400 years. Indices. 493pp. 6½ × 9¼. 24523-3 Pa. $10.95

THE FABULOUS INTERIORS OF THE GREAT OCEAN LINERS IN HISTORIC PHOTOGRAPHS, William H. Miller, Jr. Some 200 superb photographs capture exquisite interiors of world's great "floating palaces"—1890's to 1980's: *Titanic, Ile de France, Queen Elizabeth, United States, Europa,* more. Approx. 200 black-and-white photographs. Captions. Text. Introduction. 160pp. 8⅞ × 11¾. 24756-2 Pa. $9.95

THE GREAT LUXURY LINERS, 1927–1954: A Photographic Record, William H. Miller, Jr. Nostalgic tribute to heyday of ocean liners. 186 photos of Ile de France, Normandie, Leviathan, Queen Elizabeth, United States, many others. Interior and exterior views. Introduction. Captions. 160pp. 9 × 12. 24056-8 Pa. $10.95

A NATURAL HISTORY OF THE DUCKS, John Charles Phillips. Great landmark of ornithology offers complete detailed coverage of nearly 200 species and subspecies of ducks: gadwall, sheldrake, merganser, pintail, many more. 74 full-color plates, 102 black-and-white. Bibliography. Total of 1,920pp. 8⅜ × 11¼. 25141-1, 25142-X Cloth. Two-vol. set $100.00

THE SEAWEED HANDBOOK: An Illustrated Guide to Seaweeds from North Carolina to Canada, Thomas F. Lee. Concise reference covers 78 species. Scientific and common names, habitat, distribution, more. Finding keys for easy identification. 224pp. 5⅜ × 8½. 25215-9 Pa. $6.95

THE TEN BOOKS OF ARCHITECTURE: The 1755 Leoni Edition, Leon Battista Alberti. Rare classic helped introduce the glories of ancient architecture to the Renaissance. 68 black-and-white plates. 336pp. 8⅜ × 11¼. 25239-6 Pa. $14.95

MISS MACKENZIE, Anthony Trollope. Minor masterpieces by Victorian master unmasks many truths about life in 19th-century England. First inexpensive edition in years. 392pp. 5⅜ × 8½. 25201-9 Pa. $8.95

THE RIME OF THE ANCIENT MARINER, Gustave Doré, Samuel Taylor Coleridge. Dramatic engravings considered by many to be his greatest work. The terrifying space of the open sea, the storms and whirlpools of an unknown ocean, the ice of Antarctica, more—all rendered in a powerful, chilling manner. Full text. 38 plates. 77pp. 9¼ × 12. 22305-1 Pa. $4.95

THE EXPEDITIONS OF ZEBULON MONTGOMERY PIKE, Zebulon Montgomery Pike. Fascinating first-hand accounts (1805–6) of exploration of Mississippi River, Indian wars, capture by Spanish dragoons, much more. 1,088pp. 5⅜ × 8½. 25254-X, 25255-8 Pa. Two-vol. set $25.90

A CONCISE HISTORY OF PHOTOGRAPHY: Third Revised Edition, Helmut Gernsheim. Best one-volume history—camera obscura, photochemistry, daguerreotypes, evolution of cameras, film, more. Also artistic aspects—landscape, portraits, fine art, etc. 281 black-and-white photographs. 26 in color. 176pp. 8⅜ × 11¼. 25128-4 Pa. $13.95

THE DORÉ BIBLE ILLUSTRATIONS, Gustave Doré. 241 detailed plates from the Bible: the Creation scenes, Adam and Eve, Flood, Babylon, battle sequences, life of Jesus, etc. Each plate is accompanied by the verses from the King James version of the Bible. 241pp. 9 × 12. 23004-X Pa. $9.95

HUGGER-MUGGER IN THE LOUVRE, Elliot Paul. Second Homer Evans mystery-comedy. Theft at the Louvre involves sleuth in hilarious, madcap caper. "A knockout."—Books. 336pp. 5⅜ × 8½. 25185-3 Pa. $5.95

FLATLAND, E. A. Abbott. Intriguing and enormously popular science-fiction classic explores the complexities of trying to survive as a two-dimensional being in a three-dimensional world. Amusingly illustrated by the author. 16 illustrations. 103pp. 5⅜ × 8½. 20001-9 Pa. $2.50

THE HISTORY OF THE LEWIS AND CLARK EXPEDITION, Meriwether Lewis and William Clark, edited by Elliott Coues. Classic edition of Lewis and Clark's day-by-day journals that later became the basis for U.S. claims to Oregon and the West. Accurate and invaluable geographical, botanical, biological, meteorological and anthropological material. Total of 1,508pp. 5⅜ × 8½.
21268-8, 21269-6, 21270-X Pa. Three-vol. set $26.85

LANGUAGE, TRUTH AND LOGIC, Alfred J. Ayer. Famous, clear introduction to Vienna, Cambridge schools of Logical Positivism. Role of philosophy, elimination of metaphysics, nature of analysis, etc. 160pp. 5⅜ × 8½. (Available in U.S. and Canada only) 20010-8 Pa. $3.95

MATHEMATICS FOR THE NONMATHEMATICIAN, Morris Kline. Detailed, college-level treatment of mathematics in cultural and historical context, with numerous exercises. For liberal arts students. Preface. Recommended Reading Lists. Tables. Index. Numerous black-and-white figures. xvi + 641pp. 5⅜ × 8½.
24823-2 Pa. $11.95

HANDBOOK OF PICTORIAL SYMBOLS, Rudolph Modley. 3,250 signs and symbols, many systems in full; official or heavy commercial use. Arranged by subject. Most in Pictorial Archive series. 143pp. 8⅛ × 11. 23357-X Pa. $6.95

INCIDENTS OF TRAVEL IN YUCATAN, John L. Stephens. Classic (1843) exploration of jungles of Yucatan, looking for evidences of Maya civilization. Travel adventures, Mexican and Indian culture, etc. Total of 669pp. 5⅜ × 8½.
20926-1, 20927-X Pa., Two-vol. set $11.90

DEGAS: An Intimate Portrait, Ambroise Vollard. Charming, anecdotal memoir by famous art dealer of one of the greatest 19th-century French painters. 14 black-and-white illustrations. Introduction by Harold L. Van Doren. 96pp. 5⅜ × 8½.
25131-4 Pa. $4.95

PERSONAL NARRATIVE OF A PILGRIMAGE TO ALMANDINAH AND MECCAH, Richard Burton. Great travel classic by remarkably colorful personality. Burton, disguised as a Moroccan, visited sacred shrines of Islam, narrowly escaping death. 47 illustrations. 959pp. 5⅜ × 8½. 21217-3, 21218-1 Pa., Two-vol. set $19.90

PHRASE AND WORD ORIGINS, A. H. Holt. Entertaining, reliable, modern study of more than 1,200 colorful words, phrases, origins and histories. Much unexpected information. 254pp. 5⅜ × 8½. 20758-7 Pa. $5.95

THE RED THUMB MARK, R. Austin Freeman. In this first Dr. Thorndyke case, the great scientific detective draws fascinating conclusions from the nature of a single fingerprint. Exciting story, authentic science. 320pp. 5⅜ × 8½. (Available in U.S. only) 25210-8 Pa. $6.95

AN EGYPTIAN HIEROGLYPHIC DICTIONARY, E. A. Wallis Budge. Monumental work containing about 25,000 words or terms that occur in texts ranging from 3000 B.C. to 600 A.D. Each entry consists of a transliteration of the word, the word in hieroglyphs, and the meaning in English. 1,314pp. 6⅜ × 10. 23615-3, 23616-1 Pa., Two-vol. set $31.90

THE COMPLEAT STRATEGYST: Being a Primer on the Theory of Games of Strategy, J. D. Williams. Highly entertaining classic describes, with many illustrated examples, how to select best strategies in conflict situations. Prefaces. Appendices. xvi + 268pp. 5⅜ × 8½. 25101-2 Pa. $5.95

THE ROAD TO OZ, L. Frank Baum. Dorothy meets the Shaggy Man, little Button-Bright and the Rainbow's beautiful daughter in this delightful trip to the magical Land of Oz. 272pp. 5⅜ × 8. 25208-6 Pa. $5.95

POINT AND LINE TO PLANE, Wassily Kandinsky. Seminal exposition of role of point, line, other elements in non-objective painting. Essential to understanding 20th-century art. 127 illustrations. 192pp. 6½ × 9¼. 23808-3 Pa. $4.95

LADY ANNA, Anthony Trollope. Moving chronicle of Countess Lovel's bitter struggle to win for herself and daughter Anna their rightful rank and fortune—perhaps at cost of sanity itself. 384pp. 5⅜ × 8½. 24669-8 Pa. $8.95

EGYPTIAN MAGIC, E. A. Wallis Budge. Sums up all that is known about magic in Ancient Egypt: the role of magic in controlling the gods, powerful amulets that warded off evil spirits, scarabs of immortality, use of wax images, formulas and spells, the secret name, much more. 253pp. 5⅜ × 8½. 22681-6 Pa. $4.50

THE DANCE OF SIVA, Ananda Coomaraswamy. Preeminent authority unfolds the vast metaphysic of India: the revelation of her art, conception of the universe, social organization, etc. 27 reproductions of art masterpieces. 192pp. 5⅜ × 8½. 24817-8 Pa. $5.95

CHRISTMAS CUSTOMS AND TRADITIONS, Clement A. Miles. Origin, evolution, significance of religious, secular practices. Caroling, gifts, yule logs, much more. Full, scholarly yet fascinating; non-sectarian. 400pp. 5⅜ × 8½.
23354-5 Pa. $6.95

THE HUMAN FIGURE IN MOTION, Eadweard Muybridge. More than 4,500 stopped-action photos, in action series, showing undraped men, women, children jumping, lying down, throwing, sitting, wrestling, carrying, etc. 390pp. 7⅞ × 10⅝.
20204-6 Cloth. $21.95

THE MAN WHO WAS THURSDAY, Gilbert Keith Chesterton. Witty, fast-paced novel about a club of anarchists in turn-of-the-century London. Brilliant social, religious, philosophical speculations. 128pp. 5⅜ × 8½. 25121-7 Pa. $3.95

A CEZANNE SKETCHBOOK: Figures, Portraits, Landscapes and Still Lifes, Paul Cezanne. Great artist experiments with tonal effects, light, mass, other qualities in over 100 drawings. A revealing view of developing master painter, precursor of Cubism. 102 black-and-white illustrations. 144pp. 8¾ × 6⅜. 24790-2 Pa. $5.95

AN ENCYCLOPEDIA OF BATTLES: Accounts of Over 1,560 Battles from 1479 B.C. to the Present, David Eggenberger. Presents essential details of every major battle in recorded history, from the first battle of Megiddo in 1479 B.C. to Grenada in 1984. List of Battle Maps. New Appendix covering the years 1967–1984. Index. 99 illustrations. 544pp. 6½ × 9¼. 24913-1 Pa. $14.95

AN ETYMOLOGICAL DICTIONARY OF MODERN ENGLISH, Ernest Weekley. Richest, fullest work, by foremost British lexicographer. Detailed word histories. Inexhaustible. Total of 856pp. 6½ × 9¼.
21873-2, 21874-0 Pa., Two-vol. set $17.00

WEBSTER'S AMERICAN MILITARY BIOGRAPHIES, edited by Robert McHenry. Over 1,000 figures who shaped 3 centuries of American military history. Detailed biographies of Nathan Hale, Douglas MacArthur, Mary Hallaren, others. Chronologies of engagements, more. Introduction. Addenda. 1,033 entries in alphabetical order. xi + 548pp. 6½ × 9¼. (Available in U.S. only)
24758-9 Pa. $13.95

LIFE IN ANCIENT EGYPT, Adolf Erman. Detailed older account, with much not in more recent books: domestic life, religion, magic, medicine, commerce, and whatever else needed for complete picture. Many illustrations. 597pp. 5⅜ × 8½.
22632-8 Pa. $8.95

HISTORIC COSTUME IN PICTURES, Braun & Schneider. Over 1,450 costumed figures shown, covering a wide variety of peoples: kings, emperors, nobles, priests, servants, soldiers, scholars, townsfolk, peasants, merchants, courtiers, cavaliers, and more. 256pp. 8⅜ × 11¼. 23150-X Pa. $9.95

THE NOTEBOOKS OF LEONARDO DA VINCI, edited by J. P. Richter. Extracts from manuscripts reveal great genius; on painting, sculpture, anatomy, sciences, geography, etc. Both Italian and English. 186 ms. pages reproduced, plus 500 additional drawings, including studies for *Last Supper, Sforza* monument, etc. 860pp. 7⅞ × 10¾. (Available in U.S. only) 22572-0, 22573-9 Pa., Two-vol. set $31.90

THE ART NOUVEAU STYLE BOOK OF ALPHONSE MUCHA: All 72 Plates from "Documents Decoratifs" in Original Color, Alphonse Mucha. Rare copyright-free design portfolio by high priest of Art Nouveau. Jewelry, wallpaper, stained glass, furniture, figure studies, plant and animal motifs, etc. Only complete one-volume edition. 80pp. 9⅜ × 12¼. 24044-4 Pa. $9.95

ANIMALS: 1,419 COPYRIGHT-FREE ILLUSTRATIONS OF MAMMALS, BIRDS, FISH, INSECTS, ETC., edited by Jim Harter. Clear wood engravings present, in extremely lifelike poses, over 1,000 species of animals. One of the most extensive pictorial sourcebooks of its kind. Captions. Index. 284pp. 9 × 12. 23766-4 Pa. $9.95

OBELISTS FLY HIGH, C. Daly King. Masterpiece of American detective fiction, long out of print, involves murder on a 1935 transcontinental flight—"a very thrilling story"—NY Times. Unabridged and unaltered republication of the edition published by William Collins Sons & Co. Ltd., London, 1935. 288pp. 5⅜ × 8½. (Available in U.S. only) 25036-9 Pa. $5.95

VICTORIAN AND EDWARDIAN FASHION: A Photographic Survey, Alison Gernsheim. First fashion history completely illustrated by contemporary photographs. Full text plus 235 photos, 1840-1914, in which many celebrities appear. 240pp. 6½ × 9¼. 24205-6 Pa. $6.95

THE ART OF THE FRENCH ILLUSTRATED BOOK, 1700-1914, Gordon N. Ray. Over 630 superb book illustrations by Fragonard, Delacroix, Daumier, Doré, Grandville, Manet, Mucha, Steinlen, Toulouse-Lautrec and many others. Preface. Introduction. 633 halftones. Indices of artists, authors & titles, binders and provenances. Appendices. Bibliography. 608pp. 8⅜ × 11¼. 25086-5 Pa. $24.95

THE WONDERFUL WIZARD OF OZ, L. Frank Baum. Facsimile in full color of America's finest children's classic. 143 illustrations by W. W. Denslow. 267pp. 5⅜ × 8½. 20691-2 Pa. $7.95

FRONTIERS OF MODERN PHYSICS: New Perspectives on Cosmology, Relativity, Black Holes and Extraterrestrial Intelligence, Tony Rothman, et al. For the intelligent layman. Subjects include: cosmological models of the universe; black holes; the neutrino; the search for extraterrestrial intelligence. Introduction. 46 black-and-white illustrations. 192pp. 5⅜ × 8½. 24587-X Pa. $7.95

THE FRIENDLY STARS, Martha Evans Martin & Donald Howard Menzel. Classic text marshalls the stars together in an engaging, non-technical survey, presenting them as sources of beauty in night sky. 23 illustrations. Foreword. 2 star charts. Index. 147pp. 5⅜ × 8½. 21099-5 Pa. $3.95

FADS AND FALLACIES IN THE NAME OF SCIENCE, Martin Gardner. Fair, witty appraisal of cranks, quacks, and quackeries of science and pseudoscience: hollow earth, Velikovsky, orgone energy, Dianetics, flying saucers, Bridey Murphy, food and medical fads, etc. Revised, expanded In the Name of Science. "A very able and even-tempered presentation."—The New Yorker. 363pp. 5⅜ × 8. 20394-8 Pa. $6.95

ANCIENT EGYPT: ITS CULTURE AND HISTORY, J. E Manchip White. From pre-dynastics through Ptolemies: society, history, political structure, religion, daily life, literature, cultural heritage. 48 plates. 217pp. 5⅜ × 8½. 22548-8 Pa. $5.95

SIR HARRY HOTSPUR OF HUMBLETHWAITE, Anthony Trollope. Incisive, unconventional psychological study of a conflict between a wealthy baronet, his idealistic daughter, and their scapegrace cousin. The 1870 novel in its first inexpensive edition in years. 250pp. 5⅜ × 8½.   24953-0 Pa. $5.95

LASERS AND HOLOGRAPHY, Winston E. Kock. Sound introduction to burgeoning field, expanded (1981) for second edition. Wave patterns, coherence, lasers, diffraction, zone plates, properties of holograms, recent advances. 84 illustrations. 160pp. 5⅜ × 8¼. (Except in United Kingdom)   24041-X Pa. $3.95

INTRODUCTION TO ARTIFICIAL INTELLIGENCE: SECOND, EN-LARGED EDITION, Philip C. Jackson, Jr. Comprehensive survey of artificial intelligence—the study of how machines (computers) can be made to act intelligently. Includes introductory and advanced material. Extensive notes updating the main text. 132 black-and-white illustrations. 512pp. 5⅜ × 8½.   24864-X Pa. $8.95

HISTORY OF INDIAN AND INDONESIAN ART, Ananda K. Coomaraswamy. Over 400 illustrations illuminate classic study of Indian art from earliest Harappa finds to early 20th century. Provides philosophical, religious and social insights. 304pp. 6⅜ × 9⅜.   25005-9 Pa. $9.95

THE GOLEM, Gustav Meyrink. Most famous supernatural novel in modern European literature, set in Ghetto of Old Prague around 1890. Compelling story of mystical experiences, strange transformations, profound terror. 13 black-and-white illustrations. 224pp. 5⅜ × 8½. (Available in U.S. only)   25025-3 Pa. $6.95

ARMADALE, Wilkie Collins. Third great mystery novel by the author of *The Woman in White* and *The Moonstone*. Original magazine version with 40 illustrations. 597pp. 5⅜ × 8½.   23429-0 Pa. $9.95

PICTORIAL ENCYCLOPEDIA OF HISTORIC ARCHITECTURAL PLANS, DETAILS AND ELEMENTS: With 1,880 Line Drawings of Arches, Domes, Doorways, Facades, Gables, Windows, etc., John Theodore Haneman. Sourcebook of inspiration for architects, designers, others. Bibliography. Captions. 141pp. 9 × 12.   24605-1 Pa. $7.95

BENCHLEY LOST AND FOUND, Robert Benchley. Finest humor from early 30's, about pet peeves, child psychologists, post office and others. Mostly unavailable elsewhere. 73 illustrations by Peter Arno and others. 183pp. 5⅜ × 8½.
                    22410-4 Pa. $4.95

ERTÉ GRAPHICS, Erté. Collection of striking color graphics: *Seasons, Alphabet, Numerals, Aces* and *Precious Stones*. 50 plates, including 4 on covers. 48pp. 9⅜ × 12¼.   23580-7 Pa. $6.95

THE JOURNAL OF HENRY D. THOREAU, edited by Bradford Torrey, F. H. Allen. Complete reprinting of 14 volumes, 1837–61, over two million words; the sourcebooks for *Walden*, etc. Definitive. All original sketches, plus 75 photographs. 1,804pp. 8½ × 12¼.   20312-3, 20313-1 Cloth., Two-vol. set $120.00

CASTLES: THEIR CONSTRUCTION AND HISTORY, Sidney Toy. Traces castle development from ancient roots. Nearly 200 photographs and drawings illustrate moats, keeps, baileys, many other features. Caernarvon, Dover Castles, Hadrian's Wall, Tower of London, dozens more. 256pp. 5⅜ × 8¼.
                    24898-4 Pa. $6.95

AMERICAN CLIPPER SHIPS: 1833–1858, Octavius T. Howe & Frederick C. Matthews. Fully-illustrated, encyclopedic review of 352 clipper ships from the period of America's greatest maritime supremacy. Introduction. 109 halftones. 5 black-and-white line illustrations. Index. Total of 928pp. 5⅜ × 8½.

25115-2, 25116-0 Pa., Two-vol. set $17.90

TOWARDS A NEW ARCHITECTURE, Le Corbusier. Pioneering manifesto by great architect, near legendary founder of "International School." Technical and aesthetic theories, views on industry, economics, relation of form to function, "mass-production spirit," much more. Profusely illustrated. Unabridged translation of 13th French edition. Introduction by Frederick Etchells. 320pp. 6⅛ × 9¼. (Available in U.S. only)

25023-7 Pa. $8.95

THE BOOK OF KELLS, edited by Blanche Cirker. Inexpensive collection of 32 full-color, full-page plates from the greatest illuminated manuscript of the Middle Ages, painstakingly reproduced from rare facsimile edition. Publisher's Note. Captions. 32pp. 9⅜ × 12¼.

24345-1 Pa. $4.95

BEST SCIENCE FICTION STORIES OF H. G. WELLS, H. G. Wells. Full novel *The Invisible Man,* plus 17 short stories: "The Crystal Egg," "Aepyornis Island," "The Strange Orchid," etc. 303pp. 5⅜ × 8½. (Available in U.S. only)

21531-8 Pa. $6.95

AMERICAN SAILING SHIPS: Their Plans and History, Charles G. Davis. Photos, construction details of schooners, frigates, clippers, other sailcraft of 18th to early 20th centuries—plus entertaining discourse on design, rigging, nautical lore, much more. 137 black-and-white illustrations. 240pp. 6⅛ × 9¼.

24658-2 Pa. $6.95

ENTERTAINING MATHEMATICAL PUZZLES, Martin Gardner. Selection of author's favorite conundrums involving arithmetic, money, speed, etc., with lively commentary. Complete solutions. 112pp. 5⅜ × 8½.

25211-6 Pa. $2.95

THE WILL TO BELIEVE, HUMAN IMMORTALITY, William James. Two books bound together. Effect of irrational on logical, and arguments for human immortality. 402pp. 5⅜ × 8½.

20291-7 Pa. $7.95

THE HAUNTED MONASTERY and THE CHINESE MAZE MURDERS, Robert Van Gulik. 2 full novels by Van Gulik continue adventures of Judge Dee and his companions. An evil Taoist monastery, seemingly supernatural events; overgrown topiary maze that hides strange crimes. Set in 7th-century China. 27 illustrations. 328pp. 5⅜ × 8½.

23502-5 Pa. $6.95

CELEBRATED CASES OF JUDGE DEE (DEE GOONG AN), translated by Robert Van Gulik. Authentic 18th-century Chinese detective novel; Dee and associates solve three interlocked cases. Led to Van Gulik's own stories with same characters. Extensive introduction. 9 illustrations. 237pp. 5⅜ × 8½.

23337-5 Pa. $4.95

Prices subject to change without notice.
Available at your book dealer or write for free catalog to Dept. GI, Dover Publications, Inc., 31 East 2nd St., Mineola, N.Y. 11501. Dover publishes more than 175 books each year on science, elementary and advanced mathematics, biology, music, art, literary history, social sciences and other areas.